PLAY BETTER GOLF: The Swing From A–Z

Put your game on tournament level.

Strip away the mistakes that lead to slicing and hooking—and a bad game score.

Golf's great, Jack Nicklaus, shows you how to make every shot count by generously offering a comprehensive look at how to execute and achieve a "professional swing."

Here are his ten basics of good technique:

- Swing the same with every club
- Strive for a full arc
- Never try for "topspin"
- Focus strongly on the ball
- Develop a preferred shot "shape"
- Beware of overexperimenting
- Don't be too "position" conscious
- Always fully "wind your spring"
- Use all your resources
- Never forget to *hit* the ball

PLAY BETTER GOLF

THE SWING FROM A–Z

Jack Nicklaus

With Ken Bowden
Illustrated by Jim McQueen

PUBLISHED BY POCKET BOOKS NEW YORK

All drawings contained in this work have been previously published by King Features, Inc.

Another *Original* publication of POCKET BOOKS

POCKET BOOKS, a Simon & Schuster division of
GULF & WESTERN CORPORATION
1230 Avenue of the Americas, New York, N.Y. 10020

ISBN: 0-671-83522-X

First Pocket Books printing July, 1980

10 9 8 7 6 5 4 3 2 1

POCKET and colophon are trademarks of Simon & Schuster.

Printed in the U.S.A.

Contents

Introduction

Will this book *really* help you play better golf?

Well, to improve at this marvelous but maddening game you must first know what you are doing wrong and then how to make it right. Unless you've got enough time and energy to work things out purely by trial and error, that requires information. The best way to get that information is from a skilled teacher in one-on-one lessons—as I was fortunate to be able to do as a youngster. If that's impractical or unappealing, the next best way is via the printed page—especially when each piece of information is self-contained, to the point and well illustrated, as I hope we've achieved here.

Within these pages I've tried to present all I know about the tee-to-green golf swing as clearly, crisply and logically as possible. That's the most exciting part of golf, and the most demanding. Improving at it even a little bit will give you great inner satisfaction, as well as lower scores. (That's why I'm still always trying to improve, even after thirty years in the game.) In future volumes, we plan to deal in similar style and scope with the art of scoring, which includes the short game, and then with faults, cures and trouble shots.

One word of warning. If you choose to read the book first time around from cover to cover, you'll quickly realize that it contains a large amount of information. Don't try to put everything into effect at once, or even to absorb it all at one reading. Be selective in relation to your own present golfing capabilities and problems, and try always to work on one thing at a time, preferably in a properly ordered sequence. Remember that improving a golf swing or mastering a particular type of shot always takes time and patience, as well as mental know-how and physical effort.

Hopefully, you'll also find the book easy to use for quick refreshers and reminders on specific points, as well as for self-correction.

Finally, a word of appreciation. All the articles herein were originally created for distribution to newspapers worldwide by King Features Syndicate of New York, and I would like to thank my friends at King for their fine efforts in that direction.

Jack Nicklaus

PART ONE

Some Fundamentals

1

Thinking Your Way to a Better Game

Learn and Stick to Fundamentals

IF YOU **REALLY** WANT TO PLAY BETTER GOLF, LEARN THE FUNDAMENTALS OF THE GAME, THEN STICK TO THEM THROUGH THICK AND THIN.

RESIST TRYING **B**AND-**A**ID REMEDIES ANY TIME YOU HIT A BAD PATCH —

THEY NEVER LAST.

START WITH GRIP AND SET-UP, THEN WORK THROUGH THE REST OF THE BASICS — IN YOUR GENERAL GOLF THINKING, YOUR PLAY, AND ESPECIALLY DURING YOUR **PRACTICE**.

IF YOU DON'T KNOW WHAT THE FUNDAMENTALS ARE, GO SEE A GOOD TEACHING PRO.

JM

Review Your Game Honestly

TAKE THE TIME EVERY ONCE IN A WHILE, IF YOU'RE SERIOUS ABOUT GOLF, TO SIT DOWN AND HONESTLY REVIEW YOUR GAME.

IDENTIFYING YOUR WEAKNESSES IS OBVIOUSLY THE VITAL FIRST STEP IN DESIGNING ANY MEANINGFUL IMPROVEMENT PROGRAM.

I DO THIS AT LEAST ONCE A YEAR, BREAKING MY GAME DOWN INTO DRIVING, APPROACHING, RECOVERY PLAY, PUTTING, COURSE-MANAGEMENT AND SELF-MANAGEMENT. HAVING DETERMINED WHERE MY PROBLEMS LIE, I THEN DESIGN AN ACTION PLAN TO TRY TO SOLVE THEM — OFTEN BEGINNING WITH A LESSON FROM MY LIFE-LONG TEACHER, **JACK GROUT.** A SIMILAR APPROACH MIGHT BRING YOU A LOT MORE SATISFACTION FROM GOLF.

Develop Key Swing Thoughts

STRAIGHT LEFT ARM
TURN SHOULDERS 90°
EYES ON BALL
START DOWN WITH LOWER BODY
RIGHT ELBOW IN
STAY BEHIND BALL
FIRM L. GRIP

IT'S VIRTUALLY IMPOSSIBLE TO THINK OF MORE THAN ONE OR TWO THINGS DURING THE LESS-THAN-TWO-SECONDS IT GENERALLY TAKES TO COMPLETE A GOLF SWING.

SO DON'T CONFUSE YOURSELF BY TRYING TO!

THE TWO THINGS I'VE MOSTLY THOUGHT ABOUT DURING THE EXECUTION OF THE SWING ARE: 1) TAKING THE CLUB STRAIGHT BACK FROM THE BALL AS DELIBERATELY AS POSSIBLE CONSISTENT WITH SWINGING IT AWAY; AND 2) KEEPING MY HEAD STEADY. WHENEVER I'VE BEEN ACHIEVING ONE OF THESE WITHOUT HAVING TO THINK ABOUT IT, I'VE GENERALLY REPLACED IT WITH THE THOUGHT: "COMPLETE THE BACKSWING."

EVERY YEAR I'VE COMPETED AT GOLF, AS AMATEUR AND PROFESSIONAL, I'VE PREFACED THE CAMPAIGN WITH A LESSON FROM MY LIFELONG TEACHER, JACK GROUT.

"JACK," I SAY TO HIM, "I'D LIKE TO TAKE UP GOLF. SHOW ME HOW TO HOLD THE CLUB, HOW TO ADDRESS THE BALL, AND HOW TO SWING." IN OTHER WORDS, WHAT I'M AFTER IS A COMPLETE REFRESHER COURSE IN THE BASIC FUNDAMENTALS TO ENSURE I'M PROPERLY ON TRACK IN MY UPCOMING PRACTICE SESSIONS. I HAVE TO BELIEVE THE SAME EXERCISE WOULD DO YOU GOOD, TOO.

Be Prepared to Practice

HOW WELL YOU PLAY GOLF ISN'T ENTIRELY A MATTER OF HOW MUCH YOU PRACTICE, BUT THE TWO ARE CLOSELY RELATED.

ONE THING IS FOR SURE: THERE'S NEVER BEEN A GREAT PLAYER WHO DID NOT HIT HUNDREDS OF THOUSANDS OF PRACTICE SHOTS, AT LEAST WHILE HE OR SHE WAS LEARNING THE GAME.

NO TIME OR OPPORTUNITY TO PRACTICE? WELL, WHERE THERE'S A WILL THERE'S A WAY. AS A YOUNGSTER, I'D EVEN PRACTICE IN THE SNOW, CLEARING A SPOT OR HITTING OFF COMPACTED SNOW IF I COULDN'T GET TO GROUND LEVEL. NOT MANY AMATEURS WOULD GO THAT FAR, I ADMIT, BUT THERE'S NOTHING TO STOP YOU AT LEAST SWINGING A CLUB FOR FIVE OR SO MINUTES A DAY WHEN YOU CAN'T GET OUT TO THE COURSE.

9

Never Hit a "Quit" Shot

PEOPLE OFTEN COMMENT ON MY ABILITY TO CONCENTRATE AND COMPETE HARD EVEN WHEN NOT PLAYING MY BEST.

ONE FACTOR BEHIND THESE ASSETS IS A LIFELONG HABIT OF NEVER HITTING SHOTS CARELESSLY, HALF-HEARTEDLY, OR BAD-TEMPEREDLY.

PERHAPS THE SAME HABIT WOULD HELP YOUR GAME – AND YOUR MENTAL APPROACH. RESOLVE TO GIVE EVERY SINGLE STROKE YOU PLAY YOUR **ABSOLUTE** BEST TRY, IN PRACTICE AS WELL AS IN PLAY.

IN OTHER WORDS, NEVER HIT A "QUIT" SHOT.

2

Ten Basics of Good Technique

Swing the Same with Every Club

THE FULL
GOLF SWING
REMAINS BASICALLY
THE SAME
WITH EVERY CLUB
IN THE BAG.

YOU'LL
AUTOMATICALLY
STAND CLOSER
TO THE BALL
THE SHORTER THE
CLUB YOU'RE
PLAYING, AND
THUS SWING
PROGRESSIVELY
MORE UPRIGHT.

BUT THERE
SHOULD BE NO
CONSCIOUS CHANGE
IN YOUR
OVERALL SWING
PATTERN ON
ALL NORMAL
SHOTS.

Strive for a Full Arc

ONE REASON FULL SWINGERS GENERALLY LAST LONGER THAN SHORT SWINGERS IS THAT THEY CAN STILL MAKE A GOOD, BIG ARC EVEN AS AGE INEVITABLY REDUCES MUSCULAR AGILITY.

ANOTHER REASON IS THAT THE LONGER THE SWING — SO LONG AS IT IS CONTROLLED — THE MORE ROOM YOU HAVE TO ACHIEVE PROPER TIMING AND RHYTHM.

THAT'S WHY I ENCOURAGE MY BOYS TO SWING AS FULLY AS POSSIBLE AS SOON AS POSSIBLE. I ALSO ENCOURAGE THEM TO HIT THE BALL HARD NOW, AND WORRY ABOUT CONTROL LATER.

Never Try for "Topspin"

JACK, WOULD I GET MORE DISTANCE IF I HIT MY DRIVES WITH TOPSPIN OR OVERSPIN?

NO, YOU WOULDN'T. WHAT YOU'D GET IS A SHORT GROUND BALL.

WITH THE DRIVER YOU WANT MINIMUM BACKSPIN AND MAXIMUM FORWARD IMPETUS. TEEING THE BALL WELL OFF THE GROUND AND CATCHING IT RIGHT AT THE BOTTOM OF THE SWING ARC PRODUCES BOTH.

SOME BACKSPIN IS NECESSARY TO MAKE ANY GOLF SHOT RISE IN THE AIR. THAT'S WHY WE HIT IRONS SLIGHTLY DOWNWARD.

JM

Focus Strongly on the Ball

Develop a Preferred Shot "Shape"

REMEMBER THAT THE REAL SECRET OF GOOD GOLF IS **REPETITION**, AND THAT THE TOUGHEST SHOT TO REPEAT CONSISTENTLY IS A DEAD STRAIGHT ONE.

THAT'S WHY THE PROS EITHER **DRAW** OR **FADE** THE BALL ON MOST SHOTS — OR, IN THE CASE OF THE BETTER ONES, HIT IT EITHER WAY AT WILL.

YOU'LL SCORE MORE EFFECTIVELY, TOO, IF YOU CAN LEARN TO CONSISTENTLY FLIGHT THE BALL EITHER FROM LEFT TO RIGHT OR RIGHT TO LEFT.

Beware of Overexperimenting

THINK TWICE BEFORE YOU MAKE RADICAL SWING CHANGES. OVER-EXPERIMENTATION IS A MAJOR CAUSE OF ERRATIC PLAY AMONG AMATEURS.

IF YOUR SHOTS START GOING BADLY ASTRAY, DON'T SEARCH FOR DESPERATE SOLUTIONS BY TRYING SOMETHING DIFFERENT ON EVERY SWING — ESPECIALLY NOT ON THE GOLF COURSE ITSELF. RETIRE TO THE PRACTICE TEE AND METHODI-CALLY CHECK YOUR OWN PERSONAL BASICS, ONE BY ONE, ONE AT A TIME.

IF THIS DOESN'T OFFER A SOLUTION, TAKE A LESSON FROM A PRO WHO KNOWS YOUR GAME.

Don't Be Too "Position" Conscious

IN SEEKING IMPROVEMENT BY ANALYZING THE GOLF SWING, AND PARTICULARLY YOUR OWN FORM, BEWARE OF BECOMING TOO "POSITION" CONSCIOUS.

JM

REMEMBER THAT YOU SWING **THROUGH**, NOT TO, THE VARIOUS POSITIONS THAT REPRESENT GOOD FORM, AND THAT TO BE EFFECTIVE YOUR ACTIONS MUST BE A CONTINUOUS AND RHYTHMICAL FLOW OF MOVEMENT. ABOVE ALL, THINK AND FEEL **SWING** ESPECIALLY IN THE CLUBHEAD.

Always Fully "Wind Your Spring"

I BELIEVE THE FARTHER A GOLFER CAN SWING THE CLUB BACK AND STILL RETAIN CONTROL OVER IT, THE MORE POWERFULLY HE'LL PLAY THE GAME — AND THE LONGER HE'LL GO ON PLAYING WELL.

SAM SNEAD'S THE PERFECT EXAMPLE OF THAT.

HOWEVER, NOT EVERYONE HAS THE PHYSIQUE TO SWING BACK AS FULLY AS SAM. IF YOU DON'T, FORGET THE ACTUAL LENGTH OF YOUR BACKSWING ARC AND WORK INSTEAD ON **MAXIMUM COILING** OF YOUR UPPER HALF AGAINST THE RESISTANCE OF YOUR LOWER HALF.

EVEN IF THE CLUB ONLY GETS HALF AS FAR BACK AS SAM'S, YOU'LL STILL GIVE THE BALL A FINE RIDE IF YOU "WIND THE SPRING" AS HARD AS YOU CAN.

19

Use All Your Resources

THERE'S A LOT OF TALK THESE DAYS IN GOLFING CIRCLES ABOUT "LEFT-SIDEDNESS" AND "RIGHT-SIDEDNESS" IN THE SWING.

TO ME, THE GAME DEMANDS FULL USE OF **BOTH** SIDES OF THE BODY.

JM

I DON'T BELIEVE A GOLFER CAN USE HIS RIGHT SIDE TOO MUCH SO LONG AS HIS LEFT SIDE **LEADS AND CONTROLS** THE SWING. FOR EXAMPLE, ONCE MY LEFT SIDE HAS INITIATED THE DOWNSWING, WHEN DRIVING I HIT JUST ABOUT AS HARD AS I CAN WITH MY RIGHT SIDE GOING THROUGH THE BALL.

PLAYING WITH ONLY HALF THE BODY, I FEEL, WOULD PRODUCE ONLY HALF THE DISTANCE I NEED ON TEE SHOTS.

Never Forget to <u>Hit</u> The Ball

DON'T GET SO BOUND UP IN SWING THEORY AND 'POSITIONS' THAT YOU FORGET TO **HIT** THE BALL WITH THE <u>CLUBHEAD</u>.

YOU MUST <u>RELEASE</u> THE CLUBHEAD TO HIT THE BALL FAR AND TRUE. WAY TO DO THAT IS START DOWN WITH YOUR LEGS OFF A GOOD, TORQUE-PACKED BACKSWING. THEN **LET GO** FULLY AND FREELY WITH YOUR <u>ARMS</u>, <u>WRISTS</u> AND <u>HANDS</u>.

3

Golf's "Geometry"

Don't Try to Play a Dead Straight Game

YOU'LL RARELY SEE A PRO TRY TO HIT THE BALL DEAD STRAIGHT. REASON IS THAT THE ABSOLUTELY STRAIGHT SHOT IS SO DIFFICULT AS TO BE ALMOST A FLUKE.

HERE'S WHAT YOU MUST DO AT IMPACT TO ACHIEVE THAT FLUKE:
1. YOUR CLUBHEAD MUST MOVE <u>DIRECTLY</u> ALONG YOUR TARGET LINE.
2. YOUR CLUBFACE MUST BE <u>PERFECTLY</u> SQUARE TO YOUR TARGET.
3. YOU MUST HIT THE BALL <u>ABSOLUTELY</u> ON THE CENTER OF THE CLUBFACE.

1.　　2.　　3.

...AND ALL THAT WITH THE CLUBHEAD TRAVELING AT AROUND 100 M.P.H.!
BECAUSE OF THE IMPOSSIBILITY OF ALWAYS REPEATING THOSE IDEALS, MOST TOUR PROS FAVOR EITHER A DELIBERATE **FADE** OR **DRAW** — THE BEST OF THEM BEING CAPABLE OF EITHER 'SHAPE' AT ANY TIME. THAT SHOULD BE YOUR APPROACH, TOO.

JM

Know What Causes Slices, Hooks...

GOOD GOLF STARTS WITH KNOWING WHAT CAUSES YOUR SHOTS TO CURVE.

SLICING COMES FROM IMPACTING THE BALL WITH YOUR CLUBFACE LOOKING RIGHT OF THE DIRECTION IN WHICH YOUR CLUBHEAD IS TRAVELING.

A FADE — MY BASIC SHOT — COMES FROM THE SAME INTERACTION, ONLY THE ANGLE BETWEEN CLUBFACE AND SWING PATH IS SMALLER.

HOOKING COMES FROM IMPACTING THE BALL WITH THE CLUBFACE LOOKING LEFT OF THE DIRECTION IN WHICH YOUR CLUBHEAD IS TRAVELING.

A DRAW — THE IDEAL SHOT FOR THE AMATEUR — COMES FROM THE SAME INTERACTION, BUT AGAIN THE CLUBFACE SWING PATH ANGLE IS SMALLER.

Understand These Spin Effects

IN BUILDING YOURSELF A GOLF GAME, KEEP THE FOLLOWING IN MIND.

1) A FADE GIVES MORE CONTROL THAN A DRAW BECAUSE THE BALL FLIES HIGHER, LANDS MORE SOFTLY, AND BREAKS LESS SHARPLY ON IMPACT. HOWEVER, A DRAW GIVES YOU MORE DISTANCE BECAUSE THE BALL FLIES LOWER, LANDS FASTER, AND RUNS FARTHER.

2) IF A FADE TURNS INTO A SLICE, IT WILL SEVERELY REDUCE YOUR DISTANCE. HOWEVER, IF A DRAW TURNS INTO A HOOK, IT WILL OFTEN RUN INTO TROUBLE MORE READILY.

3) GOLF IS EASIEST WHEN YOU PLAY **WITH**, RATHER THAN AGAINST, YOUR NATURAL SHOT-FLIGHTING TENDENCIES.

Fit Your Plane to Your Build

DON'T LET ALL THE TALK AND LITERATURE ABOUT "FLAT" AND "UPRIGHT" SWING PLANES THROW YOU OUT OF YOUR OWN NATURAL SHAPE OF SWING. ACTUALLY, THE DIFFERENCE BETWEEN SO-CALLED FLAT AND UPRIGHT PLANES AMONG GOOD PLAYERS IS GENERALLY ONLY A FEW DEGREES.

IF YOU'RE TALL, YOU'LL NATURALLY STAND FAIRLY CLOSE TO THE BALL AND THUS NATURALLY SWING ON A FAIRLY UPRIGHT PLANE. IF YOU'RE SHORTER, STANDING FARTHER FROM THE BALL WILL NATURALLY CREATE A SOMEWHAT FLATTER PLANE. GO WITH WHAT'S NATURAL, AND DON'T EXAGGERATE.

Have These Angles Checked Out

SHOULD YOU TRY TO SWING ON AN UPRIGHT OR A FLAT PLANE?

THE SHORT ANSWER IS: DO WHAT COMES MOST NATURALLY, BUT DON'T EXAGGERATE ONE WAY OR THE OTHER.

BEYOND THAT, IT DEPENDS WHAT KIND OF GOLF SHOTS YOU PRIMARILY WANT TO HIT. GENERALLY, THE MORE UPRIGHT YOUR SWING, THE HIGHER YOU WILL HIT THE BALL AND THE MORE EASILY YOU WILL BE ABLE TO FADE IT. CONVERSELY, THE FLATTER YOU SWING, THE LOWER YOU'LL HIT THE BALL AND THE MORE EASILY YOU WILL BE ABLE TO DRAW IT.

Know the Proper Clubhead Path

MANY GOLFERS GET BACKACHE AND BAD SCORES THROUGH A FUNDAMENTAL MISCONCEPTION OF THE PATH THE CLUBHEAD SHOULD FOLLOW THROUGH IMPACT.

JM

THE CORRECT PATH IS FROM INSIDE THE TARGET LINE, TO <u>MOMENTARILY ALONG IT,</u> TO **INSIDE** AGAIN.

TRYING TO FORCE THE CLUBHEAD TO GO FROM INSIDE TO OUTSIDE THROUGH IMPACT, OR FOLLOW THE TARGET LINE FOR ANY APPRECIABLE DISTANCE, IS A SURE WAY TO HURT BOTH YOUR-SELF AND YOUR SCORE.

WHEN THE CLUB POINTS **LEFT** OF THE TARGET LINE AT THE TOP OF THE BACKSWING, IT WILL GENERALLY SWING ACROSS THAT LINE FROM OUT TO IN AT IMPACT.

CONVERSELY, WHEN THE CLUB POINTS RIGHT OF THE TARGET LINE AT THE TOP, IT WILL USUALLY BE MOVING FROM **IN TO OUT** AT IMPACT.

THAT'S WHY I ALWAYS STRIVE NOT TO "CROSS THE LINE" AT THE TOP. WHEN THE CLUB SHAFT PARALLELS THE TARGET LINE THERE, ITS NATURALLY POSITIONED TO SWING ON LINE THROUGH IMPACT.

Don't Manipulate the Clubface

IN A PROPER GOLF SWING, THE CLUBFACE <u>APPEARS</u> TO OPEN AS THE CLUB MOVES AWAY FROM THE BALL, AND <u>APPEARS</u> TO CLOSE AS IT TRACKS THE BALL INTO THE FOLLOW-THROUGH.

ACTUALLY, IT DOES NEITHER UNLESS YOU MANIPULATE IT IN SOME WAY WITH YOUR HANDS AND ARMS.

TO PROVE THE POINT, SWING BACK TO WAIST HEIGHT, THEN TURN SO THAT YOUR BODY FACES DIRECTLY DOWN THE CLUBSHAFT. DO THE SAME AFTER SWINGING TO WAIST HEIGHT IN THE FOLLOW-THROUGH.

IN BOTH CASES, YOU'LL FIND THE CLUBFACE IS IN THE SAME **SQUARE** RELATIONSHIP TO YOUR HANDS AND BODY AS IT WAS AT ADDRESS.

4

Your
Equipment

Let a Pro Help You Pick Clubs

BUYING NEW CLUBS?

UNLESS YOU'RE A GOOD ENOUGH GOLFER TO KNOW FROM EXPERIENCE EXACTLY WHAT YOU WANT, GET THE HELP OF A GOOD TEACHING PRO WHO KNOWS YOUR GAME IN DETERMINING THEIR PLAYABILITY CHARACTERISTICS.

PROPERLY MATCHING YOUR TOOLS TO YOUR TRAITS AND TALENTS — ESPECIALLY IN THE AREAS OF WEIGHT AND SHAFT FLEX — COULD DEFINITELY SAVE YOU A SHOT OR TWO. THAT'S WHY, IF YOU HAVE A FAVORITE CLUB, IT'S A GOOD IDEA TO KNOW ITS SPECIFICATIONS AND USE THOSE AS A GUIDE WHENEVER YOU'RE RE-EQUIPPING YOURSELF.

Understand the Technology

MANY GOLFERS TALK OF SWINGWEIGHT WITHOUT REALLY UNDERSTANDING WHAT IT MEANS.

ESSENTIALLY, SWINGWEIGHT IS A CONCEPT RELATING THE WEIGHT OF THE GRIP END OF A GOLF CLUB TO ITS HEAD WEIGHT.

JM

BASICALLY, THE HIGHER THE SWINGWEIGHT DESIGNATION THE HEAVIER THE CLUBHEAD WILL FEEL IN RELATION TO THE GRIP END AS YOU SWING. USE THIS CONCEPT AS A GUIDE IN SELECTING CLUBS, BUT DON'T STOP THERE. DEADWEIGHT AND SHAFT FLEXIBILITY ARE ALSO IMPORTANT FACTORS, AND YOU SHOULD OBTAIN PROFESSIONAL HELP IN MATCHING ALL THREE TO YOUR OWN PHYSIQUE AND SWING STYLE.

Match Your Set to Your Ability

THE RULES ALLOW YOU 14 CLUBS. SELECT THEM TO MATCH YOUR PERSONAL ABILITIES, NOT SOME THEORETICAL IDEAL. FOR EXAMPLE, I CARRY A DRIVER, 3-WOOD, IRONS 1 THROUGH 9, PITCHING WEDGE, MODERATELY-FLANGED SAND-WEDGE, AND PUTTER. THAT'S A MIX PERHAPS SUITABLE FOR ANYONE WHO SHOOTS 75 OR BETTER.

IF YOU SCORE MORE THAN A FEW SHOTS HIGHER THAN THAT, HOWEVER, YOU NEED AN "EASIER" SET — SUCH AS, FOR EXAMPLE, DRIVER, 3-, 4-, AND 5- (OR 6-) WOODS, IRONS 3 THROUGH 9, PITCHING WEDGE, DEEP-FLANGED SAND-WEDGE, AND PUTTER.

DON'T LET EGO PREVENT YOU FROM CARRYING CLUBS THAT YOU CAN ACTUALLY PLAY, RATHER THAN ONES THAT SIMPLY LOOK GOOD IN THE BAG.

SELECT YOUR CLUBS TO MATCH YOUR PHYSIQUE. BASICALLY, THE HEAVIER A CLUB, THE STRONGER YOU HAVE TO BE TO CONTROL IT AND GENERATE MAXIMUM HEAD SPEED.

SQUARE IMPACT IS AS IMPORTANT TO BOTH DISTANCE AND ACCURACY AS CLUBHEAD SPEED.

LESS POWERFUL SWINGERS OFTEN ACHIEVE BOTH MORE EASILY WITH LIGHTER-SWINGING CLUBS. IF YOU TAKE THE GAME SERIOUSLY, EXPERIMENT WITH VARIOUS FORMULAS OF SHAFT FLEX AND WEIGHT TO FIND YOUR OWN IDEAL "MEAN."

Take Your Height into Account

DOES A TALL GOLFER NEED LONGER-THAN-STANDARD CLUBS?

IT MIGHT BE WORTH EXPERIMENTING. BUT THE DANGER IS THAT LONGER CLUBS CAN CAUSE A TALL PLAYER TO LOSE CONTROL BY LENGTHENING HIS ALREADY LARGE SWING ARC. PROFESSIONAL COUNSEL IS ADVISABLE.

SHORT GOLFERS, ON THE OTHER HAND, CAN SOME-TIMES GAIN VALUABLE DISTANCE FROM THE BIGGER ARC THAT RESULTS FROM LONGER-THAN-STANDARD CLUBS.... ONCE THEY ARE ABLE TO CONTROL THE EXTRA LENGTH.

GARY PLAYER IS A CASE IN POINT — HIS CLUBS ARE AN INCH LONGER THAN STANDARD.

AGAIN, TALK TO YOUR PRO BEFORE YOU DECIDE.

Consider Lighter Clubs

ALTHOUGH I'M NOT REALLY FAMILIAR WITH THE SPECIAL PROBLEMS OF SENIOR MEN AND LADY GOLFERS, I'VE OFTEN FELT BOTH MIGHT ENJOY THE GAME MORE BY USING LIGHTER-THAN-NORMAL CLUBS.

VELOCITY HAVING TWICE THE VALUE OF MASS IN TERMS OF DISTANCE, IT SEEMS LOGICAL THAT BOTH GROUPS COULD HIT THE BALL FARTHER WITH CLUBS THEY COULD SWING FASTER.

ALSO, THE LIGHTER THE CLUBS, THE LESS THEY'RE GOING TO TAKE OUT OF YOU PHYSICALLY, WHICH CAN BE IMPORTANT TOWARD THE END OF A ROUND.

18
350 YDS
PAR 4

Know the Importance of "Lie"

IN SELECTING GOLF CLUBS, BE PARTICULARLY METICULOUS ABOUT THE ANGLE BETWEEN CLUBHEAD AND HOSEL — IN OTHER WORDS, ABOUT THE WAY THEY LIE. SMALL ERRORS HERE CAN CAUSE BIG ONES ON THE COURSE.

JM

SHOULD THE TOE BE OFF THE GROUND AS YOU ADDRESS THE BALL, CHANCES ARE IT WILL BE THAT WAY AT IMPACT, CAUSING THE CLUBFACE TO CLOSE AND THE BALL TO HOOK AS THE HEEL TOUCHES DOWN FIRST.

CONVERSELY, A HEEL-UP CLUB AT ADDRESS WILL GENERALLY TOUCH DOWN TOE FIRST, CAUSING THE CLUBFACE TO OPEN AND THE BALL TO SLICE.

Go for Good Quality

YOU CAN'T "BUY" A GOLF GAME IN THE CLUBS YOU CHOOSE. BUT YOU CAN SAVE YOURSELF SHOTS BY SEEKING OUT GOOD-QUALITY EQUIPMENT... AND ESPECIALLY THE FINE WORKMANSHIP THAT PRODUCES COMPATABILITY OF EACH CLUB TO ALL THE OTHERS IN A SET.

IN WOODS, LOOK FOR SIMILARITY IN GRAIN PATTERN IN PERSIMMON OR LAMINATIONS IN BONDED-WOOD HEADS, AND ALSO FOR CONSISTENCY OF FACE BULGE AND ROLL. WITH IRONS, CHECK PARTICULARLY LIE, LEADING-EDGE CONFIGURATION, GRADATIONS OF OFFSET, AND GRIP THICKNESS.

WELL-MADE CLUBS WILL ALL LOOK LIKE MEMBERS OF THE SAME HAPPY FAMILY.

Join the Pros—Use a Glove

YOU HAVE NOTICED PERHAPS THAT ALMOST EVERY GOLFER ON THE P G A TOUR WEARS A GLOVE ON HIS LEADING HAND (WHICH IS USUALLY THE LEFT, OF COURSE).

THERE ARE TWO REASONS.

THE FIRST IS THAT A GLOVE ON THIS PRIMARY SWING—CONTROLLING HAND IS THE GREATEST AID TO SECURE GRIPPING ALLOWED UNDER THE GAME'S RULES.

THE SECOND REASON IS THAT A GLOVE HELPS GREATLY IN AVOIDING THE BLISTERS AND CALLUSES THAT CAN RESULT FROM EXTENSIVE PRACTICE.

Try to "Custom-Fit" Your Driver

BECAUSE THE CLUB IS SO IMPORTANT IN PLACING THE BALL IN PLAY, TOUR GOLFERS GO TO GREAT LENGTHS TO "CUSTOM FIT" THEIR DRIVERS TO THEIR INDIVIDUAL SWING STYLES. YOU MIGHT BENEFIT FROM SOME EXPERIMENT IN THIS DIRECTION IF YOU'RE A SERIOUS AND REASONABLY CAPABLE GOLFER.

IF DISTANCE IS YOUR BIGGEST PROBLEM, EXPERIMENT WITH SOFTER SHAFTS, MORE FACE LOFT, AND PERHAPS LIGHTER CLUBS.

IF DIRECTION IS YOUR MAIN DIFFICULTY, TRY STIFFER SHAFTS AND/OR DIFFERENT CLUB FACINGS — SAY A DEGREE OR SO CLOSED IF YOU HABITUALLY SLICE, OR A DEGREE OR SO OPEN IF YOU HOOK.

Play the Ball You Can Really Handle

DON'T LET EGO DETERMINE THE COMPRESSION OF GOLF BALL YOU USE. A VERY POWERFUL SWING IS NECESSARY TO GET MAXIMUM DISTANCE FROM A HIGH COMPRESSION (100) BALL.

EVEN SOME OF THE TOUR PLAYERS PREFER A SLIGHTLY SOFTER BALL, ESPECIALLY IN COLD WEATHER.

MOST AMATEURS SEEM TO DO BEST WITH MEDIUM COMPRESSION (90) BALLS. THE VERY EASY SWINGER MIGHT FIND HE OR SHE DOES BETTER YET WITH EVEN LESS COMPRESSION — SAY 70 TO 80. EXPERIMENT TO FIND YOUR OWN IDEAL "AMMUNITION."

PART TWO

The Swing Step-by-Step

5

Building a Sound Grip

Meet These Three Goals

AN EFFECTIVE GRIP MUST DO THREE THINGS...

(1) AUTOMATICALLY DELIVER THE CLUBFACE SQUARE AT IMPACT.

(2) SUSTAIN THE SHOCK OF IMPACT WITHOUT THE HANDS SLIPPING ON THE CLUB.

(3) ALLOW THE WRISTS TO HINGE EFFICIENTLY AT CERTAIN POINTS IN THE SWING.

Place Your Hands Naturally

HAND ALIGNMENT DETERMINES CLUBFACE IMPACT ANGLE.

TO FIND YOUR MOST NATURAL GRIP, SIMPLY LET YOUR LEFT ARM HANG NORMALLY AT YOUR SIDE, THEN WRAP THE HAND SECURELY AROUND THE CLUB.

NEXT, EXTEND THE CLUB AND WRAP YOUR RIGHT HAND AROUND IT IN THE SAME ALIGNMENT IT HAD WHEN HANGING NATURALLY AT YOUR SIDE.

JM

Hold the Club like This

THE CLUB SHOULD SIT WELL INTO THE PALM OF THE LEFT HAND. MAXIMUM PRESSURE EXERTED BY THE LAST TWO OR THREE FINGERS THEN WEDGES IT SNUGLY UNDER THE HEEL PAD.

THE CLUB SITS ACROSS THE ROOTS OF THE FINGERS OF THE RIGHT HAND, WITH THE THUMB PAD SNUG AGAINST THE TOP OF THE LEFT THUMB. MAXIMUM PRESSURE IS IN THE MIDDLE TWO FINGERS.

Set Your Hands in Parallel

WHATEVER STYLE OF GRIP YOU CHOOSE — OVERLAPPING, INTERLOCKING OR 10-FINGER — KEEP IT AS **NATURAL** AS POSSIBLE. NATURALNESS COMES FROM SETTING THE HANDS PARALLEL WITH EACH OTHER, RATHER THAN LOOKING IN OPPOSING DIRECTIONS.

FOR MOST GOLFERS, THE MORE THE ALIGNMENT OF THE HANDS MATCHES THE CLUBFACE ALIGNMENT, THE STRAIGHTER THEY'LL HIT THE BALL. HOWEVER, IF YOU'RE SLICING, ALIGN YOUR HANDS MORE TO THE RIGHT OF THE CLUB FACING (AND IF YOU'RE HOOKING ALIGN THEM MORE TO THE LEFT). BUT KEEP YOUR HANDS PARALLEL TO EACH OTHER AT **ALL** TIMES.

Meld Your Hands Together

EFFICIENT WRIST HINGING AND RESISTANCE TO IMPACT SHOCK COME FROM LINKING THE HANDS AS A UNIT. HAVING SMALL HANDS, I FAVOR THE <u>INTERLOCKING</u> GRIP.

MOST POPULAR MEANS OF UNIFYING THE HANDS IS THE OVERLAP, BUT GOLFERS WITH VERY WEAK HANDS MIGHT TRY THE 10-FINGER GRIP.

WHATEVER STYLE YOU FAVOR, THE HANDS MUST BE AS <u>CLOSE TOGETHER</u> AS POSSIBLE.

Wedge Shaft into Left Palm

HOWEVER YOU GRIP — OVERLAP, INTERLOCK OR 10-FINGER STYLE — YOUR LEADING HAND NEEDS TO HANG ON VERY FIRMLY, FIRST TO GUIDE THE CLUB THROUGHOUT THE SWING, AND SECOND TO PROVIDE A BUTTRESS AGAINST THE HITTING ACTION OF THE TRAILING HAND.

I FIND WEDGING THE CLUB VERY SOLIDLY INTO THE PALM OF MY LEFT HAND BEST HELPS ME ACHIEVE THOSE BASICS.

THE ILLUSTRATIONS HERE SHOW WHAT I MEAN.

TRY THIS TECHNIQUE IF YOU FEEL YOUR LEADING HAND IS "BREAKING" DOWN AT SOME POINT IN THE SWING.

Beware of Too "Strong" a Grip

MOST PEOPLE STARTING GOLF TEND TO TAKE A VERY "STRONG" GRIP ON THE CLUB, BECAUSE THEY INSTINCTIVELY FEEL THIS WILL GIVE THEM MORE POWER.

UNFORTUNATELY, IT DOESN'T ALWAYS WORK THAT WAY.

JM

THE BETTER PLAYER DEVELOPS POWER WITH HIS **ENTIRE SWING**, NOT WITH JUST HIS HANDS AND WRISTS.

TOO STRONG A GRIP ACTUALLY INHIBITS THE FULL CLUBHEAD RELEASE NECESSARY FOR GOOD DISTANCE, SO WORK ON DEVELOPING A MORE "NEUTRAL" HOLD ON THE CLUB AS YOUR SWING SKILLS DEVELOP.

Maintain Consistent Pressure

TOO TIGHT A GRIP CAN DESTROY TEMPO AND RHYTHM BY FORCING YOU TO SWING JERKILY — ESPECIALLY DURING THE TAKEAWAY.

EVEN PRESSURE

HOLD THE CLUB LIGHTLY AT ADDRESS, FIRM UP YOUR HANDS SLIGHTLY JUST BEFORE YOU START BACK, THEN MAINTAIN THE SAME PRESSURE THROUGHOUT THE BACKSWING.

BIG THING TO AVOID IS GRABBING HARDER WITH EITHER HAND ONCE THE CLUB'S IN MOTION.

Test Your Grip like This

HERE'S A TEST OF YOUR ABILITY TO HANG ONTO THE CLUB THROUGHOUT THE SWING WITHOUT CHANGING YOUR HAND POSITION -- A MAJOR SOURCE OF INCONSISTENCY.

PLACE THREE OR MORE BALLS IN A LINE AND TRY TO HIT THEM ALL WITH-OUT REGRIPPING THE CLUB. IF YOU CAN'T, YOUR HANDS HAVE SLIPPED AT SOME POINT IN THE SWING. CHECK FOR LOOSENESS PARTICULARLY DURING THE TAKEAWAY AND AT THE TOP OF THE BACKSWING.

6

How to Aim Accurately

Select a _Specific_ Target

THE MORE SPECIFICALLY YOU SIGHT AND MENTALLY FOCUS ON A TARGET IN SETTING UP TO PLAY ANY SHOT, THE BETTER YOUR CHANCE OF HITTING WHERE YOU INTEND.

FOR THAT REASON, I ALWAYS TARGET TO A SPECIFIC POINT, RATHER THAN A VAGUE GREEN AREA, ON ALL APPROACH SHOTS. USUALLY THAT POINT IS THE PIN, BUT IF IT'S HIDDEN OR I CAN'T SHOOT DIRECTLY AT IT FOR SOME REASON, THEN I'LL SELECT A MOUND OR A TREE IN THE BACKGROUND. MAKE A SPECIAL POINT OF DOING THIS WHENEVER YOUR APPROACH PLAY BECOMES LESS SHARP THAN YOU'D LIKE.

Use This 3-Point Aiming System

INCORRECT AIM AND ALIGNMENT LIES BEHIND PROBABLY 80 PER CENT OF GOLF'S MISDIRECTED SHOTS, ESPECIALLY AMONG HIGH HANDICAPPERS. HERE'S A ROUTINE THAT WILL HELP SOLVE THAT PROBLEM FOR YOU.

1. SELECT YOUR TARGET LINE FROM BEHIND THE BALL, AND USE A MARK ON THE GROUND A FEW FEET AHEAD OF IT AS A REFERENCE POINT. 2. SET THE CLUBFACE BEHIND THE BALL LOOKING SQUARELY AT YOUR MARK AND THUS DOWN YOUR TARGET LINE, BEFORE YOU FINALIZE YOUR GRIP AND STANCE. 3. ALIGN YOUR BODY PARALLEL TO THE TARGET LINE — PARTICULARLY YOUR SHOULDERS.

PLACING YOUR FEET PARALLEL TO THE TARGET LINE AT ADDRESS WILL HELP YOU SWING THE CLUB ALONG THAT LINE THROUGH IMPACT, BUT SETTING YOUR **SHOULDERS** SQUARE TO THE LINE WILL HELP YOU DO SO EVEN MORE.

REASON IS THAT THE CLUBHEAD PATH AT IMPACT USUALLY MATCHES THE ALIGNMENT OF THE SHOULDERS AT THAT MOMENT, AND THE ANGLE OF THE SHOULDERS AT IMPACT USUALLY MATCHES THEIR ANGLE AT ADDRESS. THUS IF YOU START WITH AN OPEN OR CLOSED SHOULDER LINE, YOU ALMOST GUARANTEE AN OUT-TO-IN OR IN-TO-OUT SWING PATH.

. . . and the Clubface

MOST GOLFERS INSTINCTIVELY LINE THEMSELVES UP PARALLEL TO WHERE THE <u>CLUBFACE LOOKS</u> AT ADDRESS.

MOST GOLFERS ALSO INSTINCTIVELY DELIVER THE CLUB-HEAD TO THE BALL ON A PATH PARALLEL TO THEIR <u>SHOULDER ALIGNMENT</u> AT ADDRESS.

SO A SQUARE CLUBFACE AT ADDRESS ESTABLISHES YOUR BEST CHANCE OF SWINGING ALONG THE TARGET LINE AT IMPACT.

Never Neglect Your Alignment

CHECK YOUR ADDRESS ALIGNMENT FIRST ANY TIME YOU BEGIN TO MIS-DIRECT MORE SHOTS THAN NORMAL.

FAULTY AIMING CAUSES MORE BOGEYS THAN ANY OTHER SINGLE ERROR AMONG EXPERIENCED PLAYERS.

AND IT'S EASY TO SLIP INTO UNKNOWINGLY.

YOU'LL NOTICE AT TOUR EVENTS THAT THE PLAYERS ARE CONSTANTLY CHECKING THEIR OWN AND EACH OTHERS' SET-UPS.

HAVE A PRO OR A PAL CHECK YOURS PERIODICALLY, OR DO IT YOURSELF IN PRACTICE BY ALIGNING TO A CLUB LAID ON THE GROUND. REMEMBER, THE GREATEST SWING IN THE WORLD WON'T SCORE IF IT'S MIS-AIMED.

7

Posture, Stance
and Ball Position

Don't Exaggerate Your Posture

KEY TO GOOD POSTURE IS TO <u>AVOID EXAGGERATION</u>.

FORCE ANYTHING AT ADDRESS AND INSTINCTIVELY IT WILL COME APART DURING YOUR SWING.

YOUR <u>BASIC</u> POSTURAL ADDRESS OBJECTIVE IS SIMPLY TO **MIRROR** YOUR IDEAL IMPACT POSITION. YOU'LL DO THAT MOST EFFECTIVELY BY BEING AS <u>NATURAL</u> AS POSSIBLE WITHIN GOOD SET-UP FUNDAMENTALS.

Set Shaft and Left Arm in Line

BY SETTING-UP WITH YOUR LEFT ARM AND CLUBSHAFT IN A <u>STRAIGHT LINE</u> FROM LEFT SHOULDER TO BALL, YOU'LL AUTOMATICALLY POSITION YOUR HANDS <u>SLIGHTLY AHEAD OF THE CLUBHEAD</u> — WHICH IS WHERE THEY SHOULD BE THROUGH IMPACT.

ANOTHER ADVANTAGE OF SETTING UP "IN LINE" LIKE THIS IS THAT IT AUTOMATICALLY PUTS THE RIGHT SIDE <u>UNDER</u> AND <u>INSIDE</u> THE LEFT SIDE. THAT'S ANOTHER IMPACT "MUST."

JM

Flex Your Knees _Slightly_

A <u>SLIGHT</u> FLEX IN BOTH KNEES IS CRITICAL TO GOOD LEG ACTION, SO BUILD IT INTO YOUR ADDRESS POSTURE.

BUT DON'T OVER-BEND YOUR KNEES, BECAUSE THAT LEADS TO SLOPPY LEG ACTION ON THE THROUGH-SWING.

SEEK THE FEELING OF <u>FIRM RESILIENCE</u> WITH JUST A LITTLE "GIVE" AT THE KNEES.

Let Your Arms Hang Freely

RIGIDITY OR EXCESS MUSCULAR STRESS IN ANY PART OF THE BODY AT ADDRESS IS A SURE SWING INHIBITOR, BUT PARTICULARLY IN THE ARMS.

THEY MUST BE "LOOSE" ENOUGH TO BE ABLE TO SWING FREELY IN RESPONSE TO YOUR SHOULDER, HIP AND LEG ACTION.

TO ENSURE THAT THEY ARE, LET THEM HANG FREELY FROM YOUR SHOULDERS IN A RELAXED AND NATURAL POSITION AS YOU SET UP TO THE BALL. AVOID ANY POSTURE THAT CREATES A FEELING OF TENSION, PARTICULARLY IN YOUR FOREARMS. IF THIS MEANS EASING YOUR GRIP PRESSURE A LITTLE, DO SO — IT WILL NATURALLY FIRM UP AS THE SWING PROCEEDS.

Be as Natural as You Can

WHERE SHOULD YOUR ELBOWS POINT AT ADDRESS?

THERE HAVE BEEN ALL SORTS OF THEORIES OVER THE YEARS — — SOME OF THEM REQUIRING CONTORTIONISTS SKILLS.

MY RECOMMENDATION IS THAT YOU TRY TO PLAY GOLF AS NATURALLY AS POSSIBLE, WHICH MEANS IN THIS RESPECT NOT CONSCIOUSLY TWISTING OR TURNING YOUR ELBOWS IN ANY PARTICULAR DIRECTION. UNFORCED IN ANY DIRECTION, THEY'LL PROBABLY BE IN THE SAME ALIGNMENT AT ADDRESS AS WHEN YOUR ARMS HANG NATURALLY AT YOUR SIDES, WHICH IS JUST FINE.

Strike a Balance in Stance Width

THE WIDTH OF YOUR STANCE HAS QUITE AN INFLUENCE ON THE QUALITY OF YOUR SWING.

IF IT'S TOO **WIDE**, TURNING FREELY AND FULLY BECOMES DIFFICULT.

IF IT'S TOO **NARROW**, YOU'LL LACK STABILITY AND BALANCE.

WEDGE

DRIVER

SETTING THE INSIDES OF THE HEELS APART ABOUT THE WIDTH OF THE SHOULDERS SEEMS TO BE THE IDEAL FOR MOST TOUR PLAYERS ON FULL SHOTS.

MOSTLY THEY THEN NARROW THE STANCE GRADUALLY AS THE CLUBS SHORTEN — IN MY CASE TO ABOUT SIX INCHES FOR A SHORT WEDGE SHOT.

Distribute Your Weight Evenly

SOME MODERN INSTRUCTORS SUGGEST SETTING MOST OF THE WEIGHT ON THE REAR FOOT AT ADDRESS, TO PRE-ESTABLISH THE WEIGHT TRANSFER AND ENSURE GOOD LEG ACTION INTO THE DOWNSWING.

I PREFER TO ACHIEVE THAT EFFECT BY DIVIDING MY WEIGHT EVENLY AT ADDRESS, THEN BY BRACING MYSELF BY **PUSHING** SLIGHTLY TOWARDS THE TARGET FROM THE <u>INSIDE</u> OF MY RIGHT FOOT.

THIS WAY THERE'S LESS CHANCE OF SWAYING THE UPPER BODY THAN WHEN MOST OF THE WEIGHT IS CONSCIOUSLY SET ON THE BACK FOOT.

JM

Angle Feet to Suit Swing Style

IF YOU'RE SUPPLE ENOUGH TO EASILY MAKE A FULL BACKSWING TURN, SETTING YOUR RIGHT FOOT AT 90 DEGREES TO THE TARGET GUARDS AGAINST OVERSWINGING. CONVERSELY, POINTING IT AWAY FROM THE TARGET MAKES IT EASIER TO TURN.

HIPS

SHOULDERS

ANGLING THE LEFT FOOT TOWARDS THE TARGET — AS I DO — ENCOURAGES FAST DOWNSWING HIP CLEARANCE.

BUT DON'T OVERDO THIS IF YOU HAVE A TENDENCY TO "SPIN OUT" WITH YOUR HIPS OR "COME OVER" THE BALL WITH YOUR SHOULDERS.

Distance Yourself from Ball like This

TO FIND YOUR PROPER DISTANCE FROM THE BALL WITH ANY CLUB, STAND UPRIGHT BUT RELAXED, THEN <u>FLEX</u> YOUR KNEES SLIGHTLY AND <u>SLUMP</u> YOUR SHOULDERS DOWNWARD.

NOW BEND FROM THE <u>WAIST</u> UNTIL YOU CAN SET THE CLUB COMFORTABLY BEHIND THE BALL WITH YOUR ARMS HANGING ALMOST <u>STRAIGHT DOWN</u>.

YOUR LEFT ARM AND THE CLUB SHOULD <u>DIP</u> <u>SLIGHTLY</u> BENEATH AN IMAGINARY LINE RUNNING FROM YOUR LEFT SHOULDER TO THE BALL.

Position Ball at Bottom of Swing Arc

I PLAY ALL <u>NORMAL</u> SHOTS WITH THE BALL OPPOSITE MY LEFT HEEL. WHY?

BECAUSE, IN MY SWING, THAT'S WHERE THE CLUBHEAD IS MOMENTARILY TRAVELING <u>DIRECTLY ALONG</u> THE TARGET LINE.

IF I HAD THE BALL <u>BACK</u>, THE CLUBHEAD WOULD STILL BE COMING FROM <u>INSIDE</u>, AND I'D PUSH OR HOOK DEPENDING ON CLUBFACE ALIGNMENT.

IF I HAD THE BALL <u>FORWARD</u>, THE CLUBHEAD WOULD BE COMING FROM <u>OUTSIDE</u>, AND I'D PULL OR SLICE THE BALL.

EXPERIMENT TO FIND <u>YOUR</u> IDEAL BALL POSITION.

Center Clubface Behind Ball

CHECK PERIODICALLY THAT YOU ARE CENTERING THE CLUBFACE AGAINST THE BALL AT ADDRESS. MANY GOLFERS FAIL TO DO SO, WHICH CREATES EITHER TOE OR HEEL CONTACT OR NEEDLESS COMPENSATIONS AT SOME POINT IN THE SWING.

IF YOU FAIL TO MEET THE BALL SQUARELY AFTER HAVING ADDRESSED IT CORRECTLY, THERE IS A FLAW IN EITHER YOUR SET-UP OR YOUR SWING.

MOST OFTEN YOU'LL FIND THAT YOU'RE STANDING EITHER TOO FAR FROM OR TOO CLOSE TO THE BALL.

8

Starting Back

Stay in Motion to Avoid "Freezing"

STARTING BACK 1

A LOT OF JERKY SWINGS, AND VISITS TO THE WOODS, ARE THE RESULT OF "FREEZING" OVER THE BALL AT ADDRESS.

ALL GOOD GOLFERS STAY IN MOTION IN SOME PART OF THE BODY AS THEY GET READY TO SWING.

JM

MOST POPULAR TENSION-PREVENTER IS THE WAGGLE, BUT I ALSO LIKE TO KEEP MY LEGS LOOSE BY SHIFTING MY WEIGHT SLIGHTLY FROM FOOT TO FOOT AS I GET SET TO SWING.

Find Yourself a Swing "Trigger"

STARTING BACK 2

EVERY GOLFER NEEDS AN EFFECTIVE SWING "TRIGGER," AND THERE ARE PLENTY TO CHOOSE FROM. FOR EXAMPLE, **GARY PLAYER** "KICKS IN" HIS RIGHT KNEE —

— WHEREAS **JULIUS BOROS** GETS GOING OFF THE FINAL SHUFFLING OF HIS FEET INTO POSITION.

MOST POPULAR "TRIGGER" ON THE TOUR — AND THE ONE I FAVOR — IS THE FORWARD PRESS: A SLIGHT INCLINATION OF THE HANDS TOWARDS THE TARGET, FROM WHICH YOU "REBOUND" INTO THE TAKEAWAY.

STARTING
BACK
3

YOU CAN'T START A GOLF CLUB BACK TOO SLOWLY, PROVIDED YOU SWING RATHER THAN TAKE OR LIFT IT AWAY FROM THE BALL.

I TRY ON EVERY SHOT TO SWING INTO MOTION VERY DELIBERATELY — JUST FAST ENOUGH TO AVOID JERKINESS.

OBVIOUSLY THE MOTION SPEEDS UP AS THE BACKSWING PROGRESSES.

BUT THE SLOWER YOU CAN KEEP THOSE FIRST TWO OR THREE FEET, THE BETTER YOU'LL PLAY — ESPECIALLY WHEN YOU WANT DISTANCE.

Let Club Path Follow Body Turn

Start Back in "One Piece"

STARTING BACK 5

I FAVOR A "ONE-PIECE" TAKEAWAY, WHICH MEANS KEEPING ALL MOVING PARTS OF THE BODY IN STEP WITH EACH OTHER DURING THE INITIAL BACKSWING MOTION.

A ONE-PIECE START-BACK SETS UP A WIDE SWING ARC, FORCES THE BODY TO TURN, PREVENTS "PICKING UP" THE CLUB WITH THE HANDS AND ARMS ONLY, AND PROMOTES A SMOOTH AND WELL-PACED OVERALL SWING TEMPO.

Watch Out for Those Wrists!

STARTING
BACK
6

OVER-
ACTIVE
HANDS
AND
WRISTS
AT THE
START
OF THE
SWING ARE
RESPONSIBLE
FOR A LOT OF
GOLF'S FOUL BALLS.

MY LEFT ARM AND CLUB
SHAFT RETAIN THE STRAIGHT-
LINE RELATIONSHIP THEY
FORM AT ADDRESS
UNTIL MY HANDS
REACH ABOUT
HIP HEIGHT.

THEN THE WEIGHT
OF THE RISING
CLUBHEAD
NATURALLY BEGINS
TO COCK THE
WRISTS WITHOUT
ANY CONSCIOUS
EFFORT ON
MY PART.

Feel Left Shoulder Pushing Club Back

STARTING BACK 7

JACK, WHAT'S YOUR MAIN <u>FEELING</u> DURING THE EARLY PART OF THE BACKSWING?

THAT THE LEFT ARM AND CLUB ARE BEING **PUSHED** BACK BY MY LEFT SHOULDER AS IT BEGINS TO TURN <u>DOWN</u> AND AROUND UNDER MY CHIN.

A HELPFUL FEELING IS THAT YOUR LEFT ARM'S SWINGING MOTION NEVER GETS AHEAD OF YOUR LEFT SHOULDER'S <u>PUSHING</u> MOTION EARLY IN THE BACKSWING. THIS WILL ENCOURAGE YOU TO <u>TURN FULLY</u>, RATHER THAN JUST LIFTING THE CLUB WITH YOUR ARMS.

Don't Manipulate the Clubface

STARTING BACK 8

A SURE WAY TO GET ALL PRETZELED UP AT GOLF IS TO TRY TO FORCE THE CLUBFACE TO STAY "SQUARE" TO THE TARGET TOO LONG INTO THE BACK- SWING.

AS THE SHOULDERS TURN, THE CLUB- FACE WILL APPEAR TO "OPEN" — LOOK INCREASINGLY RIGHT OF TARGET. BUT WHEN YOU GO BACK IN "ONE PIECE," WITHOUT INDEPENDENT HAND/ARM MANIPULATION, IT WILL STILL BE CORRECTLY SQUARE TO THE ARC THE CLUB IS DESCRIBING.

To the
Top

Know Your Options

BACKSWING 1

THE MORE UPRIGHT THE SWING, THE LESS THE CLUB MOVES AWAY FROM THE TARGET LINE.

JM

THE LESS THE CLUBHEAD MOVES AWAY FROM THE TARGET LINE, THE BETTER ITS CHANCE OF SWINGING **ALONG** THAT LINE AT IMPACT.

THAT'S WHY I'VE ALWAYS FAVORED A FAIRLY UPRIGHT SWING PLANE.

FLAT

UPRIGHT

Coil Shoulders, Swing Hands High

BACKSWING 2

DANGER OF BECOMING <u>TOO</u> UPRIGHT IS THAT THE CLUB WON'T STAY AT GROUND LEVEL LONG ENOUGH THROUGH IMPACT TO MEET THE BALL SOLIDLY.

JM

WAY TO AVOID THAT IS TO COMBINE A **FULL COILING** OF YOUR UPPER BODY WITH THE UPWARD SWINGING OF YOUR ARMS.

ATTEMPTING TO SWING UPRIGHT WITHOUT FULLY TURNING AND TILTING THE SHOULDERS RESULTS IN <u>LIFTING</u> THE CLUB TO THE TOP -- AND A WEAK CHOPPING ACTION AT IMPACT.

Extend Arms but Stay "Centered"

BACK-SWING 3

FIRST ESSENTIAL FOR A WIDE ARC IS <u>MAXIMUM EXTENSION</u> OF YOUR ARMS **AWAY** FROM YOU AS THEY SWING BACK AND UP, <u>WITHOUT SWAYING YOUR BODY</u>.

A <u>WIDE</u> SWING ARC IS ESSENTIAL TO GENERATE MAXIMUM CLUBHEAD SPEED THROUGH MAXIMUM LEVERAGE.

SECOND ESSENTIAL IS THE FULLEST POSSIBLE <u>COILING</u> OF YOUR UPPER BODY, CONSISTENT WITH KEEPING THE TOP OF YOUR SPINE "CENTERED" AND YOUR RIGHT KNEE SLIGHTLY FLEXED.

Play from the Insides of Your Feet

BACKSWING 4

MANY GOLFERS' POOR SWINGS ORIGINATE IN WEAK FOOT AND ANKLE ACTION.

BASICALLY, THE MORE YOU CAN SWING FROM THE <u>INSIDES</u> OF YOUR FEET, AND THE MORE OF YOUR FEET YOU CAN KEEP ON THE GROUND, THE BETTER YOU'LL PLAY.

THE FARTHER I GO BACK, THE MORE MY WEIGHT MOVES TO THE <u>INSIDE</u> OF MY RIGHT FOOT, AND THE MORE THE REMAINING WEIGHT ON THE LEFT FOOT <u>ROLLS</u> TO THE <u>INSIDE</u> THROUGH A **HINGING** OF THE ANKLE.

MY LEFT HEEL COMES SLIGHTLY OFF THE GROUND AT THE TOP ONLY ON FULL WOOD AND LONG-IRON SHOTS.

JM

Anchor Swing with Flexed Right Knee

BACKSWING 5

YOUR RIGHT KNEE IS YOUR BACKSWING "ANCHOR".

KEEPING IT _FLEXED_ AND _RESILIENT_ IS THE KEY TO A STRONG WIND-UP AND PROPER DOWNSWING INITIATION.

AS YOU SWING BACK, YOUR RIGHT KNEE CAN MOVE REARWARD A LITTLE IF IT HAS TO, IN RESPONSE TO YOUR SHOULDER AND HIP TURN.

BUT _NEVER_ LET IT STRAIGHTEN OR MOVE LATERALLY AWAY FROM THE TARGET.

Let Left Knee Move Behind Ball

BACKSWING 6

TURNING FULLY IN THE SHOULDERS AND HIPS REQUIRES THAT YOUR LEFT KNEE FLEX <u>INWARD</u>, TOWARDS THE BALL, AS THE BACKSWING PROGRESSES.

BEWARE SIMPLY BENDING THE LEFT KNEE <u>FORWARD</u> BY LIFTING YOUR LEFT HEEL HIGH OFF THE GROUND.

PROPER LEG WORK CALLS FOR THE KNEE TO BE <u>PULLED</u> TOWARDS THE BALL BY THE FORCE OF YOUR BODY WIND-UP.

Beware Too Much Heel Lift

LIFTING THE LEFT HEEL HIGH OFF THE GROUND IS A DANGEROUS MOVE, FOR TWO REASONS.

FIRST, THE RAISING ACTION MAY CAUSE AN INVOLUNTARY LIFTING OF THE ENTIRE BODY, WHICH WILL OBVIOUSLY DISTORT YOUR SWING ARC.

SECOND, THE HIGHER YOUR LEFT HEEL RISES, THE MORE DIFFICULT IT IS TO GET IT FIRMLY BACK TO EARTH AS THE INITIATING MOVE OF THE DOWNSWING — A FREQUENT CAUSE OF "THROWING" THE CLUB WITH THE HANDS AND SHOULDERS.

BACKSWING 8

THERE'S A SCHOOL OF THOUGHT THAT SAYS THE HIPS SHOULD TURN VERY SLIGHTLY, IF AT ALL, ON THE BACKSWING.

I DON'T SUBSCRIBE TO IT, BECAUSE IF I DON'T LET MY HIPS TURN I CAN'T TURN MY SHOULDERS -- AND IF I DON'T TURN MY SHOULDERS I CAN'T GENERATE LEVERAGE.

THUS, GOING BACK, I ALLOW MY HIPS TO TURN AS FAR AROUND AS THEY'LL GO WITHOUT FORCING MY RIGHT LEG TO STRAIGHTEN OR COLLAPSE, OR MY WEIGHT TO MOVE TO THE OUTSIDE OF MY RIGHT FOOT.

YOU SHOULD, TOO.

BACKSWING 9

MODERN GOLFERS
ALLOW THEIR
HIPS TO TURN
GOING BACK
IN <u>RESPONSE</u>
TO THE <u>PULL</u> OF
THE SHOULDER
TURN, NOT AS
A CONSCIOUS OR
INDEPENDENT ACT.

IN MY CASE, THE HIPS
ONLY BEGIN TO BE
TURNED BY THE SHOULDER
WIND-UP AFTER THE
CLUB REACHES
ABOUT HIP-HIGH.

BE SURE TO
MAKE THE HIPS
<u>FOLLOWERS</u>,
NOT LEADERS,
IN YOUR
WIND-UP.

JM

Make Your Spine Your Swing "Hub"

BACKSWING 10

TO BE SURE YOU **TURN** YOUR BODY GOING BACK, RATHER THAN SWAY IT, THINK OF YOUR **SPINE** AS YOUR SWING "HUB".

MAKE THE **TOP** OF THE SPINE (THE NECK AREA) THE "AXIS" AROUND WHICH YOU TURN YOUR SHOULDERS, AND TURN YOUR HIPS AROUND YOUR LOWER SPINE.

"CENTERING" YOUR SWING THUS WILL IMPROVE YOUR WIND-UP, AS WELL AS ELIMINATING ANY TENDENCY TO SWAY.

JM

Coil Your Shoulders as Fully as You Can

BACKSWING 11

FLAILING <u>AT</u> THE BALL WITH THE HANDS AND ARMS, INSTEAD OF **LEVERING** THE CLUB <u>THROUGH</u> IT VIA A FULL UPPER-BODY TURN, IS ONE OF GOLF'S COMMONEST FAULTS.

JM

CURE IS TO TURN YOUR SHOULDERS <u>AS FAR AROUND</u> AS THEY'LL GO SHORT OF FORCING YOUR RIGHT KNEE TO STIFFEN, YOUR WEIGHT TO MOVE TO THE OUTSIDE OF YOUR RIGHT FOOT, OR YOUR LEFT HEEL TO RISE MORE THAN ABOUT AN INCH OFF THE GROUND.

Practice These 3 "Feels"

HERE ARE THREE PRACTICE-TEE THOUGHTS TO HELP YOU MAXIMIZE YOUR UPPER-BODY TURN.

FOR THE FIRST THIRD OF THE BACKSWING, DEVELOP THE FEELING THAT YOUR SHOULDERS ARE **PUSHING** YOUR ARMS BACK AND UP.

AS THE CLUB GETS HIP-HIGH, AND FOR THE NEXT THIRD OF THE BACKSWING, SWITCH TO A FEELING OF YOUR UP-SWINGING ARMS **PULLING** YOUR SHOULDERS AROUND.

DURING THE FINAL PART OF THE BACKSWING, CONCEN-TRATE ON THRUSTING YOUR HANDS AS HIGH AS THEY'LL GO BEHIND YOUR HEAD — REALLY "REACH FOR THE CLOUDS."

Keep Left Arm Straight but Not Stiff

BACKSWING 13

GOLFERS OF OLD PLAYED WELL WITH BENT LEFT ARMS, BUT YOU DON'T SEE MANY ON TOUR TODAY.

REASON IS THE DIFFICULTY OF CONSISTENTLY REPRODUCING THE PROPER SWING PATH THROUGH IMPACT WHEN THE ARC-CONTROLLING ARM BENDS GOING BACK AND THEN STRAIGHTENS COMING DOWN.

A STRAIGHT-BUT-NOT-STIFF LEFT ARM IS MOST TOUR PROS' GOAL, INCLUDING ME.

KEY TO ATTAINING IT IS A FIRM LEFT-HAND GRIP, AND A ONE-PIECE MOVEMENT AWAY FROM THE BALL FROM THE LEFT SHOULDER TO THE CLUBHEAD.

Never Loosen Your Grip

BACKSWING 14

LOOSENING THE GRIP AT THE TOP OF THE BACKSWING IS A SURE ROUTE TO DISASTER.

MANY GOLFERS DO IT INVOLUNTARILY IN TRYING TO SWING LONGER WITHOUT MAKING A FULLER BODY TURN.

CHECK THIS POINT IF YOU ARE SPRAYING SHOTS.

CURE LIES IN ESTABLISHING A SECURE GRIP AT ADDRESS, AND SUSTAINING IT BY USING THE BODY TURN AS WELL AS THE HAND-AND-ARM SWING TO GET THE CLUB FULLY BACK.

BACKSWING 15

KEEPING THE BACK OF YOUR LEFT HAND IN LINE WITH YOUR FOREARM THROUGHOUT THE BACKSWING HAS THREE BENEFITS.

1) IT PREVENTS INDEPENDENT MANIPULATION OF THE CLUBFACE BY THE HANDS AND WRISTS DURING THE TAKEAWAY.

2) IT KEEPS THE WRISTS FIRM, AND ENSURES THAT THEY COCK AT THE CORRECT ANGLE IN RESPONSE TO THE SWINGING WEIGHT OF THE CLUBHEAD.

3) IT KEEPS THE CLUBFACE CORRECTLY SQUARE TO THE ARC THE CLUB IS DESCRIBING THROUGHOUT THE SWING.

JM

Don't Rush from the Top

BACKSWING 16

SHOULD YOU "PAUSE" AT THE TOP? A FEW FINE GOLFERS HAVE — NOTABLY TWO-TIME U.S. OPEN CHAMPION **CARY MIDDLECOFF.**

I HAVE NO DISCERNIBLE PAUSE, BECAUSE MY LOWER BODY ACTUALLY BEGINS THE DOWNSWING JUST AS MY UPPER BODY IS COMPLETING THE BACKSWING.

HOWEVER, I DO HAVE A SENSE OF "WAITING" AT THE TOP IN MY HANDS, ARMS AND SHOULDERS UNTIL MY FEET, LEGS AND HIPS HAVE STARTED THE UNWINDING MOTION.

IT'S A FEELING YOU SHOULD CULTIVATE, TOO.

Swing as "Long" as You Can

BACK-SWING 17

HOW FAR SHOULD I SWING BACK, JACK?

AS FAR AS YOU CAN WITHOUT STIFFENING YOUR RIGHT KNEE, FORCING YOUR WEIGHT TO THE OUTSIDE OF YOUR RIGHT FOOT, LIFTING YOUR LEFT HEEL HIGH, BENDING YOUR LEFT ARM, OR LOOSENING YOUR GRIP.

WITHIN THOSE CONDITIONS, THE LONGER YOUR SWING THE BETTER YOU'LL PLAY -- AND THE LONGER YOU'LL GO ON PLAYING WELL.

YOU DON'T SEE MANY SENIOR CHAMPIONS WITH SHORT SWINGS — AS WITNESS **SAM SNEAD.**

10

Down and Through

Look for Downswing Fault
in Backswing

THROUGH - SWING 1

BECAUSE IT HAPPENS TOO FAST TO BE CONSCIOUSLY DIRECTED, THE DOWNSWING MUST BE LARGELY A <u>REFLEXIVE</u> ACTION.

SO, IF YOU'RE FAULTY COMING DOWN, THE FIRST PLACE TO LOOK FOR THE PROBLEM IS IN HOW YOU GO BACK.

BUILD A GOOD BACKSWING AND YOU'LL AUTOMATICALLY DEVELOP A GOOD THROUGH - SWING PATTERN.

Reverse "Halves" Coming Down

THROUGH-SWING 2

HERE'S THE BASIC FACTOR TO ALWAYS REMEMBER ABOUT GOLF'S BACKWARD AND FORWARD MOTIONS.

GOING BACK, YOUR LOWER BODY WORKS IN RESPONSE TO THE COILING OF YOUR UPPER BODY. EXACTLY THE REVERSE MUST HAPPEN COMING DOWN — YOUR UPPER BODY MUST RESPOND ONLY TO THE UNCOILING OF YOUR LOWER BODY.

THAT'S FUNDAMENTAL WHATEVER YOUR PERSONAL SWING STYLE.

JM

Maximize Your Leverage

THROUGH-SWING 3

VERY FEW GOLFERS (GOOD ONES) ACTUALLY PAUSE — HALT ALL MOTION — AT THE TOP OF THE BACKSWING.

WHAT HAPPENS IS THAT THE LOWER BODY STARTS THE DOWNSWING JUST BEFORE THE UPPER BODY COMPLETES THE BACKSWING.

THAT WAY YOU ACHIEVE BOTH MAXIMUM LEVERAGE AND A SMOOTH TRANSITION FROM BACKWARD TO FORWARD MOTION.

JM

Swing Down from Feet Up

THROUGH - SWING 4

MOST GOLFERS WOULD IMPROVE IMMENSELY BY LEARNING TO START DOWN WITH THEIR FEET RATHER THAN THEIR HANDS.

GET THE FEELING OF YOUR LEFT HEEL REPLANTING SOLIDLY AS YOU PUSH HARD OFF THE INSIDE OF YOUR RIGHT FOOT.

DO THAT BEFORE ANYTHING UP TOP UNWINDS AND YOU'RE 90 PER CENT OF THE WAY TO PROPER LOWER-BODY ACTION.

Never Hurry Your Shoulders

THROUGH - SWING 5

HERE'S A TIP TO HELP YOU INITIATE THE DOWNSWING MOTION WITH YOUR FEET AND LEGS RATHER THAN YOUR UPPER BODY.

JM

SLOW

AS YOU START BACK TO THE BALL, TRY TO KEEP THE UPWARD MOVEMENT OF YOUR LEFT SHOULDER AS <u>SLOW</u> AS POSSIBLE.

THE SLOWER THIS HAPPENS, THE MORE TIME YOUR LEGS HAVE TO MOVE TARGETWARDS BEFORE YOUR SHOULDERS UNWIND.

Flex—and Use—Those Knees

CORRECT FOOT ACTION STARTING DOWN PULLS BOTH KNEES <u>LATERALLY</u> TOWARDS THE TARGET.

THROUGH SWING 6

IN MY CASE, THE LEFT KNEE MOVES WELL FORWARD OF THE BALL BEFORE MY HANDS HAVE DESCENDED MORE THAN A FEW INCHES.

KEY TO ACHIEVING AND SUSTAINING THIS STRONG LEG ACTION IS TO KEEP <u>BOTH</u> KNEES FLEXED THROUGH IMPACT.

STIFFENING THE LEFT LEG TOO FAST IS A FREQUENT CAUSE OF SPINNING THE SHOULDERS OVER THE BALL.

S-t-r-e-t-c-h That Left Side

THROUGH - SWING 7

MANY GOLFERS HAVE A PROBLEM COMBINING A FLEXED LEFT KNEE THROUGH IMPACT WITH A FIRM LEFT SIDE.

FEELING TO STRIVE FOR IS ONE OF STRETCHING FROM YOUR LEFT FOOT TO YOUR LEFT SHOULDER WITHOUT STRAIGHTENING YOUR LEFT LEG — OR RAISING YOUR HEAD — UNTIL THE BALL HAS BEEN STRUCK.

THE BETTER SHAPE YOUR LEGS ARE IN, THE EASIER THIS BECOMES.

Don't Think About Wrist Action

Keep Legs Moving Ahead of Arms

THROUGH – SWING 9

MANY TEACHERS FAVOR STARTING THE THROUGH - SWING WITH A DOWNWARD PULLING OF THE LEFT ARM — A "TOLLING THE BELL" ACTION.

THAT'S FINE SO LONG AS YOUR LEGS WORK IN HARNESS WITH YOUR ARM SWING.

IF YOUR LEGS DON'T MOVE JUST A LITTLE AHEAD OF YOUR ARMS, CHANCES ARE YOUR ARMS WILL PULL YOUR SHOULDERS FORWARD 'OVER' THE BALL.

JM

Avoid These 3 Errors

THROUGH SWING 10

RAISING THE BODY UP AS THE CLUB SWINGS DOWN CAUSES MANY HORROR SHOTS. IT COMES MAINLY FROM THE FOLLOWING:

1. CROUCHING OVER THE BALL AT ADDRESS, USUALLY WITH STIFF LEGS.

2. THROWING THE CLUB FROM THE TOP WITH THE HANDS AND WRISTS.

3. FAILING TO START DOWN WITH THE FEET AND KNEES, WHICH KEEPS THE WEIGHT ON THE RIGHT SIDE AND STIFFENS THE LEGS.

Let Hips Follow Knees...

THROUGH-SWING 11

ONCE YOUR KNEES HAVE MOVED TARGETWARDS COMING DOWN, YOUR HIPS MUST TURN TOWARDS THE TARGET TO CLEAR A PATH FOR YOUR ARMS TO SWING PAST YOUR BODY.

KEY HERE IS NEVER TO LET YOUR HIPS TURN AHEAD OF YOUR TARGETWARDS KNEE MOTION.

LETTING YOUR HIPS UNCOIL AHEAD OF YOUR LEG ACTION — "SPINNING OUT," THE PROS CALL IT — IS A SURE WAY TO SWING "OVER" THE BALL.

JM

... but Keep Lower-Body Action <u>Smooth</u>

THROUGH SWING 12

IN TRYING TO IMPROVE YOUR LOWER-BODY ACTION, BE CAREFUL NOT TO OVER-DO YOUR LEG/HIP MOTION TO THE POINT WHERE YOU LURCH YOUR ENTIRE BODY FORWARD.

JM

KEY IS TO THRUST YOUR KNEES <u>SMOOTHLY</u> TOWARDS THE TARGET, AND YOUR HIPS GRADUALLY AROUND TO FACE IT, WHILE KEEPING YOUR HEAD WELL <u>BEHIND</u> THE BALL.

Prefer "Left-Side" Thoughts

THROUGH - SWING 13

I BASICALLY CONTROL THE SWING WITH MY <u>LEFT SIDE</u>, BUT IF THINGS AREN'T GOING WELL I'LL TRY EMPHASIZING RIGHT-SIDE ACTION.

FOR EXAMPLE, MY PREFERRED THOUGHT COMING DOWN IS "MOVE THE LEFT SHOULDER UP AND THE LEFT HIP AROUND."

BUT IF THAT DOESN'T SEEM TO BE WORKING, I'LL TRY "MOVE THE <u>RIGHT</u> SHOULDER <u>DOWN</u> AND THE RIGHT HIP AROUND."

BALANCING OUT SWING "FEELS" THUS MIGHT HELP YOU PLAY BETTER.

JM

Work Lower Body—Then Release!

THROUGH - SWING 14

JOE, YOU'RE LETTING ALL THAT STUFF ABOUT HITTING "LATE" WITH THE HANDS AND WRISTS PREVENT YOU FROM RELEASING THE CLUBHEAD THROUGH THE BALL!

AS LONG AS YOU START DOWN WITH YOUR LOWER BODY AND KEEP IT MOVING AHEAD OF YOUR UPPER HALF, YOU CAN'T HIT TOO "EARLY" WITH YOUR HANDS AND WRISTS.

SO GET THOSE LEGS GOING, AND THEN LET THAT CLUBHEAD **FLY**!

Meld Hip and Hand/Wrist Action

THROUGH - SWING 15

IF YOUR BASIC SWING PATTERN IS SOUND BUT YOU START TO SLICE SHOTS, CHANCES ARE YOUR HIP ACTION IS GETTING AHEAD OF YOUR HAND/WRIST ACTION.

EITHER SLOWING DOWN YOUR HIP UNWIND OR SPEEDING UP YOUR CLUBHEAD RELEASE SHOULD STRAIGHTEN YOU OUT.

IF THE PROBLEM'S A HOOK, CHANCES ARE THAT YOUR HANDS/WRISTS ARE RELEASING THE CLUB BEFORE YOU'VE ACHIEVED SUFFICIENT HIP CLEARANCE.

ANSWER HERE IS TO EITHER SPEED UP YOUR HIP ACTION OR HOLD BACK A LITTLE ON YOUR CLUBHEAD RELEASE.

Check for This Sign of "Spinning"

THROUGH - SWING 16

RISING UP ON THE RIGHT TOE WELL BEFORE IMPACT IS A SURE SIGN OF SPINNING THE UPPER BODY "OVER AND AROUND" INSTEAD OF SWINGING "UNDER AND THROUGH."

ONE WAY TO CURE THIS UGLY MOVE IS TO PRACTICE HITTING SHOTS WHILE KEEPING THE RIGHT HEEL ANCHORED AND THE RIGHT KNEE FACING THE BALL.

IT'LL BE A WHOLE NEW FEEL, SO START WITH THE SHORT IRONS AND WORK UP.

Let Right Arm Straighten

THROUGH SWING 17

IN MOST GOOD GOLF SWINGS THE RIGHT ELBOW STAYS SLIGHTLY BENT, AND POINTING TOWARDS THE RIGHT SIDE, RIGHT UP UNTIL IMPACT.

ONCE THE BALL IS STRUCK, HOWEVER, A QUICKLY STRAIGHTENING AND EXTENDING RIGHT ARM IS A SIGN OF FULL CLUBHEAD RELEASE. FEELING I LIKE AT THAT POINT IS OF ALMOST BEING ABLE TO REACH OUT AND RETRIEVE THE FLYING BALL WITH MY RIGHT HAND.

Chase Ball with Clubface

THROUGH SWING 18

GREATER ARM EXTENSION THROUGH THE BALL WOULD HELP MANY GOLFERS WITH DIRECTIONAL PROBLEMS.

JM

FEELING I OFTEN SEEK WHEN I NEED MAXIMUM ACCURACY IS THAT OF KEEPING THE CLUBFACE ON THE BALL AS LONG AS POSSIBLE AFTER IMPACT.

FIRM WRISTS AND STAYING WELL DOWN AND BACK ON THE SHOT ARE ESSENTIAL TO PROMOTE IT.

Think "Acceleration"

SCIENTISTS SAY IT'S IMPOSSIBLE TO ACTUALLY KEEP ON ACCELERATING THE CLUBHEAD THROUGH THE BALL — THAT IT ALWAYS REACHES MAXIMUM SPEED <u>BEFORE</u> IMPACT.

THROUGH - SWING 19

NEVERTHELESS, I THINK IT PAYS TO HAVE THE FEELING OF **TRYING** TO ACCELERATE THROUGH THE BALL AND BEYOND. DANGER IS THAT, IF YOU DO NOT <u>THINK</u> ACCELERATION, YOU'LL PROBABLY DECELERATE BEFORE IMPACT.

ACCELERATION!

Strive for a Fine Follow-through

THROUGH SWING 20

BIG DOWN-SWING FAULT OF HIGH HANDICAP GOLFERS IS HITTING <u>AT</u> THE BALL INSTEAD OF SWINGING THE CLUBHEAD FREELY <u>THROUGH</u> IT.

ONE WAY TO OVERCOME THIS IS TO PRACTICE WHILE IMAGINING THE BALL SIMPLY ISN'T THERE.

IF THAT DOESN'T WORK, FOCUSING MENTALLY ON ACHIEVING A SPECIFIC FOLLOW-THROUGH PATTERN OR "FEEL" WILL REDUCE YOUR BALL CONSCIOUSNESS.

11

Tempo, Rhythm and Timing

Understand What "Timing" Is

TIMING IS A WORD FOR THE WAY ALL YOUR SWING MOTIONS MELD TOGETHER.

WHEN THE MELD PRODUCES MAXIMUM SQUARENESS OF CLUBFACE AND CLUBHEAD SPEED AT IMPACT, YOUR TIMING IS PERFECT.

SLOW

SMOOTH

GOOD TIMING REQUIRES GOOD SWING FORM, SO WHEN YOUR TIMING GOES OFF LOOK BACK INTO THE FUNDAMENTALS OF YOUR ACTION — PARTICULARLY YOUR TAKEAWAY TEMPO AND TRANSITION FROM BACKSWING TO THROUGH-SWING.

Swing Rhythmically Within Natural Tempo

YOUR TEMPO, OR SPEED OF SWING, IS LARGELY DETERMINED BY YOUR PERSONALITY.

DELIBERATE PEOPLE NATURALLY TEND TO SWING SLOWLY, HYPERACTIVE PEOPLE QUICKLY.

RATHER THAN TAMPER WITH WHAT COMES NATURALLY, STRIVE TO SWING RHYTHMICALLY WHATEVER YOUR PACE.

RHYTHM IS THE QUALITY WITH WHICH YOU MELD ALL THE MOVING PARTS OF THE SWING, AND THE SMOOTHER IT IS THE BETTER YOUR TIMING WILL BE.

Use Bigger Muscles for Smoother Action

A SLOWER SWING ISN'T NECESSARILY GOING TO IMPROVE YOUR GAME, BUT A **SMOOTHER TEMPO** ALMOST ALWAYS WILL.

IT'S MY EXPERIENCE THAT THE BIGGER THE MUSCLES YOU USE TO PROPEL THE CLUB, THE MORE FLUIDLY AND SMOOTHLY YOU CAN SWING IT.

SO, IN WORKING ON YOUR TEMPO, BE WARY OF OVER-DOING THE HAND AND WRIST ACTION AT THE EXPENSE OF YOUR BACK AND LEGS.

USE A FULL UPPER BODY TURN TO GET THE CLUB BACK, AND A STRONG LEG DRIVE TO GET IT STARTED DOWN – AND ONLY **THEN** BRING THE HANDS AND WRISTS INTO MAXIMUM PLAY.

Work on Rhythm When Timing Is Off

BEWARE OF TRYING TO CHANGE YOUR OVERALL SPEED OF SWING, BECAUSE THIS ALMOST CERTAINLY IS A PRODUCT OF YOUR PERSONALITY, AND AS SUCH PRETTY DIFFICULT TO CHANGE EFFECTIVELY.

INSTEAD, WHEN YOU FEEL YOUR TIMING IS "OFF" CONCENTRATE ON THE **RHYTHM** OF YOUR ACTION RATHER THAN ITS OVERALL PACE.

WHETHER YOU NATURALLY SWING FAST OR SLOW, STRIVE FOR **SMOOTHNESS** OF MOTION FROM TAKEAWAY TO COMPLETION OF FOLLOW-THROUGH.

ALSO, THINKING OF SWINGING THE CLUBHEAD **THROUGH** THE BALL, NOT **AT IT**, IS OFTEN HELPFUL IN IMPROVING TIMING.

BEGINNERS AT GOLF OFTEN SEEM TO THINK THEY NEED A DIFFERENT SWING FOR EVERY CLUB IN THE BAG. THAT ISN'T TRUE — AND ESPECIALLY NOT IN TERMS OF TEMPO.

HIGH-SPEED FILMS OF ME HAVE SHOWN THAT, WHEN PLAYING WELL, MY SWING POSITIONS ARE THE SAME WHETHER SWINGING A ONE-IRON OR AN 8-IRON.... WHICH MEANS MY TEMPO IS PRETTY MUCH IDENTICAL.

THAT'S A GOAL I THINK EVERY GOLFER SHOULD STRIVE FOR.

Make Driver Swing Your Tempo Model

OBVIOUSLY THE SHORTER THE CLUB, THE SHORTER THE ELAPSED TIME OF THE SWING.

BUT YOU SHOULDN'T _FEEL_ THAT YOU SWING A WEDGE ANY FASTER THAN YOU SWING A DRIVER.

WHEN I'M PLAYING WELL, I FEEL THAT THE _PACE_ OF MY SWING IS EXACTLY THE SAME WITH EVERY CLUB IN THE BAG — EVEN THE PUTTER. AND THE IDEAL PACE IN MY CASE IS THE DRIVER SWING — THE SLOWEST.

JM

Try This to Smooth Out Takeaway

I'M ONE OF A SMALL NUMBER OF TOUR PLAYERS WHO NEVER GROUND THE CLUB AT ADDRESS.

THE TECHNIQUE BEGAN IN MY CASE AS A GUARD AGAINST ACCIDENTALLY MOVING THE BALL OR STUBBING THE CLUB STARTING BACK, BUT ITS BIGGEST VALUE HAS LONG BEEN ITS SMOOTHING EFFECT ON MY TAKEAWAY.

IT TAKES A WHILE TO GET USED TO STARTING BACK FROM AN UNGROUNDED POSITION, BUT IT'S A CERTAIN WAY TO SMOOTH OUT A JERKY TAKEAWAY, AND A BIG HELP IN BUILDING A ONE-PIECE BACKSWING.

BEGIN WITH THE SHORT IRONS AND WORK UP IF YOU DECIDE TO GIVE IT A TRY.

SMOOTH

Beware of a Dead Halt at Top

IS "PAUSE AT THE TOP" A GOOD THOUGHT?

NOT, IN MY VIEW, IF IT CAUSES YOU TO LITERALLY COME TO A DEAD STOP BEFORE YOU START DOWN AGAIN, BECAUSE THAT'S A SURE WAY TO WRECK YOUR TEMPO AND MOMENTUM — NOT TO MENTION YOUR BALANCE.

A BETTER THOUGHT TO ME WOULD BE "WAIT FOR THE LEGS TO WORK BEFORE THE HANDS START DOWN." OR "CHANGE DIRECTIONS SMOOTHLY." OR — MY FAVORITE — "START DOWN AT THE SAME SPEED YOU STARTED BACK."

IN OTHER WORDS, ANYTHING THAT PROMOTES GOOD TIMING — WHICH A DEAD HALT DOESN'T, IN MY VIEW.

Sense Swinging Weight of Clubhead

CONSCIOUSLY FEELING THE WEIGHT OF THE CLUBHEAD AGAINST THE TENSION OF THE SHAFT HELPS ME TO SWING RHYTHMICALLY.

AS THE BACKSWING DEVELOPS, I LIKE TO FEEL THE CLUBHEAD'S WEIGHT <u>PULLING</u> MY HANDS AND ARMS BACK AND UP.

STARTING DOWN, I LIKE TO FEEL THE CLUBHEAD WEIGHT LAGGING BACK — RESISTING — AS MY LOWER-BODY ACTION PULLS MY ARMS DOWN.

WHEN I CAN WAIT FOR THESE "FEELS," I'M USUALLY GIVING MYSELF TIME TO MOVE EVERYTHING IN PROPER SEQUENCE. AND THUS MY TEMPO IS EXCELLENT.

12

Power!

Never Hit for Distance Only

IS DISTANCE AS BIG A GOLFING ASSET AS MOST PLAYERS SEEM TO THINK IT IS ??

ONLY IF YOU CAN HIT LONG **AND STRAIGHT** — AND ONLY THEN IF YOU USE LENGTH INTELLIGENTLY.

FOR EXAMPLE, YOUR PRINCIPAL GOAL ON A DRIVE IS TO PLACE THE BALL IN THE EASIEST POSSIBLE POSITION FOR THE NEXT SHOT. NEARNESS TO THE HOLE ISN'T THE BEST POSITION IF THE BALL ENDS UP IN A LAKE OR A FOREST — OR EVEN ON A SHARP DOWNHILL LIE. SO DRIVE FOR THE BEST APPROACH ANGLES COMBINED WITH THE MOST LEVEL LIES — **NOT** FOR SHEER YARDAGE ALONE.

Beware the "Steering" Tendency

AS A KID I WAS TAUGHT BY JACK GROUT TO HIT HARD FIRST AND DEVELOP ACCURACY LATER.

MANY GOLFERS LACK DISTANCE BECAUSE THEY'VE HABITUALIZED "BABYING" OR "STEERING" THE BALL STRAIGHT.

INCREASED BODY TURN AND ARM EXTENSION WILL LET YOU TAKE A BIGGER CUT AT IT.

BUT TRY FIRST ON A DRIVING RANGE. AND KEEP YOUR HEAD STILL AND YOUR TEMPO **SMOOTH**.

THERE'S NO DOUBT SOME OF THE GAME'S LONGEST HITTERS SWING FLAT OUT ON MANY OF THEIR DRIVES. PERHAPS THAT'S WHY A NUMBER OF THEM ALSO SPEND SO MUCH TIME IN THE TALL GRASS!

UNLESS CIRCUMSTANCES ABSOLUTELY FORCE ME TO GO FOR MAXIMUM DISTANCE, I RARELY SWING WHEN DRIVING AT MORE THAN 90 PER CENT OF MY FULL PHYSICAL CAPACITY. THAT'S BECAUSE I'VE FOUND DISTANCE TO BE OF VALUE **ONLY** IN A FORWARD DIRECTION. ALSO, THE LESS DIRECTLY FORWARD I'M DRIVING THE BALL, THE MORE I'LL EASE BACK ON THE GAS PEDAL IN ORDER TO ACHIEVE MORE SOLID CONTACT THROUGH GREATER CONTROL.

Work on a Square Hit

THE WOMEN PROFESSIONALS ARE LIVING PROOF THAT STRENGTH ALONE DOESN'T PRODUCE DISTANCE IN GOLF.

QUITE A NUMBER OF THE **LPGA** PROFESSIONALS DRIVE THE BALL FARTHER THAN MOST MALE CLUB GOLFERS.

HOW?

ONE IMPORTANT FACTOR IS ACCURACY OF STRIKE. THE TOP GIRLS HIT THE BALL VERY **SQUARELY**, WHICH IN THEIR CASE IS A PRODUCT OF SWING CONTROL AND COORDINATION MUCH MORE THAN STRENGTH. SO NEVER BE AFRAID OF TRADING A LITTLE CLUBHEAD SPEED FOR A MORE SOLID HIT — FREQUENTLY IT WILL INCREASE YOUR DISTANCE.

THERE ARE BASICALLY TWO WAYS TO GET DISTANCE! ONE IS VIA A LONG, HIGH, FLOATING CARRY --- WHICH IS THE WAY I FAVOR BECAUSE IT OFFERS THE GREATEST CONTROL. BUT IT TAKES A CERTAIN AMOUNT OF STRENGTH AND AN UPRIGHT SWING PLANE.

THE OTHER WAY IS VIA A LOWER, MORE BORING SHOT GIVEN MAXIMUM RUN BY A TOUCH OF DRAW. THIS TAKES LESS STRENGTH AND A FLATTER SWING PLANE, BUT BOTH REQUIRE GOOD BASIC SWING MECHANICS.

KEY IS TO DETERMINE WHICH TECHNIQUE IS WITHIN YOUR CAPABILITIES, THEN STICK TO IT.

Don't Cramp Your Style

TOO MANY GOLFERS CRAMP OR OVER-FLATTEN THEIR SWINGS BY TRYING TO AVOID A "FLYING" RIGHT ELBOW.

YOU CAN'T GET FULL ARM EXTENSION — AND THUS MAXIMUM DISTANCE-PRODUCING LEVERAGE — IF YOU OVER-CONSTRICT YOUR RIGHT ELBOW.

MY RIGHT ARM MOVES WELL AWAY FROM AND BEHIND MY BODY ON THE BACKSWING, BUT IT'S NOT "FLYING."

TO DO THAT IT WOULD HAVE TO POINT OUTWARD — BEHIND ME — WHEREAS IT ACTUALLY POINTS TOWARD THE GROUND.

SO, LONG AS YOURS DOES THE SAME, IT WON'T BE "FLYING" EITHER.

139

LOSING DISTANCE AS THOSE BIRTHDAYS KEEP COMING ALONG FASTER AND FASTER ??

TRY LETTING YOUR HIPS TURN A LITTLE MORE FULLY GOING BACK IN RESPONSE TO YOUR ARM SWING AND SHOULDER WIND-UP.

JM

IT'S TRUE THAT MANY OF THE YOUNGER OR MORE FLEXIBLE TOUR PLAYERS DON'T TURN THEIR HIPS MUCH -- BUT IT'S ALSO TRUE THAT **BOBBY JONES** WON HIS 13 MAJORS TURNING HIS HIPS ALMOST AS MUCH AS HIS SHOULDERS.

IN MY VIEW, A LOT OF HIP TURN IS BETTER THAN NONE — ESPECIALLY FOR SENIORS AND STOCKY PLAYERS.

Move Faster from the Hips Down

MOST AMATEURS WHEN TRYING FOR EXTRA DISTANCE INSTINCTIVELY TRY TO HIT HARDER WITH THEIR HANDS AND ARMS FROM THE TOP OF THE BACKSWING. IT'S A SURE WAY TO BOTH DIMINISH CLUBHEAD SPEED AND DISTORT CLUBFACE ALIGNMENT.

NO. 5
570 yds
PAR 5

MY PRIMARY THOUGHT IN GOING FOR A BIG ONE IS A FASTER HIP UNWIND THROUGHOUT THE DOWNSWING. SO LONG AS YOU CAN KEEP THE ACTION SMOOTH AND FLUID, THE FASTER YOU UNCOIL YOUR HIPS THE GREATER THE LEVERAGE YOU CREATE, AND THUS THE FASTER YOU'LL WHIP THE CLUBHEAD THROUGH THE BALL.

CHECK THE HEIGHT YOU TEE THE BALL IF YOUR DRIVES ARE STOPPING SHORTER THAN YOU'D LIKE.

TEEING THE BALL LOW ENCOURAGES HITTING DOWN ON IT, WHICH INCREASES BACKSPIN, WHICH DECREASES ROLL.

TEEING THE BALL SO THAT ITS CENTER IS ABOUT EVEN WITH THE TOP EDGE OF THE DRIVER WILL ENCOURAGE YOU TO SWEEP THE CLUBHEAD THROUGH ON A MORE LEVEL PATH AT IMPACT. THAT'LL GIVE YOU BOTH MAXIMUM CARRY AND ROLL.

Extend That Arc!

No. **7**
572 YDS
PAR 5

USUAL RESULT OF AN ATTEMPT TO DRIVE FARTHER IS A VICE-LIKE GRIP, AN EXCESSIVE PIVOT, A SWAYING HEAD, A BENT LEFT ARM, AND A SHOULDER-SPINNING LUNGE AT THE BALL COMING DOWN.

NEXT TIME YOU NEED A BIG ONE, FORGET TRYING TO 'FORCE' THE SHOT.

INSTEAD, STAY WITH YOUR BASIC SWING MOVES AND TEMPO, BUT SIMPLY TRY TO EXTEND THE ARC BY GETTING YOUR ARMS HIGHER AT THE TOP. DON'T START DOWN UNTIL YOU'VE FELT YOUR HANDS REACH **ABOVE** YOUR SHOULDERS.

Try This Stance Adjustment...

CONSIDER YOUR RIGHT FOOT PLACEMENT IF YOU'RE HAVING TROUBLE MAKING A GOOD, FULL BODY TURN.

CURRENT PRO TOUR FASHION IS TO SET THE REAR FOOT AT 90 DEGREES TO THE TARGET LINE, BUT THAT'S TOO RESTRICTIVE FOR MANY SENIOR AND LESS SUPPLE GOLFERS.

THE FARTHER THE RIGHT FOOT POINTS AWAY FROM THE TARGET, THE FARTHER THE HIPS CAN BE ROTATED, AND THE FARTHER THE HIPS CAN BE ROTATED, THE MORE FULLY THE SHOULDERS CAN BE COILED.

SO POINT YOUR FOOT FOR POWER, NOT FOR APPEARANCES.

JM

WHEN I'M REALLY GOING FOR A BIG HIT, I MAKE A SLIGHT STANCE ADJUSTMENT THAT HELPS ME SPEED UP MY LEG THRUST AND HIP CLEARANCE.

15th HOLE
PAR 5 520 YDS.
AUGUSTA NATIONAL

BY TURNING MY LEFT FOOT TARGETWARDS A LITTLE MORE, I GIVE MYSELF A RUNNING START ON SHIFTING MY HIPS OUT OF THE WAY FASTER ON THE FORWARD SWING.

IF YOU TRY THIS, BE SURE TO START DOWN WITH YOUR LEGS — OTHERWISE YOU RISK SPINNING OUT WITH YOUR SHOULDERS.

JM

Set Right Hand to "Sling" Club

IF YOU LACK DISTANCE ON DRIVES OR "ZIP" IN YOUR LONG-IRON SHOTS, CHECK HOW YOU'RE HOLDING THE CLUB WITH YOUR **RIGHT** HAND. GRIPPING TOO MUCH IN THE PALM INHIBITS A FULL, FREE RELEASE OF THE CLUBHEAD THROUGH THE BALL.

JM

TRY TO THROW A BALL HELD IN THE PALM OF YOUR HAND AND YOU WON'T MOVE IT VERY FAR.

GRIP THE BALL TOWARDS THE END OF YOUR FINGERS AND YOU CAN REALLY SLING IT.

LONG-HITTING AT GOLF REQUIRES THE SAME SORT OF SLINGING ACTION THROUGH IMPACT.

FOR THE CLUBHEAD TO BE FULLY RELEASED, THE RIGHT HAND AND WRIST MUST ROLL OVER THE LEFT SOMETIME BEYOND IMPACT.

JM

BLOCKING OR OVER-DELAYING THAT ACTION IN AN EFFORT TO HOLD THE CLUBFACE SQUARE TO THE TARGET TOO LONG IS ONE REASON MANY GOLFERS LACK REAL "ZIP" IN THEIR SHOTS.

THE KEY IS TO LET THE FOREARMS ROTATE NATURALLY INTO THE FOLLOW-THROUGH, **WITHOUT** (A) THE LEFT WRIST BREAKING DOWN BY CUPPING INWARD (B).

A.

B.

PART THREE

Special Factors and Situations

13

The Lower-Body Action

Allow Your Weight to Shift

THE MORE YOU CAN KEEP THE WEIGHT ON THE **INSIDES** OF YOUR FEET DURING THE SWING, THE MORE "CENTERED" YOUR BODY WILL BE AND THE LESS CHANCE YOU'LL HAVE OF SWAYING OFF THE BALL.

AT THE TOP I FEEL I HAVE ABOUT 80 PER CENT OF MY WEIGHT ON THE INSIDE OF MY RIGHT FOOT AND THE REST ON THE INSIDE OF MY LEFT.

AT **IMPACT**, THESE PROPORTIONS ARE REVERSED, WITH ALMOST ALL THE WEIGHT EVENTUALLY GOING OVER TO THE OUTSIDE EDGE OF THE LEFT FOOT AS THE FOLLOW-THROUGH PROGRESSES.

Practice "Rolling" with Heels Down

THE MORE YOU CAN ROLL RATHER THAN "DANCE" ON YOUR FEET, THE BETTER GOLF YOU'LL PLAY.

SOME OF THE BEST PRACTICE I EVER SPENT AS A YOUNGSTER WAS HITTING SHOTS WITHOUT ALLOWING MY HEELS TO LEAVE THE GROUND.

GOING BACK, ROLLING THE LEFT ANKLE AWAY FROM THE TARGET MOVES THE WEIGHT ONTO THE **INSIDE** OF THE RIGHT FOOT. COMING DOWN, ROLLING THE RIGHT ANKLE **TOWARDS** THE TARGET MOVES THE WEIGHT SOLIDLY BACK ONTO THE LEFT FOOT.

PRACTICE THESE MOTIONS WITH A MEDIUM-IRON AND A FAIRLY NARROW STANCE IF YOU WANT TO IMPROVE YOUR LEG ACTION. YOU'LL FIND YOUR BALANCE IMPROVING, TOO.

WHETHER YOUR LEFT HEEL LIFTS ON A FULL SWING DEPENDS ON YOUR SUPPLENESS. IF IT <u>HAS</u> TO COME OFF THE GROUND TO FACILITATE A FULL BODY TURN — AS IN MY CASE WITH THE LONGER CLUBS — THEN LET IT.

IF YOU CAN MAKE A GOOD WIND-UP WITHOUT RAISING THE LEFT HEEL, THEN YOU'VE GOT <u>TWO</u> ADVANTAGES OVER THOSE WHO MUST LET IT LIFT.

ONE IS THAT YOU'LL GET BACK FASTER ONTO YOUR LEFT SIDE COMING DOWN.

THE OTHER IS THAT YOUR LEFT FOOT WILL NOT MOVE OUT OF POSITION AS YOU SHIFT YOUR WEIGHT — AS SOMETIMES HAPPENS IN MY CASE.

Check Your Knee Flex

HOW MUCH SHOULD YOUR KNEES BEND OR FLEX AT ADDRESS AND THROUGHOUT THE SWING?

THE EXACT DEGREE DEPENDS ON YOUR BUILD AND SWING STYLE, BUT YOU SHOULD WORK WITHIN CERTAIN LIMITS.

SETTING-UP AND SWING-ING WITH THE LEGS TOO STRAIGHT OR STIFF BREEDS TENSION AND RESTRICTS TURN BY LOCKING THE BODY.

TOO MUCH SAG IN THE KNEES UNDERMINES SOLID ANCHORING AND LOWER BODY RESILIENCE.

SO TRY TO FIND A HAPPY MEDIUM, COMBINING COMFORT WITH A SENSE OF SPRINGY 'READINESS' IN THE LEGS.

SWAYING AND/OR STIFFENING THE RIGHT LEG GOING BACK CAUSES MUCH HEARTACHE FOR WEEKEND GOLFERS. REASON IS THAT SUCH MOVES PREVENT BOTH PROPER <u>WEIGHT-SHIFTING</u> AND <u>HIP CLEARANCE</u> COMING DOWN.

FLEX YOUR RIGHT KNEE SLIGHTLY AT ADDRESS AND KEEP IT THAT WAY THROUGHOUT THE BACKSWING. DEVELOP THE FEELING OF COILING AROUND A <u>FIXED BUT FLEXED</u> RIGHT KNEE.

PRACTICING WITH A GOLF BALL UNDER THE OUTER EDGE OF THE FOOT WILL QUICKLY TEACH YOU THE PROPER RIGHT LEG ACTION.

JM

Learn Proper Weight Shift like This

BECAUSE IT CAN'T BE DONE WITHOUT THE LEGS MOVING TARGETWARDS, LEARNING TO SHIFT THE WEIGHT FROM THE RIGHT TO THE LEFT FOOT STARTING THE DOWNSWING IS A GREAT WAY TO DEVELOP GOOD LOWER-BODY ACTION.

PRACTICE THE MOTION USING A SHORT-IRON WITH THE BALL TEED AND THE FEET FAIRLY CLOSE TOGETHER. START WITH A LEISURELY HALF-SWING AND BUILD UP, CONCENTRATING ON A DISTINCT TO-AND-FRO WEIGHT SHIFT BY ROLLING THE ANKLES.

TRY TO FINISH EACH SWING WITH 90 PER CENT OF YOUR WEIGHT ON THE OUTSIDE EDGE OF YOUR LEFT FOOT.

90%

14

The Role of the Hands and Wrists

Let Your Hands Follow, Not Lead

WHAT'S THE ROLE OF THE HANDS AND WRISTS IN GOLF?

THAT'S BEEN A SUBJECT OF GREAT DEBATE EVER SINCE THE GAME BEGAN, AND PROBABLY WILL BE AS LONG AS IT'S PLAYED.

JM

BEING ESSENTIALLY A "BODY" RATHER THAN A "HANDS" PLAYER, THE HANDS AND WRISTS IN MY SWING ARE FOLLOWERS RATHER THAN LEADERS. BASICALLY, THEY WORK SIMPLY AS A HINGE TO STORE AND THEN TRANSMIT THE FORCE CREATED BY MY LEG AND BODY ACTION. AS SUCH, THEY COME INTO PLAY REFLEXIVELY RATHER THAN CONSCIOUSLY.

Allow Your Wrists to Cock Reflexively

WRIST-COCKING IS A NATURAL RESPONSE TO THE <u>MOMENTUM</u> OF THE CLUBHEAD.

MY WRISTS BEGIN TO COCK AUTOMATICALLY AS THE CLUB PASSES HORIZONTAL GOING BACK.

THE FARTHER BACK I GET, THE MORE MY WRISTS COCK IN RESPONSE TO THE <u>SWINGING WEIGHT</u> OF THE CLUBHEAD.

YOU'LL NEVER HAVE TO THINK ABOUT YOUR WRISTS IF YOU GRIP THE CLUB FIRMLY AND MAKE A FULL BODY TURN AND ARM SWING — THEY'LL COCK REFLEXIVELY.

JM

"Reach for the Sky" with Your Hands

THE HIGHER THE HANDS AT THE TOP, THE BETTER THE GOLF SWING AS I SEE IT.

IF YOU HAVE DIFFICULTY CREATING THE FULL BODY TURN AND ARM EXTENSION THAT HIGH HANDS SIGNIFY, HERE'S A TIP THAT MIGHT HELP YOU.

JM

GOING BACK, STRIVE FOR THE FEELING THAT YOUR LEFT ARM AND THE CLUB SHAFT REMAIN IN A STRAIGHT LINE UNTIL THE WEIGHT OF THE SWINGING CLUBHEAD CAUSES YOUR WRISTS TO HINGE INVOLUNTARILY. SWING SMOOTHLY AND DELIBERATELY AND YOU'LL FIND IT MUCH EASIER TO "REACH FOR THE SKY" WITH THIS ONE-PIECE TAKEAWAY FEELING.

Guide with Left, Hit with Right

IS THERE SUCH A THING AS "TOO MUCH RIGHT HAND" IN GOLF?

NOT IN MY VIEW!

IF THE RIGHT HAND OVERPOWERS THE LEFT, IT'S BECAUSE THE LEFT HAS BEEN USED IMPROPERLY.

JM

THE LEFT HAND SHOULD CERTAINLY BE THE DOMINANT FACTOR IN GUIDING AND DIRECTING THE CLUB TO THE BALL. BUT IF IT DOES THAT CORRECTLY, YOU CAN — AND SHOULD — HIT AS HARD AS POSSIBLE WITH THE RIGHT HAND.

IN OTHER WORDS, YOU CAN USE **BOTH** HANDS TO THE UTMOST, SO LONG AS YOU USE THEM <u>PROPERLY</u>.

Try Bigger Muscles for Better Timing

"HANDS" PLAYERS SEEM TO HAVE MORE TIMING PROBLEMS THAN "BODY" GOLFERS, PERHAPS BECAUSE SMALL MUSCLES OPERATE FASTER AND MORE SPONTANEOUSLY THAN BIG ONES.

THUS LEARNING TO MAKE MORE USE OF THE LEGS AND BACK, AND LESS OF THE HANDS AND WRISTS, IS ONE WAY TO IMPROVE AT GOLF.

IT TAKES TIME AND EFFORT, BUT THE GREATER CONSISTENCY MAY BE WORTH THE PRICE FOR THE AMBITIOUS PLAYER.

15

The All-Important Head

Copy the Masters—Stay Steady

THERE ARE A LOT OF WAYS TO PLAY GOOD GOLF, BUT THEY ALL HAVE ONE THING IN COMMON: A **STEADY HEAD**.

KEEPING YOUR HEAD STEADY ISN'T THE SAME THING AS "KEEPING YOUR EYE ON THE BALL"—I CAN SWAY MY HEAD TWO FEET AND STILL SEE THE BALL.

THE KEY TO HEAD STEADINESS IS NOT ALLOWING THE BACK OF YOUR NECK TO MOVE UP, DOWN OR SIDEWAYS AT ANY POINT FROM TAKEAWAY TO IMPACT.

THAT TAKES DISCIPLINE — AND <u>PRACTICE</u>.

Avoid These 3 Shot-Wreckers

YOUR HEAD IS YOUR SWING FULCRUM. IF IT MOVES SUBSTANTIALLY ONE OR ALL OF THE FOLLOWING WILL HAPPEN:

1. YOUR ARC AND PLANE WILL CHANGE.

2. YOUR EYES WILL RELATE INCORRECTLY TO YOUR TARGET LINE.

3. YOU'LL LOSE BALANCE.

JM

LEARNING TO KEEP THE HEAD STEADY IS ONE OF GOLF'S TOUGHEST CHALLENGES, BUT IT'S AN ABSOLUTE **MUST** IF YOU WISH TO PLAY THE GAME WELL. THE ONLY ANSWERS ARE WILLPOWER AND PRACTICE — SUFFICIENT PRACTICE TO AUTOMATE SWINGING **AROUND** YOUR HEAD, NOT WITH IT.

Swivel Your Chin Going Back...

YOU'LL NEVER HIT THE BALL **SOLIDLY FORWARD** IF YOUR HEAD ISN'T SOLIDLY **BEHIND** IT AT IMPACT. MY HEAD AT THAT POINT STAYS BEHIND A VERTICAL LINE DRAWN UP FROM THE BALL.

I ENSURE THIS BY POSITIONING MY HEAD **BEHIND** THE BALL AT ADDRESS.

THEN I ENSURE IT EVEN MORE BY **SWIVELING** MY CHIN **AWAY** FROM THE TARGET ON THE TAKEAWAY AND **LEAVING** IT THERE UNTIL WELL AFTER IMPACT.

. . . and Going Through

A STEADY HEAD IS THE NO. 1 FUNDAMENTAL OF GOLF, BUT IT <u>CAN</u> BE OVERDONE.

IN FACT, TRYING TO LOOK AT THE BALL POSITION TOO LONG AFTER IMPACT ON A FULL SWING CAN ACTUALLY CAUSE YOUR HEAD TO BE FORCED UPWARD BY THE UNWINDING MOTION OF YOUR BODY.

TRICK IS TO LET YOUR HEAD <u>SWIVEL</u> SLOWLY SIDEWAYS, <u>WITHOUT LIFTING</u>, AS THE BODY SWINGS UNDER IT INTO THE FOLLOW-THROUGH.

THAT WAY YOU CAN STILL KEEP YOUR HEAD <u>DOWN AND CENTERED</u> WITHOUT INHIBITING YOUR ARM AND BODY ACTION THROUGH THE BALL.

Beware of Up-and-Down Movement

ALTHOUGH EVEN THE BEST GOLFERS' HEADS DO MOVE A LITTLE DURING THE SWING, I BELIEVE **THINKING** OF KEEPING THE HEAD IN ONE PLACE, AT LEAST UNTIL IMPACT, DEFINITELY HELPS IN STRIKING THE BALL SOLIDLY.

AVOID UP-AND-DOWN HEAD MOVEMENT AS WELL AS SIDE-TO-SIDE. IF YOUR HEAD GOES DOWN ON THE BACKSWING AND UP ON THE THROUGH-SWING, YOU'LL TOP A LOT OF SHOTS.

IF THE REVERSE HAPPENS — UP IN THE BACKSWING AND DOWN IN THE THROUGH-SWING — YOU'LL HIT A LOT OF SHOTS "FAT" (GROUND BEFORE BALL).

Check Your Head Action the Hard Way

THE BEST WAY TO CHECK HEAD MOVEMENT IS TO HAVE SOMEONE WATCH YOUR HEAD AGAINST A BACKGROUND POINT.

IF YOU HAVE TROUBLE KEEPING THE TOP HALF STEADY, HIT A FEW SHOTS WHILE SOMEONE GRABS YOUR HAIR.

IT MAY BRING TEARS TO YOUR EYES, BUT IT'LL GET THE MESSAGE ACROSS FASTER THAN ANYTHING I KNOW!

SWIVELING THE CHIN TO MAKE ROOM FOR MAXIMUM SHOULDER TURN — AS I DO — IS O.K., SO LONG AS THE BACK OF YOUR NECK REMAINS STEADY.

JM

16

Angled
Lies

Stay Cool in Uneven Situations

YOU DON'T LIKE HILLY LIES?

WELL, I'VE HAD MY HOT MOMENTS ABOUT THEM TOO, BUT I'VE ALWAYS COOLED DOWN WHEN I THOUGHT HOW DULL THE GAME WOULD BE IF THE WORLD WAS DEAD FLAT.

TREAT ANGLED LIES AS AN INTEGRAL CHALLENGE OF THE GAME AND YOU'LL APPROACH THEM A LOT MORE POSITIVELY. YOU'LL PLAY THEM EVEN MORE POSITIVELY YET IF YOU INCLUDE A VARIETY OF THEM IN YOUR PRACTICE SESSIONS AS I DO — ESPECIALLY ON CHIPPING AND PITCHING.

WHAT IS THE MOST IMPORTANT ADJUSTMENT TO MAKE WHEN FACED WITH AN UPHILL OR DOWNHILL LIE?

MY ANSWER WOULD BE TO TAKE SPECIAL CARE OVER <u>CLUB SELECTION</u>.

NORMALLY HIT, THE BALL WILL FLY HIGHER AND THUS SHORTER FROM AN UPHILL LIE, AND LOWER AND THUS FARTHER FROM A DOWNHILL LIE.

THE MORE THE GROUND SLOPES, THE GREATER THESE EFFECTS ON THE BALL'S FLIGHT, THUS THE MORE CRITICAL CLUBBING BECOMES.

173

Weight Back When Ground Slopes Down

A SEVERE DOWNHILL LIE IS TOUGH BECAUSE IT PRESENTS A BALANCE PROBLEM AS WELL AS REQUIRING SWING ADJUSTMENTS. TO TAKE CARE OF THE BALANCE FACTOR, OPEN YOUR STANCE AND SET MOST OF YOUR WEIGHT ON YOUR BACK FOOT.

TAKE A MORE LOFTED CLUB, TOO, SO THAT YOU CAN GET ADEQUATE HEIGHT WITHOUT PRESSING TOO HARD.

REGARDING SWING ADJUSTMENTS, PLAY THE BALL MORE TOWARD YOUR RIGHT FOOT AND OPEN THE CLUBFACE A LITTLE TO OFFSET A PULLING TENDENCY.

THEN BREAK YOUR WRISTS EARLY ON THE BACKSWING, HIT FIRMLY, AND TRY TO DELAY THE ROLL OF YOUR WRISTS UNTIL WELL AFTER IMPACT.

Allow for Hook When Ball's Higher

A SIDEHILL SHOT WITH THE BALL HIGH ABOVE YOUR FEET IS ONE OF THE TOUGHEST IN GOLF. BEST POLICY IS TO AVOID SUCH LIES BY SHOOTING FOR LEVEL FAIRWAY AREAS.

WHEN THE SHOT DOES PRESENT ITSELF, CHOKE WELL DOWN ON THE CLUB, STAND MORE UPRIGHT THAN NORMAL, AND KEEP YOUR WEIGHT MORE ON YOUR TOES TO OFFSET THE TENDENCY TO FALL BACKWARDS. TRY TO SWING AS SMOOTHLY AND COMPACTLY AS POSSIBLE, WITH A SWEEPING RATHER THAN A PUNCHING ACTION.

ALSO, AIM TO THE RIGHT TO ALLOW FOR THE INEVITABLE HOOK.

Allow for Slice When Ball's Lower

A SIDEHILL SHOT WITH THE BALL WELL BELOW YOUR FEET IS ALWAYS A TESTER.

CAREFUL SHOT-PLANNING FROM THE TEE IS THE BEST WAY TO ENSURE YOU DON'T ENCOUNTER TOO MANY OF THESE POTENTIAL SCORE-WRECKERS.

WHEN YOU DO, GRIP THE CLUB AS CLOSE TO THE END AS POSSIBLE, GET WELL DOWN TO THE SHOT BY FLEXING YOUR KNEES, AND PROTECT YOUR BALANCE BY "SITTING ON YOUR HEELS."

SWING COMPACTLY AND RHYTHMICALLY, **STAY DOWN**, AND AIM LEFT TO ALLOW FOR THE LIKELY FADE.

17

Finessing
the Ball

Swing Steeper for Extra "Bite"

MANY CLUB GOLFERS LACK "BITE" ON THEIR APPROACH SHOTS BECAUSE THEY LACK BACKSPIN.

A SURE REDUCER OF BACKSPIN IS GRASS COMING BETWEEN CLUBFACE AND BALL AT IMPACT, SO CLEAN STRIKING IS YOUR FIRST GOAL.

ANOTHER MIGHT BE TO SWING A LITTLE MORE UPRIGHT, IN THAT THE STEEPER THE ANGLE OF CLUB APPROACH THE MORE POWERFULLY THE BALL WILL BE SPUN UP AND OFF THE CLUBFACE.

HOWEVER, IF YOU GO TO AN UPRIGHT PLANE, BE SURE YOU CONTINUE TO **TURN** AND **EXTEND** FULLY ON THE BACKSWING.

Swing Shorter for "Part" Shots

MANY GOLFERS NEVER TRY ANYTHING LESS THAN A FULL SWING FOR FEAR OF MISSING THE SHOT BY "LETTING UP" ON IT.

BY SO DOING THEY ARE NEEDLESSLY LIMITING THEIR STROKE-MAKING ARSENAL.

THE KEY TO A LESS-THAN-FULL EFFORT IS A <u>SHORTER</u> SWING — SAY THREE-QUARTER LENGTH — RATHER THAN THREE-QUARTERS OF NORMAL POWER.

YOU'LL ACHIEVE THIS SIMPLY BY **CHOKING DOWN** ON THE CLUB — WHICH ALSO PROVIDES BETTER "FEEL." HAVING DONE THAT, HIT AWAY AS HARD AS USUAL.

"Sweep" Ball with Long Irons

LONG-IRONS AREN'T AS DIFFICULT TO PLAY AS MANY GOLFERS BELIEVE — GIVEN THE RIGHT KIND OF SET-UP AND SWING.

FIRST KEY IS TO POSITION THE BALL FAIRLY WELL FORWARD IN YOUR STANCE, WHERE YOU CAN <u>SWEEP</u> THE CLUBHEAD <u>THROUGH</u> RATHER THAN HITTING DOWN AT THE BALL.

SECOND KEY IS TO SWING ON THE SAME SCALE AND AT THE SAME TEMPO AS YOU SWING A WOODEN CLUB.

THIRD KEY IS TO PRACTICE BOTH TECHNIQUES WITH THE BALL TEED ON A PEG UNTIL YOU BUILD ENOUGH CONFIDENCE IN THE CLUBS TO PLAY THEM FOR REAL OFF THE GROUND.

Waggle as You Want Shot to Fly

YOUR PHYSICAL EXECUTION OF EACH SHOT IS HEAVILY INFLUENCED BY HOW YOU PICTURE IT MENTALLY.

FOR THAT REASON, AND ALSO AS A FORM OF "MINI-REHEARSAL," I WAGGLE AT ADDRESS ACCORDING TO MY INTENDED FLIGHT PATH.

JM

IF I'M PLANNING TO HIT THE BALL PRETTY MUCH STRAIGHT, I WAGGLE THE CLUB STRAIGHT BACK AND FORTH ALONG MY TARGET LINE (A).

IF I'M GOING FOR A FADE, I WAGGLE ON A SLIGHTLY OUT-TO-IN LINE (B).

AND IF I'M ATTEMPTING A DRAW, I WAGGLE ON A SLIGHTLY IN-TO-OUT PATH (C).

To Slice Change Set-up, Not Swing

THERE ARE TWO WAYS TO INTENTIONALLY SLICE A SHOT. ONE IS TO GRIP WITH THE HANDS FARTHER **LEFT** THAN USUAL, THEN SWING **OUT-TO-IN**.

USE THIS IF IT WORKS FOR YOU, BUT IF NOT, TRY MY WAY.

TO SLICE A SHOT, I SIMPLY OPEN THE CLUBFACE AT ADDRESS, AIM LEFT OF TARGET, THEN SWING NORMALLY.

THE MORE SLICE I WANT, THE MORE I OPEN THE CLUBFACE AND MY SHOULDER ALIGNMENT. THIS WAY I DON'T HAVE TO CHANGE MY BASIC SWING PATTERN.

JM

Understand These "Release" Factors

THE LONGER YOU DELAY THE ROLL OF THE RIGHT FOREARM OVER THE LEFT, THE MORE OPEN THE CLUBFACE WILL BE AND THE BETTER YOUR CHANCES OF FADING OR SLICING THE BALL.

CONVERSELY, THE EARLIER THE WRISTS AND FOREARMS ROTATE THROUGH THE IMPACT ZONE, THE BETTER YOUR CHANCES OF DRAWING OR HOOKING THE BALL BECAUSE OF A CLOSING CLUBFACE. EXPERIMENTING WITH THESE ACTIONS IN PRACTICE IS A FINE WAY TO LEARN SHOT FLIGHTING AND BALL CONTROL.

JM

Use Shaft for High and Low Shots

GOLF OFTEN SEEMS A PARADOXICAL GAME, AND THAT'S NOWHERE MORE TRUE THAN WHEN YOU'RE TRYING TO HIT A HARD LOW SHOT OR A SOFT HIGH SHOT. FOLLOWING THEIR INSTINCTS, MANY GOLFERS HOLD THE CLUB EXACTLY OPPOSITE TO THE CORRECT WAY.

JM

HITTING A HARD LOW SHOT BECOMES MUCH EASIER WHEN YOU **CHOKE DOWN** (A) ON THE CLUB. CONVERSELY, USING **ALL THE SHAFT** (B) MAKES PLAYING A SOFT HIGH SHOT MUCH SIMPLER BY ALLOWING A SLOW TEMPO AND A DELIBERATE SWING.

PROVE THIS TO YOURSELF BY PRACTICING BOTH TECHNIQUES.

A

B

Move Ball and Hand Back for Less Height

MOVING THE BALL BACK IN YOUR STANCE IS CORRECT PROCEDURE ANY TIME YOU WANT TO HIT IT LOWER, BUT ANOTHER ADJUSTMENT IS NECESSARY TO BE SURE YOU GET THE DESIRED FLIGHT.

IF YOU LEAVE YOUR HANDS WHERE THEY NORMALLY ARE AT ADDRESS WHEN MOVING THE BALL BACK, THE EFFECT WILL BE TO CREATE A STEEPER DOWNSWING ARC WHICH WILL CAUSE MORE BACKSPIN AND THUS GREATER RATHER THAN LESSER HEIGHT.

SOLUTION IS TO ALSO MOVE YOUR HANDS BACK PROPORTIONATELY TO THE BALL PLACEMENT, THEN SWING NORMALLY.

7-27

Delay Release to Keep Ball Down

YOU'LL KEEP THE BALL **DOWN** MOST EFFECTIVELY WITH A SLIGHTLY CLOSED CLUBFACE DELIVERY AND A DELAYED RELEASE OF THE CLUBHEAD.

FOR A LOW SHOT, POSITION THE BALL A LITTLE FARTHER BACK IN YOUR STANCE AND HOOD THE CLUBFACE SLIGHTLY.

THEN DELAY THE CLUBHEAD RELEASE BY LEADING THE THROUGH-SWING WITH YOUR LEGS WHILE KEEPING YOUR WRISTS FIRM.

STAY DOWN ON THE SHOT, AND ALLOW FOR A DRAW.

Release Freely to Hit Ball High

HEIGHT IS MOST EASILY ACHIEVED BY A SLIGHTLY <u>OPEN</u> CLUBFACE DELIVERY, COMBINED WITH A <u>VIGOROUS RELEASE</u> OF THE CLUBHEAD THROUGH THE BALL.

WHEN YOU NEED A PARTICULARLY HIGH SHOT, SET THE BALL A LITTLE FARTHER FORWARD IN YOUR STANCE AND OPEN THE CLUBFACE A FEW DEGREES.

THEN BE SURE TO <u>RELEASE</u> THE CLUBHEAD — UNCOCK YOUR WRISTS — FULLY THROUGH IMPACT. STAY <u>BEHIND</u> THE BALL, AND ALLOW FOR A LITTLE FADE.

JM

Practice

WHAT MAKES A GOOD GOLFER?

ATHLETICISM, COORDINATION, DESIRE, INTELLIGENCE, SELF-CONTROL ARE ALL FACTORS — PERHAPS INDISPENSABLE ONES FOR ANYONE WHO SEEKS TO ACHIEVE THE HIGHEST LEVELS OF THE GAME TODAY.

BUT THERE'S ANOTHER FACTOR, TOO — PRACTICE. THERE'S NEVER BEEN A TOP PLAYER WHO DID NOT HIT TENS OF THOUSANDS OF PRACTICE SHOTS BOTH IN LEARNING AND SUSTAINING HIS OR HER GAME. THE REASON IS THAT THIS IS THE ONLY WAY TO ENSURE THAT FINE SHOTS CAN BE PRODUCED "AUTOMATICALLY"—WHICH IS THE BIG DIFFERENCE BETWEEN THE GOOD CLUB GOLFER AND THOSE WHO PLAY GOLF FOR A LIVING.

Work Most on One Basic "Shape"

WHAT SHOULD A GOLFER BEGINNING A GAME — IMPROVEMENT PROGRAM DO FIRST? IN MY VIEW, HE SHOULD CONSCIOUSLY DECIDE WHETHER HE IS BASICALLY GOING TO WORK THE BALL FROM RIGHT TO LEFT (**DRAW**) OR FROM LEFT TO RIGHT (**FADE**).

A DEAD STRAIGHT SHOT IS THE TOUGHEST TO HIT ONCE, LET ALONE TO REPEAT CONTINUALLY. FOR THAT AND ALSO FOR STRATEGICAL REASONS, ALMOST ALL TOUR PROS DELIBERATELY EITHER DRAW OR FADE MOST OF THEIR LONG SHOTS. THAT'S HOW YOU SHOULD LEARN TO PLAY GOLF, TOO.

(EVENTUALLY, OF COURSE, IF YOU'RE REALLY SERIOUS ABOUT THE GAME, YOU SHOULD LEARN TO HIT **BOTH** WAYS AT WILL.)

Keep Those Legs Strong

GOOD GOLF IS IMPOSSIBLE IF YOUR LEGS ARE IN LOUSY SHAPE, SO BEING AS ACTIVE AS YOU CAN OFF THE COURSE IS DEFINITELY GOING TO INCREASE YOUR PROWESS AND YOUR PLEASURE ON IT.

GOLF HAS NEVER PROVIDED ME WITH VIGOROUS ENOUGH EXERCISE TO STAY IN THE SHAPE I FEEL NECESSARY TO BE FULLY COMPETITIVE, SO I LIKE TO PLAY MORE STRENUOUS SPORTS AS OFTEN AS POSSIBLE. THE COMPETITION INVOLVED HELPS KEEP ME SHARP FOR GOLF, TOO.

Build Your Game off The Course

ANY TIME YOU CAN'T GET TO THE COURSE FOR A LENGTHY SPELL, DO YOUR DARNDEST TO KEEP AS MANY OF YOUR GOLFING MUSCLES AS POSSIBLE IN THE BEST SHAPE YOU CAN.

IT MIGHT MAKE YOU SWEAT A LITTLE, BUT IT'LL PAY OFF COME PAY-UP TIME!

DO A FEW STRETCHING, BENDING AND TWISTING EXERCISES EACH MORNING FOR THE LOWER BACK AND TORSO. WALK INSTEAD OF RIDING AND TAKE THE STAIRS OVER THE ELEVATOR WHENEVER YOU CAN. ABOVE ALL, TRY TO SWING A CLUB SOMEWHERE PERIODICALLY — AND PREFERABLY A WEIGHTED ONE.

Practice One Thing at a Time

YOU'LL PRACTICE MORE EFFECTIVELY IF YOU CONCENTRATE ON ONE AREA OF THE SWING AT A TIME.

THE FIRST PRIORITIES ARE WHAT MIGHT BE CALLED THE 'STATIC' FUNDAMENTALS — GRIP, AIM AND STANCE, HEAD POSITION, BALL POSITION, AND ADDRESS POSTURE.

ONLY MOVE ON TO THE "ACTION" FUNDAMENTALS WHEN YOU FEEL YOU HAVE THESE 'STATICS' RIGHT. THE ACTION FUNDAMENTALS, TO ME, ARE FULL BACKSWING TURN, HIGH HANDS AT THE TOP, BEGINNING THE DOWNSWING WITH THE LOWER BODY, RELEASING THE CLUBHEAD FULLY, AND SMOOTH OVERALL TEMPO.

JM

Practice on the Course, Too

FIND PRACTICING ON A DRIVING RANGE BORING?

OKAY, THEN DO YOUR PRACTICING ON THE COURSE.

PLAY ALONE WHENEVER THE COURSE ISN'T TOO BUSY, HITTING TWO OR THREE BALLS ON EACH HOLE.

PLAYING EACH BALL AGAINST THE OTHER IS ONE WAY TO MAINTAIN YOUR INTEREST. ANOTHER IS TO TAKE OUT ONLY A FEW CLUBS AND LEARN HOW TO "MANUFACTURE" SHOTS — A GREAT WAY TO DEVELOP FINESSE. ALSO, WALK RATHER THAN RIDE ON THESE OUTINGS, BECAUSE THE EXTRA MILEAGE YOU COVER HITTING A NUMBER OF BALLS WILL DO WONDERS FOR YOUR LEGS.

Warm Up Before You Play

YOU'LL RARELY SEE A HANDICAP GOLFER HIT WARM-UP SHOTS BEFORE HE RUSHES TO THE FIRST TEE. YOU'LL RARELY SEE A PROFESSIONAL <u>NOT</u> DO SO.

MAYBE THAT HAS A LITTLE SOMETHING TO DO WITH THE WAY EACH PLAYS.

START A WARM-UP SESSION WITH A SHORT-IRON AND THEN HIT A FEW SHOTS WITH EVERY SECOND OR THIRD CLUB.

DON'T OVERDO IT!

REMEMBER, YOU'RE WARMING UP, NOT REBUILDING YOUR SWING!

Don't Be Overambitious After Lay-off

TOUGHEST THING TO RECAPTURE AFTER A LONG LAYOFF FROM GOLF IS GOOD SWING TEMPO. GENERALLY, BEING OUT OF PRACTICE AND MAYBE LACKING CONFIDENCE, YOU'LL TEND TO BE JERKY AND FAST.

TO REFIND YOUR TEMPO — AND WITH IT "FEEL" AND CONFIDENCE — DON'T BE TOO AMBITIOUS ON THE PRACTICE RANGE: CONCENTRATE ON BASIC SWING FUNDAMENTALS RATHER THAN WHERE OR HOW FAR THE BALL GOES. AND KEEP EVERYTHING SIMPLE FOR A WHILE, TOO, SAVING THE FANCY SHOTS AND THE FINESSE STROKES UNTIL YOU'VE GOT THE BASICS DOWN PAT AGAIN.

JM

Practice "Finessing" the Ball

FIRST REQUIREMENT FOR GOOD GOLF IS A SWING THAT WILL REPEAT ONE BASIC TYPE OF SHOT TIME AND AGAIN, ALMOST AUTOMATICALLY, UNDER ALL CONDITIONS AND DEGREES OF PRESSURE.

NEXT REQUIREMENT IS THE ABILITY TO "FINESSE" THE BALL — TO FIT SPECIAL SHOTS TO SPECIAL CIRCUMSTANCES. ADDING THIS CAPABILITY TO ONE'S ARMORY TAKES IMAGINATION AND A CERTAIN AMOUNT OF TRIAL AND ERROR. BUT MOST OF ALL IT TAKES PRACTICE — LOTS AND LOTS OF PRACTICE. SO ALWAYS TRY TO INCLUDE SOME NON-STANDARD OR "TYPE" SHOTS IN YOUR GAME-BUILDING SESSIONS.

Work on Balance This Way

BEST WAY I KNOW TO DEVELOP BALANCE — AND ALSO A GOOD HEAD STEADIER — IS TO PRACTICE SWINGING FROM THE INSIDES OF THE FEET.

USING A MIDDLE-IRON AND A FAIRLY NARROW STANCE, HIT HALF- AND THREE-QUARTER SHOTS WITH YOUR WEIGHT ON THE INSIDE OF YOUR RIGHT FOOT GOING BACK AND THE INSIDE OF YOUR LEFT FOOT COMING DOWN.

KEEPING YOUR HEELS ON THE GROUND WILL TEACH YOU HOW TO ROLL YOUR FEET AND ANKLES, WHICH IS A KEY TO GOOD LEG ACTION.

Learn to Play Less Than Full Shots

THERE'S NO DOUBT AMPLE SHORT-IRON PRACTICE WILL IMPROVE YOUR SCORING FASTER THAN MOST OTHER TRAINING REGIMENS. BUT THE IMPROVEMENT WILL BE EVEN GREATER YET IF YOU INCLUDE PLENTY OF 'FINESSE' SHOTS IN THESE SESSIONS.

IN OTHER WORDS, HIT HALF- AND THREE-QUARTER AS WELL AS FULL SHOTS. PRACTICE HITTING YOUR 8-IRON AS FAR AS A FULL WEDGE, THEN YOUR 7-IRON AS FAR AS A FULL 9-IRON, AND SO ON. YOU'LL DEVELOP FEEL AND TOUCH FAST, NOT ONLY FOR REGULAR SHOTS BUT ALSO FOR BAD-WEATHER AND RECOVERY PLAY.

100 YDS

WANT TO IMPROVE FAST AT GOLF??
IF YOU CAN'T BREAK 100 BUT ARE CLOSE, A COUPLE OF LESSONS WOULD ALMOST CERTAINLY MOVE YOU INTO THE 90s.

IF YOU'RE A 90s-SHOOTER YEARNING FOR THE 80s, WORKING ON YOUR SHORT GAME WILL GET YOU THERE FASTEST.

AND THE GOLFER SEEKING THE 70s OR BETTER?

RESIGN YOURSELF TO PRACTICING A LOT MORE THAN YOU PLAY, AND MAKE TIME TO WORK ON **EVERY** FACET OF SHOTMAKING, NOT JUST THOSE YOU ENJOY THE MOST. ALSO, COMPETE AS MUCH AS YOU POSSIBLY CAN, AND AGAINST THE BEST OPPOSITION YOU CAN FIND.

The Notorious Wolfes

*A powerful dynasty, where secrets
and scandal never sleep!*

THE DYNASTY
Eight siblings, blessed with wealth, but denied the one
thing they wanted—a father's love.

A family destroyed by one man's thirst for power.

THE SECRETS
Haunted by their past and driven to succeed,
the Wolfes scattered to the far corners of the globe.
But secrets never sleep and scandal is starting to stir....

THE POWER
Now, the Wolfe brothers are back, stronger than ever,
but hiding hearts as hard as granite.
It's said that even the blackest of souls can be
healed by the purest of love....
But can the dynasty rise again?

Each month, Harlequin Presents is delighted to bring you
an exciting new installment from
The Notorious Wolfes. You won't want to miss out!

A NIGHT OF SCANDAL—*Sarah Morgan*
THE DISGRACED PLAYBOY—*Caitlin Crews*
THE STOLEN BRIDE—*Abby Green*
THE FEARLESS MAVERICK—*Robyn Grady*
THE MAN WITH THE MONEY—*Lynn Raye Harris*
THE TROPHY WIFE—*Janette Kenny*
THE GIRL THAT LOVE FORGOT—*Jennie Lucas*
THE LONE WOLFE—*Kate Hewitt*

Visit www.NotoriousWolfes.com for exclusive extras!

"You are as charming as I'd hoped. *Mucho gusto*," Stefano whispered, looking down at her. **"*Encantado.*"**

He didn't touch her, but his words were like a caress, as if he'd pressed his warm lips against her skin. She felt the power emanating off his tanned skin, the virile strength of his lean, muscular body.

She swallowed, gripping her camera bag with both hands as she muttered, "Nice to meet you."

His sensual mouth curved, as if he knew why she did not hold out her hand in greeting.

"I look forward to seven days of your company, *señorita*," he said. "I can see this week will be pleasurable indeed."

His dark eyes gleamed with the promise of untold delights, and Annabelle's breath quickened. She felt vulnerable. *Feminine.* And a strange, deep longing to let herself go, to melt her tense body into his warmth and fire.

Dear God, what madness had come over her? Even a legendary Spanish playboy couldn't have this much power, this fast!

She set her jaw. She would show both of them that she was no fool. Because she knew, however beautiful a playboy's face might be, his soul was always selfish and cold. She'd learned that long ago.

Jennie Lucas

THE GIRL THAT LOVE FORGOT

TORONTO NEW YORK LONDON
AMSTERDAM PARIS SYDNEY HAMBURG
STOCKHOLM ATHENS TOKYO MILAN MADRID
PRAGUE WARSAW BUDAPEST AUCKLAND

Recycling programs
for this product may
not exist in your area.

ISBN-13: 978-0-373-13042-9

THE GIRL THAT LOVE FORGOT

Originally published in the U.K. as THE FORGOTTEN DAUGHTER

First North American Publication 2012

Copyright © 2011 by Harlequin Books S.A.

Special thanks and acknowledgment are given to Jennie Lucas for
her contribution to *The Notorious Wolfes* series

www.Harlequin.com

Printed in U.S.A.

All about the author...
Jennie Lucas

JENNIE LUCAS had a tragic beginning for any would-be writer: a very happy childhood. Her parents owned a bookstore, and she grew up surrounded by books, dreaming about faraway lands. When she was ten, her father secretly paid her a dollar for every classic novel (*Jane Eyre, War and Peace*) that she read.

At fifteen, she went to a Connecticut boarding school on scholarship. She took her first solo trip to Europe at sixteen, then put off college and traveled around the U.S., supporting herself with jobs as diverse as gas-station cashier and newspaper advertising assistant.

At twenty-two, she met the man who would be her husband. For the first time in her life, she wanted to stay in one place, as long as she could be with him. After their marriage, she graduated from Kent State University with a degree in English, and started writing books a year later.

Jennie was a finalist in the Romance Writers of America's Golden Heart contest in 2003 and won the award in 2005. A fellow 2003 finalist, Australian author Trish Morey, read Jennie's writing and told her that she should write for Harlequin® Presents. It seemed like too big a dream, but Jennie took a deep breath and went for it. A year later Jennie got the magical call from London that turned her into a published author.

Since then, life has been hectic—juggling a writing career, a sexy husband and two young children—but Jennie loves her crazy, chaotic life. Now, if she could only figure out how to pack up her family and live in all the places she's writing about!

For more about Jennie and her books, please visit her website at www.jennielucas.com.

Other titles by Jennie Lucas available in ebook:

Harlequin Presents
2965—THE BRIDE THIEF

Harlequin Presents Extra®
158—RECKLESS NIGHT IN RIO

CHAPTER ONE

SHE'D BEEN WARNED ABOUT Stefano Cortez.

As Annabelle Wolfe climbed out of her vintage 4x4, she surveyed the sprawling white hacienda with a feeling of dread. She'd been warned constantly over the past few months: Stefano Cortez could not be trusted.

Be careful, Miss Wolfe. You won't be able to resist him. No woman can.

Guard your heart, miss. The broken hearts he's scattered are as infinite as stars.

I have nothing to worry about, Annabelle told herself fiercely. Stefano Cortez might be the equestrian world's most famous playboy, but he would have no effect on her. She wouldn't let those stupid warnings make her lose her nerve!

But her body still trembled, and she knew it wasn't just from all the coffee she'd gulped down on the long, dusty drive from Portugal to northern Spain.

Slamming her truck door with a bang, Annabelle stretched her stiff limbs, trying to shake off her nervous fear. It didn't work. Warnings about Stefano Cortez's charm had been repeated too often lately, repeated everywhere she'd visited for her photojournalism series on Europe's top-ten horse ranches for *Equestrian* magazine.

Stefano Cortez's ranch, Santo Castillo, was the final

one of her assignment. He sold the most expensive, exclusive horses in the world, and even then, only to customers he deemed worthy. Wealthy buyers fell over themselves to get the reclusive ranch owner's approval. But that was nothing compared to what women did for his attention.

The world's number-one stud farm, the current joke went, *is owned by the world's number-one stud.*

Annabelle rolled her tight shoulders. If Stefano Cortez was even a fraction of the man he was reputed to be, he would definitely try to lure her into bed. Most men usually did, unfortunately. It was a long-standing joke to all her colleagues and assistants.

But Stefano Cortez took seduction to a whole new level. According to rumor, no woman had ever turned Cortez down. *Ever.* And what if the rumors were true? What if by some horrible chance Annabelle fell into his bed like all the rest?

No way, she told herself, biting down on her lip. Annabelle didn't have a passionate bone in her body. She was cold and proud and rude—didn't men always say so after she refused their advances? At thirty-three, she was a confirmed spinster, immune to any playboy's charm. After everything she'd been through, she'd never let any man close to her.

She would be on her guard with Stefano Cortez, and if he tried any smooth moves on her, she'd laugh in his face.

Wouldn't she…?

Looking around her, Annabelle took a deep breath. So where was he? Where was the famous playboy who would apparently try to drag her into his bed the moment he saw her?

She saw half-wild horses racing across wide gold-colored fields, beneath a blue sky that stretched forever. She heard the burble of a nearby stream and birdsong rising from the forested hills. June in northern Spain. It was so beautiful here that she turned to reach through the truck's open window for her camera bag on the seat.

A man's deep voice spoke behind her.

"So you have arrived at last."

Annabelle froze. Slinging her bag on her shoulder, she braced herself and slowly turned around.

And nearly gasped.

Stefano Cortez stood before her, his eyes dark and luminous as fire beneath the Spanish sun. At five-ten, Annabelle was far from petite, but she had to tilt her head back to look into his gorgeously chiseled face.

He was even more devastating in person than in photographs. At thirty-five, he was breathtakingly handsome, dark-haired and strong with a lean, muscular physique. His worn jeans fit snugly against trim hips. The sleeves of his black shirt were rolled up, revealing tanned forearms laced with dark hair, showing he clearly was not afraid of physical labor. His chin-length dark hair was pulled back into a leather tie at the base of his neck.

He held his powerful body absolutely still as his dark eyes raked slowly over her.

Annabelle's breath disappeared from her lungs. She felt vulnerable and exposed, like a hapless gazelle beneath a lion's lazy gaze. She felt the restrained hunger of a well-fed predator who had absolute confidence in his power over her.

"Welcome to my home, Miss Wolfe," he said in softly accented English. His sensual lips curved into a half smile. "I have been waiting for you."

Their eyes locked. Heat flashed through her, heat so sudden and unexpected that she nearly stumbled back. Annabelle had to force herself to keep her face impassive, even as her trembling hands tightened around the strap of her camera bag.

"You—you have?" she said faintly.

"Your reputation precedes you." Stefano Cortez's lips curved as his gaze traced slowly down her body. "The famous Annabelle Wolfe. The beautiful photographer who travels to every corner of the world on assignment."

Struggling to hide her flushed skin and pounding heart, Annabelle lifted her chin. "And you are Stefano Cortez—the greatest stud of Santo Castillo."

She'd meant to offend him, but he only gave a low laugh. The sound of that deep, masculine amusement caused another strange flutter through her body.

He moved closer, and she licked her suddenly dry lips.

"You are as charming as I'd hoped. *Mucho gusto,*" he whispered, looking down at her. *"Encantado."*

He didn't touch her, but his words were like a caress, as if he'd kissed her hand. As if he'd pressed his warm lips against her skin. His masculine power pressed upon her consciousness from all sides. She felt the power emanating off his tanned skin, the virile strength of his lean, muscular body.

She swallowed, gripping her camera bag with both hands as she muttered, "Nice to meet you."

His sensual mouth curved, as if he knew why she did not hold out her hand in greeting, much less her cheek.

"I look forward to seven days of your company, *señorita,*" he said. "I can see this week will be pleasurable indeed."

His dark eyes gleamed with the promise of untold delights, and Annabelle's breath quickened. He was so close she could feel the heat emanating from her skin. She felt vulnerable. *Feminine.* She felt a strange, deep longing to let herself go, to melt her tense body into his warmth and fire.

Dear God, what madness had come over her? She had to get a grip! Even a legendary Spanish playboy couldn't have this much power, this fast!

She set her jaw. She would show both of them that she was no fool. Because she knew, however beautiful a playboy's face might be, his soul was always selfish and cold. She'd learned that long ago.

Annabelle drew back, glaring at him.

"How flattering," she said acidly. "But surely you don't intend to spend the entire week with me, Mr. Cortez. I've heard from multiple sources that your interest in a woman rarely lasts longer than a single night."

Annabelle waited for him to scowl at her rudeness, but to her chagrin he only looked amused.

"In your case, Miss Wolfe," he said softly, "I might make an exception."

Her heart leaped in her throat. She swallowed, trying to slow her quick, shallow breath.

Do not trust his charm. Do not, she told herself fiercely.

"I work best alone." She raised her chin. "So thanks, but I won't need your company. Or want it."

He blinked.

Annabelle took a deep breath, remembered how hard *Equestrian* had fought to get this exclusive at Santo Castillo, and tried to modulate her tone. "Forgive me if that sounds harsh. I just don't like to have anyone hovering over me as I work." She tried to smile. "And I'm sure you have a great deal to do for your charity gala this weekend...."

Abruptly, he lifted his hand toward her. She jumped back, wide-eyed and jittery as a colt.

He frowned. "Allow me to carry your bag, Miss Wolfe."

Oh. So that was why he'd reached for her. A warm blush curled her cheeks. "That's not necessary."

"You are my guest."

"Thank you, but I can manage my own equipment."

"*Por supuesto.* But it seems a great deal for one person."

"Usually I have an assistant…" Annabelle stopped, thinking of Marie who was now in Cornwall with her husband and newborn baby. She took a deep breath. "But I'll be fine. Don't worry. My photos of your ranch will be fine. The project will be fine. I work best alone," she repeated.

"So you said." Stefano looked down at her, and she felt a bead of sweat break out between her breasts.

"Why do you keep looking at me like that?"

"Like what?"

"Like you…" Her voice trailed off as she struggled to think of words that wouldn't sound ridiculous. *Like you want to rip off my clothes. Like you want to drink me for tea. Like you want to fling me over your shoulder, throw me into your bed and lick every inch of me.* She finished awkwardly, "Like you've never seen a woman before."

He barked a laugh. "I've seen many, as you know. And yet…" He paused. "I cannot stop looking at you."

"Why?"

"Because you are more beautiful than I even imagined."

She swallowed. "I…I am?"

He gave a single nod. "The photos I've seen of you hardly did you justice."

A chill went down Annabelle's spine.

The photos I've seen of you.

Which photos did he mean? Recent pictures of Annabelle at her brother's society wedding in London? Pictures of her sunburned face as she'd traveled on assignment through the Sahara and the plains of Mongolia earlier that winter?

Or…images from nearly twenty years ago, when her drunken father had tried to kill her as a teenager?

Had Stefano Cortez stumbled upon the before-and-after images that had once been in every British newspaper—the first showing Annabelle as a blonde, smiling fourteen-year-old with rosy cheeks, the second showing her with a monster's swollen face, her eyes like slits, a savage red whip slash peeling back her skin?

Annabelle searched Stefano's expression with hard eyes. But only a smile curved his sensual mouth as he looked back at her.

She exhaled with a flare of her nostrils. Good. He didn't know about her past. As juicy and notorious as the Wolfe family scandal had once been, the world had moved on. People had forgotten.

But not Annabelle. She would never forget. She still had scars to prove it. On her body. On her face. Beneath her carefully applied makeup and long blond bangs, the vestige of the violent red scar from her father's whip would always remain.

Tilting his head, Stefano frowned down at her. "You do not care for compliments."

"Why do you say that?" she evaded.

"You look almost…angry."

"It's fine." He was far too observant. Annabelle smoothed imaginary crumbs off her light-gray suit, then looked up. "But you should know I am well aware of your reputation. I do not intend to be another notch in your bedpost. You are wasting your compliments on me."

His dark eyes gleamed. "No compliment on a pretty

woman is ever wasted. And you are more than pretty. You are...*belleza*."

"You're wasting your time, Casanova," she said sharply. "I am quite impossible to seduce."

His gaze deepened with interest, as if she'd just offered him an irresistible challenge. A few strands of his chin-length black hair escaped the leather tie at the nape of his neck, falling forward to frame the brilliance of his dark eyes. "So I have heard."

Pulling the heavy camera bag up higher on her shoulder, she muttered, "Afonso Moreira told me you'd be like this."

"Ah. My Portuguese rival." He lifted a sardonic eyebrow. "What else did he say?"

"He said you're a playboy who steals women's hearts, along with their virtue. He said I should lock my door."

As she looked up at him, white sunlight lit his black hair like a halo. He looked like a dark angel as his eyes became like endless pools of night.

"Moreira is right," he said quietly.

Her mouth fell open. She hadn't expected that reply in a million years. "He—he is?"

"*Sí.*" His sensual lips curved upward. "That's exactly the kind of man I am."

Annabelle's heart pounded in her throat as she stared up into his darkly handsome face. She was dimly aware of the warm wind against her skin, loosening her chignon, blowing blond tendrils across her cheek. For an instant, she was lost in the swirling darkness of his gaze.

His eyes weren't black as she'd first thought. They were a multitude of colors as infinite as Spanish earth, obsidian and sable, coffee and burnt sienna. Full of warmth. *Full of life.*

He reached his hand toward her cheek, his fingers a

millimeter from her skin, so close she could almost feel the warmth of his finger-tips.

Annabelle felt her heart slow, then stop. She was only dimly aware of her feet turning in the dusty courtyard, ready to bolt back to her truck, back to London.

Stefano frowned, his forehead furrowed as he stared down at her. Abruptly, he pulled away, dropping his hand.

"Yes, you are a beauty, Miss Wolfe," he said almost casually. "No doubt many men find you attractive. But I…"

His voice trailed off.

Annabelle's lips parted. "But you…don't?"

Stefano gave her a half-lidded smile. "Let's just say you're not my usual type."

His words should have come as a relief to her. Instead, they felt strangely like a rejection, a low dull hurt she hadn't expected. She pressed her lips together. "Oh. Good."

"So you see," he said quietly, looking down at her, "you have no reason to be afraid of me."

Annabelle looked up at him, horrified. Had he seen her fear? Had he known she'd been briefly tempted to run away—from Santo Castillo, from her assignment, from *him*—like some terrified virgin?

But that was exactly how he made her feel. Every inch the terrified virgin she was.

But her job and reputation were on the line. Straightening her shoulders, she tossed her head and lied, "I'm not afraid of you."

"Bien." He moved closer, his eyes locked with hers as he whispered, "I promise you have no need to lock your door."

Feeling like a fool, she looked away, her cheeks hot with embarrassment. She'd been so sure that the notorious playboy would try to seduce her. But she *wasn't his type*. She was apparently the one woman on earth who left him cold.

While Annabelle felt differently. She felt…warm. More than warm. She felt hot every time he looked at her. Just being near him made her skin flush pink and her core melt.

For the first time in Annabelle's life, she felt a physical shock of awareness. Of attraction. Of…*desire*.

And he wasn't even trying to seduce her. Funny. Either Stefano Cortez didn't realize the effect he had on women, or he didn't care. Either way, no wonder he'd left a trail of broken hearts in his wake.

"You must let me help you." Reaching around her, Stefano opened the back of her truck. He pulled out her suitcase and duffel bag, then looked at all the photography equipment behind it. "I'll come back for the rest."

"It's not necessary."

"It is to me." He lifted her heavy suitcase on his shoulder, then casually added her duffel bag on top, as if the weight were nothing. "Follow me to your bedroom, *señorita*."

Balancing both bags easily on his shoulder, he started walking toward the whitewashed house on the other side of the courtyard.

Follow me to your bedroom.

Staring after him, Annabelle shivered. She tugged her camera bag up higher on her shoulder, wishing—not for the first time—that she were truly the ice queen that everyone believed her to be. Because she traveled the world for her career, people thought she was fearless. The truth was that when she wasn't behind her camera lens, she felt vulnerable. Afraid. Unable to trust anyone. *And always so alone.*

Annabelle took a deep breath. She could hear the

leaves of the shadowy trees waving in the hot wind above her. Her assignment would be over in a week and she'd never have to see Stefano Cortez again. One week with him. How hard could it be?

She watched the way he moved, his long, leonine strides as he carried her bags toward the hacienda.

Stefano Cortez was the most dangerous playboy she'd ever met.

Thank heaven he was not attracted to her. God help her if he ever really tried to seduce her. She would not survive the onslaught of that sensual charm.

If he ever chose to take her...

Would she be able to resist? Or would his fire consume her, leaving only the charred ashes of her heart behind?

Her feet shuffled in the dust, ready to run, ready to jump back in the Land Rover, start the engine and not stop till she reached London.

Instead, Annabelle forced herself to be professional and do what she must. She slowly walked across the courtyard.

He doesn't want me, she told herself. *I'm perfectly safe.*

But as Annabelle approached the doorway of the house where he waited for her, his dark eyes seared hers. And she shivered.

All the warnings about Stefano Cortez...*were true.*

CHAPTER TWO

SEDUCING ANNABELLE WOLFE was not going to be easy.

But then, Stefano Cortez thought in lazy amusement as he led her down the shadowy hallway of the hacienda, truly enjoyable experiences in life rarely were easy. It was the difficulty of a challenge that gave any goal its true flavor and delight.

"We have all tried," Afonso Moreira had growled over the phone that morning. "We tried and failed. The woman is made of ice."

"Then you have barely tried," Stefano had replied scornfully.

"I used all my best tricks. Woman is immune. No man could seduce her. Not even you, Cortez."

"I can seduce any woman," Stefano had replied arrogantly. "You've said it yourself."

The older man snorted a laugh. "Annabelle Wolfe is just what you need. The ice queen will set you down a peg or two. You will not win this time, Cortez. I'll relish your failure."

Now, Stefano glanced back at the beautiful English photographer as she followed him down the hall. Her eyes were lowered to the tile floor. She kept her distance as they walked, careful not to touch him.

No. Seducing her would not be easy. The famously

elusive Miss Wolfe had evaded most men who'd tried to hunt her. Only a few had battled their way into her bed, most famously her old tutor and mentor. Patrick Arbuthnot, a famous photographer himself, had visited Gabriel's charity event at Santo Castillo a few years ago, and he'd sung the praises of Annabelle's passion and the bliss of her body, claiming he'd been the man who broke her.

The ice queen. Stefano had heard the epithet everywhere but he couldn't understand it. From a distance, he supposed she was attractive in a cool, restrained sort of way. If he had to pick a color for Annabelle Wolfe it would be gray, gray like her suit, gray like afternoon shadows, like twilight in winter.

But from close up, he'd been astonished by the glory of her natural beauty. She wore makeup on her skin, but no lipstick or mascara. Strange. Her eyelashes were blond, as were her eyebrows. She was tall and slender and beautiful, and yet strangely the ultimate effect was to evade notice.

Icy? No. She was prickly and rude, but her body— ah. Stefano could read what her body was telling him, and it was far warmer. He'd seen the roses in her cheeks, the warmth of her creamy skin and tremble of her slender body when he'd reached toward her in the courtyard. When he even looked at her.

He wanted to break through her cool reserve. To find out how wild she could be once she lost that restraint. Once she clutched his naked body to her own with a gasp as heat and sweat and passion mingled between them.

He could hardly wait.

And…for the first time in a decade, he might actually have to wait. It would take time to woo this woman. Perhaps he might not have her in bed tonight. Perhaps not until tomorrow.

The challenge intrigued him. It offered a pleasurable distraction this week, his least favorite week of the year, when his land and home would be invaded—first by event planners, then wealthy tycoons and their fur-dripping wives. Stefano held his annual polo match and gala for a good cause, to help poverty-stricken local villages, and yet he hated it every year.

So he would think of Annabelle Wolfe instead. Looking at her willowy figure in the shadowy light of the hallway made his body tense in an entirely different way. It was delicious.

He paused, smiling down at her. "Would you care for a tour of the house?"

"A tour around the house?" She stared up at him, her brow furrowed. "While you're carrying my luggage on your back?"

"So?"

She squinted at him doubtfully, then shook her head. "It's your funeral. Sure. I would love a tour so I don't get lost. Just make it short."

Her words were abrasive, but Stefano could read her body. He saw the stiffness of her shoulders and tremble of her wrists. Beneath her cold demeanor, she was desperately trying to hide her attraction.

Testing her, Stefano placed one hand on the small of her back, as if to guide her.

He heard her intake of breath, the hiss through her teeth as she jumped away. She glared up at him with wide-set gray eyes.

He hid a smile. Maybe he wouldn't have to wait until tomorrow, after all.

He looked back at her innocently, motioning down the hall. "This way, Miss Wolfe."

She set her jaw, hitching her leather bag up her shoulder as she growled, "You're the tour guide. You go first."

She clearly didn't want him to touch her, not even briefly, not even over multiple layers of her buttoned-up, businesslike clothing. *Hostia,* the woman was aware of him. And she was skittish, in spite of her defiant words.

He'd never seen a woman who so badly needed to be kissed. With her hair in a tight blond chignon, she had the cool poise of Grace Kelly, and the same hint of simmering fire beneath the surface.

Stefano wanted her. Not just for the novelty of a challenge. He wanted her for pure pleasure.

But Afonso Moreira had been right. This was not a woman who would easily be tamed. Her guard was up far too high. If Stefano wooed her too strongly, she would flee. He'd seen that in the courtyard. So to calm her fears, he'd implied he did not want her, and allowed her to draw her own conclusions.

Let's just say you're not my usual type. It wasn't even a lie. His usual type was beautiful, willing and uncomplicated. A pretty tourist passing through the nearest village. A French socialite or New York debutante he would see once a year, or better yet, never again.

Annabelle Wolfe was unique. Special. And he would have her.

Stefano walked ahead in the hallway, listening to the clack-clack of her two-inch heels on the tile floor behind him.

"This is the main salon," he pointed out as they passed the wide arched doorway. They continued down the hall past an old suit of armor, gleaming in the dull light. "Through that door is the library. And that hallway there leads to the kitchen."

"This place is like a maze." Her voice was cool, almost sardonic. "Will I need a map?"

He slowed, walking beside her. "Somehow I doubt that. You spend your life traveling the world, do you not? From Zanzibar to the Yukon, I've heard."

"Yes."

"Don't you have a home?"

"London." Her voice was clipped, as if reluctant to give even the smallest tidbit of personal information.

"And yet are you ever there? That's hardly a home."

"The world is my home," she bit out.

"I do not envy your life," he said softly.

She lifted her chin, and her gray eyes glittered like silver shards in snow.

"For the past few months," she said, "I've visited horse ranches all over Europe. I'm curious to see how your ranch can possibly be the best. Because so far I can't see it."

He knew she was baiting him, but he still felt annoyed in spite of himself. It was one thing to criticize him, something else entirely to insult his horses or his home. "You can't?"

She shrugged. "It's a beautiful place…"

"But?" he demanded.

Her eyes met his. "You charge double for your horses as compared to other breeders, and you often refuse to sell to customers for no reason. You make your buyers jump through ridiculous hoops."

"My horses are precious and rare. The only men who should own them are those who deserve to win races. It is not just a question of money."

"And yet you charge a vast fortune." She tilted her head and said doubtfully, "Maybe your horses are worth it…"

"Or?" he said sharply.

"Or maybe…you're just a brilliant huckster who understands how to trick rich fools out of their money."

He stared down at her. She gave him a tranquil smile, as if to say, *I have more armor than you can possibly comprehend.*

His whole body tightened painfully. His interest in bedding her now went beyond desire for her cool beauty to the passion for the hunt. For the thrill of victory. He wanted to best her. He wanted to hear her cry out his name in the breathless sensual gasp of need.

He wanted her more than he'd wanted anything for a long, long time.

Narrowing his eyes, he evenly returned her smile. "I will be delighted to show you why we're the best, Miss Wolfe," he said. "I will leave you in no doubt."

Her eyes narrowed suspiciously at his tone. He kept his expression bland, then turned away. "Come."

Stefano walked through the wide, dimly lit hallway. As she followed him, he matched his pace to hers. If she increased her speed, so did he. If she slowed down, he did the same. He gave her brief touches, crowding her space—innocently, of course, and always in the context of pointing out various beautiful items in the house, some of them antiques of great value. He guided her past an old Spanish painting of a woman.…

"Is that a Goya?" she demanded breathlessly.

"Yes, I believe it is," he said.

Then he led her into a large room with high ceilings of stucco and slatted wood. "This is the dining hall." He motioned toward the long wooden table surrounded by chairs. "I eat here with the stablehands. Mrs. Gutierrez, the housekeeper, does not care for our rough manners and so often keeps to her own room. But I don't stand on ceremony. We are equals."

Annabelle's pink lips curved. "Except for the fact that you own the place."

He gave a sudden sharp grin. *"Exactamente."*

They smiled at each other for a moment before Annabelle's smile fell. Turning away, she gestured toward a faded family coat of arms painted on the high whitewashed stucco wall. "That's your family crest, I suppose."

"Mine?" He snorted a laugh. "No. My parents were servants here when this *pazo* belonged to an aristocratic family. But the family's younger generation disliked living here and moved to a flashy *palacio* in Madrid. This house was abandoned. I bought it at a bargain price, using earnings from my brief and glorious show-jumping career."

She gave him a sideways glance at his sardonic use of *brief* and *glorious*. "I heard about that."

"Did you?" he said coolly.

"All the other ranch owners couldn't wait to tell me how when you were nineteen, you stopped your horse before a jump in the middle of the London International Equestrian Show. You would have won the show-jumping prize. Instead, you dropped out of the event and never competed professionally again. No one could tell me why. Care to share?"

"Maybe some other time," he said, never intending to do so. He turned toward the coat of arms in faded paint on the wall. "When I remodeled the house, I left that painting on the wall because it amused my mother."

"That's sweet. Are you close to your parents?"

"I was. They died. My mother only lived here a year."

She looked up at him. Her gray eyes were sympathetic

and even seemed to gleam with tears. "I'm so sorry," she whispered. "My own mother died when I was just two."

"I'm sorry," he said in a low voice. "But your father? Is he alive still?"

She averted her face. Her voice was strangely muffled as she asked, "Do you have any brothers or sisters?"

She'd deliberately changed the subject. He wondered about it but just said, "I'm an only child."

"I have seven brothers," she said. "But I rarely see them."

He looked at her, trying to see her face.

"Your house is lovely," she said softly, refusing to meet his gaze. "But I've seen enough. Please take me to my room now."

Without waiting for his reply, she turned on her heel and left the dining hall.

Stefano followed her, watching Annabelle as she walked. She was graceful, like a dancer. She was quiet, he thought, but not hard or cold as people called her—at least, not when she wasn't actively trying to push back his advances. She was gentle. Wistful. Even sad.

Why did no one know this? Why had no one ever seen it in her?

Annabelle's steps floundered as she paused at the base of the stairs. He saw the pink color in her pale cheeks. "I don't know where we're going. You need to lead."

"Yes," he said soothingly. Leading was what he did best. Going up on the sweeping staircase—noting the way she shrank back when he passed her—he led her to the second floor.

He'd remodeled the house when he bought it, but he'd changed very little of the look. He liked the solid old furniture, the traditional architecture. He'd added modern wiring and wireless internet, replacing the windows and appliances to make them more environmentally sound. But he preferred the house as it was. It was not just home—it was a symbol of what mattered and what did not.

His father had been a lowly stable keeper, and now the stables belonged to Stefano. His mother had once been a maid here, and now he possessed every stick of furniture.

His parents had been proud of their son's success. They'd loved him. For one year, before his mother had died, they'd been happy here. If only Stefano had known sooner about her illness...

He froze the thought cold, and stopped abruptly in front of a door. "This is your room, Miss Wolfe."

Annabelle stared at him with eyes the swirling gray of storm clouds. For a moment, she frowned up at him, as if bewildered by his sudden change in mood. Then she walked past him.

It was the best guest bedroom in the hacienda, the largest except for his own. He entered the doorway and relaxed at the comfort all around him. The room was bathed in beams of warm sunlight from the windows. The large bed had a lathed wooden frame, and a handwoven rug covered the clay tile floor. In a separate sitting area, an old desk held framed vintage photos of flowers, and an overstuffed sofa overlooked a small fireplace.

He set down her suitcase and duffel. "Will this do?"

She blinked, setting down her camera bag as she looked slowly around her. "It's lovely." She glanced at the corner by the fireplace. "I can store the rest of my photography equipment there."

"Bien." He watched her face, waiting for the moment when she would see the magnificent view out the windows. He wasn't disappointed.

Annabelle's eyes widened. Her full pink lips parted

in astonishment as she walked across the bedroom and pushed open the French doors.

Smiling, he followed her onto the veranda. Like her, he saw horses crossing the golden fields beneath the verdant sharp mountains and blue sky. As always, his heart rose in his throat at the vision of his land.

"It's so beautiful," Annabelle whispered, leaning on the railing and staring out at the vast view. "I've never seen anything so lovely."

Stefano exhaled. He hadn't realized until then how much her earlier words about the ranch had wounded him. But of course she hadn't meant them, not truly. How could anyone not see the miraculous beauty of his home?

He leaned on the railing beside her. "Every morning I wake," he said softly, "it's like waking up in heaven. I can hardly believe Santo Castillo is mine."

"No wonder you rarely leave here." She threw him a sideways glance. "Your women must love it."

"Women?"

"Your queue of lovers."

"I don't bring any women here. If I wish to, as you say, take a lover, I go to the village tavern and rent a room for the night." Leaning his elbows against the railing, he looked up at the wide blue sky. "I do not allow strangers here."

"Except for this Saturday."

He stared at her blankly.

"Your polo match. The charity gala," she said with exaggerated patience. "The most exclusive event of the horse-racing world." She shook her head with a laugh. "Did you already forget?"

He inhaled.

"Yes," he said flatly. "I did."

For a few happy moments, he'd forgotten his land

would soon be overrun by service trucks and hired staff and white tents, by flashy cars and the sharp stiletto heels of skinny women in slinky dresses, by the flashy horse trailers of rich men who wouldn't know a good horse from an old ass.

Annabelle blinked, staring at him. "You don't like hosting the charity event?"

"No," he said, looking down. "I dread it every year."

"So why do it?"

He leaned back from her. "Perhaps I do it for publicity. Perhaps that is why my ranch is so exclusive," he said coldly. "To get good press, to charge higher prices for my horses."

"If you wanted more press, you would do the celebrity circuit in New York and London, you would do the horse-racing circuit in Kentucky and Dubai," she observed. "But you stay here. You rarely even give interviews. That's hardly the way to get press coverage."

He looked at her. "Then perhaps I do it because I'm just *a brilliant huckster who understands how to trick rich fools out of their money.*"

An awkward pause fell between them. They were side by side, inches apart, leaning over the railing on the veranda.

"Maybe," she said doubtfully. He heard her hesitate, then she added quietly, "Although I heard that you donated your fee for participating in this cover story to your charitable foundation. Most men would brag about something like that. You almost go out of your way to avoid credit."

He stiffened. "So?"

"So," she said quietly, "are you some kind of saint, Mr. Cortez?"

Snorting a laugh, he looked at her. "A saint?" He gave

her a sensual, heavy-lidded stare. "You know very well that I am not."

She frowned at him. "I'm just trying to understand. For the cover story. Who are you, Mr. Cortez? Who are you really?"

He stared down at her for a long moment, then left the railing. "I will go get the rest of your equipment while you unpack."

Abruptly, he opened the French doors and went back inside. But to his surprise, she followed.

"I'm coming with you to get the equipment," she said, lifting her chin.

He shook his head. "You are my guest. And it is silly how you fight me every time I try to do you the smallest kindness."

"I'm not your guest." She glared at him. "And you don't know anything about my equipment. You might break it."

"I won't," he said indignantly.

"I know you won't, because I'm coming with you."

Her cool gray eyes challenged him. Defied him. *Tempted him.*

In the cool shadows of her bedroom, standing so close in front of the bed, Stefano looked down at her. He heard the sound of her breath, saw the pink flush of her pale skin. They were so close. The temperature between them was already hot and rising.

He had the sudden impulse to push her back against her bed, to run his fingers through her lustrous blond hair and pull it down from its tight chignon. He wanted to rip off her prim suit and see her lingerie beneath, to kiss and lick and suckle her skin.

He wanted to show her how unlike a saint he really was.

He'd already taken a step toward her before he stopped.

Dios mío. This was not his style! He was known for his seduction—not for throwing women down on a bed like a rough brute!

His hands tightened.

The more she pushed him away, the more he wanted her. The harder he would pursue her. The more absolute became his need to possess her.

He would see those cool gray eyes turn bewildered with sensual need. She would press her lips against his skin and he would hear her soft sigh. First, her surrender. Then, her release.

She would be completely his.

But not like this. Not like a barbarian. He would take her like a civilized man—by stealth. By seduction.

This time it was his own rough breathing he heard in his ears as he turned away from her. "Unpack your suitcase," he ordered. "I often carry equipment far heavier than yours."

"Wait," she bit out.

He stopped halfway to the door. *"Si?"*

"I forgot to mention one condition of my work. One I insist upon with every assignment."

He waited, folding his arms with a guarded expression.

She gave him that small, tight smile he was starting to recognize came before an attack. "You will agree not to interfere with my work. I must be allowed to speak to anyone at Santo Castillo, and photograph anything I like."

Stefano didn't like the sound of that. He'd had one or two reporters write about him over the past decade, and though he'd always managed to gloss over questions he didn't wish to answer, he despised the thought of having his privacy invaded. He'd bargained only on having a few photos of his land taken in exchange for the magazine's generous payment that local villages so sorely needed.

Bad enough that he already had to dread the charity event invasion on Saturday. He would remain in control of all photographs of his home. Always.

He gave Annabelle a gracious smile, holding out his hands in a conciliatory gesture.

"We will compromise," he said, meaning he would win. "I'll just need the last word on all photographs, and final approval before you send anything to the magazine."

Annabelle's brow furrowed in disbelief as she snapped her camera bag shut. "Give you control over my work? Absolutely not."

Watching her from beneath hooded eyes, he shrugged with a practiced carelessness. "Then perhaps we should tell the magazine to cancel the cover story. Perhaps you should leave now."

"Agreed." To his shock, she picked up her suitcase and lifted her camera bag back onto her shoulder. "I'll drive back to London and explain to *Equestrian* that you'll be returning their fee. Grab my duffel, will you?"

Carrying her suitcase and camera bag, she headed for the door in those sturdy beige shoes.

Stefano cursed softly under his breath. A woman who not only electrified his body, who not only shied away from his pursuit, she called him on a bluff?

Who was this woman?

"Wait," he said harshly.

She stopped, then turned around in the shadowy doorway. She waited, arms folded.

He could not remember the last time he'd had to entice a woman, to lure her, to play the game, using all the skills of his body and mind to tame her. He could not remember the last time a woman had defied him—*beaten* him—and it made him want her all the more. He stalked toward her.

"*Vale.* You keep the final word," he said, then added

in a low voice, "But I ask you to consider the feelings of the younger members of my staff and villagers. Do not publish anything that will leave them feeling exposed or embarrassed."

Annabelle's eyes widened. For a moment she seemed to go pale as if in memory.

Then, throwing her head back, she glared at him. "Do I look like a celebrity gossip reporter to you?"

His eyes traced slowly over her. The truth was that she looked just like what he needed. A long, tall drink of water to a thirsty man. A mirage. Beautiful. Untouchable. And, oh, he could hardly wait to touch her. "No, you do not."

Visibly mollified, she gave a single nod. "I will give you my word not to deliberately hurt any innocent person. Is that enough? For you?"

Stefano narrowed his eyes, looking at the determined sincerity of her face. *"Sí."*

He held out his hand to seal the bargain. She hesitated, staring down at his hand outstretched hand. Biting her lip, she slowly placed her hand against his.

And it was like being struck by lightning.

Stefano felt her hand in his own, skin against skin. Shock sizzled through him as her slender fingers trembled in his rough grasp. He tightened his grip, pressing their palms together, pulling her close in a visceral reaction.

He felt staggered by sudden violent hunger. His mind filled with vivid images, of ripping off her clothes, running his hands down her bare skin. Of pulling her down on the bed, taking her, filling her as her fingernails dug into his back, as he made her scream with savage pleasure.

With a ragged intake of breath, Annabelle ripped away her hand. Her cheeks were red as she turned away.

But the damage had already been done.

Dios mío. Stefano's breath was shallow. She was the ultimate mystery. She was cold and hot, gentle and cruel.

He stared down at her, his body vibrating with need.

Soon, he vowed grimly, she would be pliant in his arms, spread naked across his bed. He would make her weep with pleasure. He would give her everything. He would *take* everything.

Nothing on earth would stop him from seducing her now.

CHAPTER THREE

ANNABELLE HADN'T WANTED to shake his hand. No way. But he'd stood there with his outstretched and left her no choice.

Touching Stefano's hand had been like touching fire.

Annabelle had nearly gasped when she'd felt his naked palm, hot and rough against her own, when she felt his calloused fingertips brush the tender spot of her wrist. Electricity sizzled up her arm and ripped through her body. Her earlobes tingled, her breasts became heavy. Tension crackled through her like a lightning storm.

Just from touching his hand.

With a harsh intake of breath, Annabelle ripped her hand away, her cheeks burning hot. Even with her limited experience, she'd never felt anything like this.

"You win," she said hoarsely, fighting to keep her voice even. "Go get my equipment. I'll unpack."

She heard something from him that sounded like a purr of satisfaction, but she was afraid to look at his face, afraid of what he might read in her eyes. Confusion. Fear. *Desire.*

"Give me the keys to your truck," he said.

"It's unlocked," she muttered, still not looking at him.

"I will park it when I'm done unloading." She heard sudden amusement in his voice. "That is, unless you fear you cannot trust me not to break your car while driving it into the garage."

Reaching into her camera bag, she tossed him her keys with the merest sideways glance. But in spite of her efforts not to meet his gaze, she could not resist one tiny peek. Their eyes locked and she held her breath, caught, unable to look away.

He was so beautiful.

Beams of sunlight from the windows illuminated his black hair as his dark eyes ripped through her. Stefano Cortez was so brutal, so masculine.

Her pulse hammered in her throat. Men had hit on her before, but they'd left her completely untouched and unmoved.

Stefano made her tremble from within.

He doesn't want me, she told herself desperately, fighting her humiliating desire to flee. *I'm not his type.*

But his dark gaze was so intense. Almost…hungry. She saw the shadow of his chiseled jawline, the silhouette of his Roman nose, the masculine beauty of his face. He was like his house, she thought suddenly. As distant and foreign to modern life as his vast, remote ranch. Like a medieval Spanish *caballero.*

A warm breeze blew in from an open window, causing the tendrils of her hair to sweep against her cheek as their eyes held.

"Bien," he whispered finally. "I'll go. But I am glad you are here, Annabelle. I look forward to it. To all of it."

As he left, it was as if he took the warm sunlight with him, leaving her in darkness and cold.

When she was alone, Annabelle sagged back against the large bed. Her knees collapsed and she sat down hard on the white down comforter. Her camera bag was still clutched in her lap as she stared blankly at the beam of sunlight against the white wall.

How was she going to get through this week?

How was she going to make it?

Every time Stefano looked at her she felt weak. Just touching his hand had made her jump out of her skin.

Did every woman feel like this? No wonder she'd been warned. But all the warnings hadn't helped. She still... burned.

Annabelle covered her face with her hands. She had to calm down. Get ahold of herself. Everywhere she traveled, from Chile to Chelsea, men of every age and social rank had thought her single status and apparent freedom was a license to make a play for her. A farmer in South Africa had once tried endlessly to entice her into his bed, but every single time she had refused his endeavors. She'd laughed when the overweight, middle-aged man had pouted like a child when he'd realized that she wasn't going to take him up on his offer. To assuage the man's hurt feelings, Annabelle had ultimately bought him a short whiskey in the bar of the hotel she was staying in before sending him on his way.

The South African farmer hadn't been a bad sort, really. At least he'd been obvious and clear about his intentions. She preferred that straightforward attitude over the slimy, underhanded things that rich tycoons had tried, such as when an American billionaire had set up a fake "photography session" on his private island in the Caribbean. Or when a married duke had invited her to a party in the Highlands, and she'd arrived at his castle to discover his party was only for two. All of them clearly thought Annabelle, with her independent status and liberated career, was fair game and an easy lay.

Of course, Patrick's ugly lies about her, so many years ago, was probably a big reason for that.

Perhaps it would have been better if she hadn't ever gone to London to study photography. After her father's death, she'd buried herself at Wolfe Manor for years, hiding there like a ghost until she was almost twenty-two. If she'd stayed there, she wouldn't have to fight so hard now in the outside world.

But she couldn't believe that. She looked down at the camera bag in her arms. Taking pictures—whether of raucous revelers after a football match in London or of hunters pursuing deer in Africa—was the only time Annabelle felt alive. Working brought her peace. And more than peace: contentment. Even joy.

She didn't want to give that up. She wouldn't. Not for all the harassing men in the world.

"You want this by the fireplace?"

Annabelle looked up with an intake of breath to see Stefano striding into her room, barely visible beneath all the photography equipment covering his shoulders and arms.

"Yes, thank you," she said, rising unsteadily to her feet.

He set down the cameras, the umbrellas and scrims, the battery packs and studio lights, her laptop and sleek portable printer, stacking them in a well-organized arrangement into the sitting area of her bedroom. It completely filled the corner between the white fireplace and the old sofa.

Turning back to her, Stefano lifted a dark eyebrow.

"Care to see if I've broken anything?"

"Um," she said incoherently, biting her lip. Staring at the equipment, she looked up at him in amazement. "You carried all of it? In a single trip?"

"It's more efficient that way, don't you think?"

"How on earth did you manage it?"

He shrugged. "Perhaps I'm not as clumsy as you thought."

"I never thought you were—"

His dark gaze went through her, and her throat closed. She forgot what she'd been saying.

Stefano's sensual lips curved into a smile. "I'll go put your truck away now. Dinner's at eight in the dining hall. By the way, meals are casual here." His dark eyes seemed to twinkle as he looked over her designer suit. "If you think you can manage *that*."

Without waiting for a reply, he turned on the worn heel of his black leather boot. It took several seconds for her to come to her senses.

"I can do casual!" she yelled after him indignantly, but he was already gone.

She exhaled, staring at the closed door. Stefano Cortez was like no other man she'd met. Beyond his masculine beauty and devil-tongued charm, he had a physical strength and power that amazed her.

He'd carried all her gear. In one trip.

Usually, it took Annabelle—even with Marie's help—four or five trips. And yet he'd carried it all on his back with ease, and then stacked it all efficiently. Looking through the equipment, she saw it was all perfectly in order. She opened the extra cases with her cameras inside, pristine and safe. She took a deep breath, trying to make her heart grow calm and her warm cheeks return to their usual cool state.

She was attracted to him, yes. But it was worse than that. She almost…liked him. And that frightened her most of all.

Annabelle exhaled.

Work. That thought calmed her as nothing else could. She glanced at her watch. She had most of the afternoon, and would make good use of it.

Not bothering to change out of her gray skirt suit, she grabbed an extra camera and put it into her bag. Going downstairs, she went out the front door.

Past the house, on the other side of the courtyard, she saw a whitewashed stable. She peeked inside. There were only twenty stalls, all filled with tall, powerful horses. The stable looked like the remnant of another era, as if she had gone back in history two hundred years to the time of carriages. Closing her eyes, she appreciatively breathed in the smell of fresh hay, horse sweat and leather.

She took a few pictures, then went on to explore the ranch farther. The fields around the sprawling, white-washed house were wide and beautiful. She saw horses galloping beneath the sun, heard the lazy buzzing of bees in the soft air. The warmth of Santo Castillo was lush and lovely as a childhood summer.

Walking past a grove of trees, Annabelle saw a huge, modern, well-lit building behind the courtyard. A second stable? Annabelle shook her head, laughing at herself. Of course there was another stable. The Cortez horses were famous, after all, and twenty antiquated stalls were hardly enough for all the animals they raised here. Of course the ranch would be modern where it counted.

Opening the door, she walked inside the second stable.

It was enormous, with endless stalls and more horses than she could count. Then she heard laughter. She peeked around the corner and saw five young stablehands, perhaps eighteen or nineteen years old, dark-haired and skinny in T-shirts and jeans. They were working hard, two shoveling hay and three brushing down the horses, but even while so industriously employed the boys were still joking and scuffling. They reminded her of what Stefano must have been like at that age.

One of the teenagers saw her, and he cleared his throat. They all straightened, greeting her respectfully in Spanish.

"Buenas tardes, señorita."

"Necesita ayuda?"

She shook her head. "I'm going to take some pictures, all right?" she replied in the same language.

They nodded, then went back to work. They seemed self-conscious under her scrutiny, but were too disciplined to do more than give her a shy glance or two beneath their dark lashes.

Annabelle took pictures of the smiling teenagers, of the vast white stable, of the beautiful horses, using her smaller camera with a portrait lens.

"Gracias." After she left, she went out and took preliminary photos of the golden fields and sharp green mountains, testing the sunlight. She used her telephoto lens on the largest digital camera to capture some shots of the dappled brown horses galloping so gracefully, tossing their heads.

Annabelle took pictures for hours, lost in her work. By the time she came back to herself, the sun was starting to fall gently into the western horizon. The light had changed to soft gold, the color of ripe peaches.

She rubbed the dust and sweat off her forehead as she looked at her watch. Seven-thirty. She looked quickly through the images she'd taken with her digital camera. They were good, but the composition didn't quite do justice to this magical place. Some critical component was still missing. But what?

She'd have to figure it out tomorrow. The sunset was deepening, the golden light slanting. She tucked her camera back in her bag. Work was over. Now she had no choice but to deal with the problems of the real world.

Like how she would be able to be around Stefano Cortez for an entire week.

Even having dinner with him tonight scared her. *We won't be alone,* she told herself. Hadn't Stefano said everyone at the ranch ate together at the long table in the dining hall? She would just sit far away from him, talk to the laughing teenagers and pretend Stefano wasn't there.

A childish action, to be sure. But it seemed her only hope. Because as much as she tried to tell herself that her body's strange reaction to Stefano had been a one-off, and all the warnings she'd heard must have just thrown her, she didn't quite believe it. She would just have to be icily polite to him from now on—a layer of ice on top of a glacier, she told herself.

But she didn't believe that, either.

Even just thinking of him caused a shiver of heat down her spine. Why did her body react this way? Why?

Annabelle hurried toward the house. As she passed the large modern stable, she saw the boys were long gone. She was going to be late.

Rushing upstairs to her bedroom, she raced down the empty hallway and jumped into the shower of her en suite bathroom. She was toweling off her hair in two minutes flat. She pulled her wet hair back into a tight ponytail. Far from optimal for scar coverage, but it was all she had time to do.

Her hands trembled as she tried to hurry with her makeup, putting on thick foundation and cover-up over the long red scar that crossed her cheek and forehead. She'd repeated this routine every day, often multiple times, for almost twenty years. She could have done it blindfolded. Drawing back to survey her face in the mirror, she exhaled. At least her scar was invisible.

But she was going to be late, and she was never late for anything. Her cheeks went hot as she imagined Stefano's darkly amused drawl: *Did it take you an hour to find something casual to wear, Miss Wolfe?*

And it might. Annabelle zipped open her carefully packed suitcase. *I can do casual,* she'd told Stefano defiantly, but as she dug through her suitcase she had a sinking feeling in her heart.

Her former assistant had always packed something casual for her on every trip just in case. Unfortunately, now Annabelle was packing for herself, and she hadn't thought casual clothes were necessary. She double-checked, but the results were the same. Her only "casual" choices were an old silken robe she'd bought in Hong Kong, or a single pair of flimsy flip-flops. Great.

Exhaling, she sat back on her haunches. She missed Marie.

Marie had been the most capable assistant she'd ever had, but she'd put her photography career on indefinite hold to raise her family. *My camera will always be there,* she'd told Annabelle, *but time with my babies will be short and precious.*

Just thinking of her assistant's happy, exhausted face when Annabelle had visited her in the hospital, remembering the way Marie had cooed to her newborn baby as her accountant husband beamed at them both with an adoring, protective smile, Annabelle felt a pain in her throat as sharp as a razor blade.

With an intake of breath, she squared her shoulders. She told herself that self-pity was ugly and ridiculous and she must stop it, she must stop it *at once.*

Fine, she thought grimly as she reached for a clean

pantsuit and pulled it over her sensible white cotton underwear. Let Stefano and his young ranch hands laugh at her in her dressy clothes. She didn't care. In fact, it would make it easier.

She stared at her expressionless face one last time in the mirror and pulled her blond bangs forward over her now-invisible scar in an automatic gesture. She glanced at her watch: 7:59.

Closing her door behind her, she walked through the darkened hallway and down the sweeping stairs. Though the hacienda had only two floors, it was deceptively large, perhaps even the size of Wolfe Manor. When she finally approached the dining hall, she knew she was late. She came almost at a run.

But when she reached the doorway, she slid to a halt. Her mouth fell open.

She'd expected the dining hall to be brightly lit and filled with the noise of hungry teenaged boys fighting over the bread basket across the long wooden table.

Instead, the upper corners of the soaring ceiling were dark. A cluster of white candles flickered against the whitewashed walls.

Stefano was alone at the table.

When he saw her, he rose slowly to his feet. He looked dark, powerful, like a conquistador from a savage, brutal age. Emotion pulsed through her, a longing that tore at her heart.

He looked at her with eyes glimmering and black as night. Pulling out a high-backed wooden chair from the table, he said in a low voice, "You're late."

Annabelle froze, unable to move.

The flickering candlelight cast shadows on his chiseled cheekbones and shadowed, sharp jawline. His dark eyes were illuminated, as if lit by a deep fire.

He walked toward her. Stopping directly in front of her, he looked her up and down. His gaze skimmed over her tight ponytail, her designer pantsuit and low sensible heels.

"You have a funny idea of the word *casual*," he murmured.

It broke the spell. She exhaled.

Folding her arms, Annabelle glared up at him. "It was either this or my pajamas."

His dark eyes glinted with amusement.

"Next time," he said, his lips curving wickedly as he looked over her body, "choose the pajamas."

His gaze made her catch her breath. She turned away sharply to look around the dining hall. The candlelight didn't quite reach the soaring ceilings, leaving the high windows the scarlet color of sunset. The stone fireplace on the other side of the room was shadowy and unlit.

Annabelle swallowed. "Did the electricity go out or something?"

"No."

"Why the candles?"

"Romance, *querida*," he said softly.

She stared at him, shocked. He looked down at her with heavy-lidded eyes, and her heart turned over in her chest.

"After all," he said, his lips turning up in a smile, "you are here to show the readers of the magazine why Santo Castillo is the top-ranked ranch in Europe. I wanted you to see my home as it might have looked three hundred years ago. I wanted you," he said in a low voice, "to see the magic."

Magic? Annabelle already saw the magic. She was looking right at him.

"Come," he said, holding out his hand. "Join me."

She stared down at his hand, remembering what had happened last time. She looked up at his handsome face with dismay. How on earth was she supposed to keep her distance with just the two of them like this? A romantic dinner with Stefano Cortez, alone together in a candlelit hall, was not on her agenda!

Keeping her hands at her sides, she licked her lips. "But where is everyone?"

His gaze fell to her mouth. "Who?"

"The stablehands. The rest of your staff. You said they always joined you for dinner."

"Oh." Dropping his hand, he shrugged. "They finished eating an hour ago."

She exhaled. "They ate early?"

"*Sí.*"

"Why?"

He looked down at her. "I wanted to be alone with you."

She stared up at him, her mouth a wide O. "But why— why would you want that?"

"So we could talk."

"Talk? Talk about what?"

He smiled. "About your photography project, of course."

"Oh." Her cheeks burned. *Of course,* she thought, angry at herself. *What else would he want to talk to me about?* "Right."

Stefano walked back to the long wooden table. Against her will, Annabelle's eyes traced his lean hips and muscular thighs in his dark jeans. He'd showered and changed his clothes before dinner, and unlike her, he was decidedly casual. And so, so sexy. His black hair was still damp, pulled back tightly with a leather tie. Her eyes traced over his curved biceps to the tanned arms peeking out from his black shirt.

Going behind the table, he pulled out a chair.

"If you please," he said.

Annabelle's legs felt as if she were wading through water as she followed him to the table. She felt his gaze on her with every step. She fell into the chair.

Courteously, he pushed her chair forward under the table. He didn't touch her at all, and for about the tenth time since she'd arrived at his ranch, she felt incredibly foolish for thinking he was coming on to her. He was just being polite. Of course he was, she yelled at herself. He'd outright told her he wasn't interested in her. So why did she keep imagining that she saw molten desire in his dark eyes?

Clearly she was going mad. When she had been ten years old, her twin brother Alex had used to tease her when she played in the woods on their estate, digging in the stream, pretending each frog was a prince, every field was a distant country and that she could fly around the world in an invisible plane. Alex had laughed himself silly, telling her she was crazy, and he feared his sister would someday go all the way around the bend. Perhaps he'd been right, and all her years of loneliness had finally caught up with her.

Annabelle jumped in her chair as Stefano sat right beside her. She'd thought he would sit across from her, not next to her. He was too close. Way too close. And he smelled so good, like saddle soap and sunlight. Woodsy and clean and masculine. She took a deep breath. He smelled like everything good. Everything *dangerous*.

Trembling, she tilted as far away from him as she could without falling out of her chair. *Subtle, very subtle,* she thought sourly, but it was the best she could do when her body was screaming for her to run.

Trying to hide her pounding heart, she grabbed a linen napkin from the table and spread it across her lap. As casually as she could manage, she said, "So, what's for dinner?"

As if he hadn't noticed her leaning diagonally away from him, Stefano opened a bottle of wine. "Mrs. Gutierrez has prepared some of my favorite dishes to welcome you to the hacienda. I hope you will enjoy them."

Pouring red wine into two antique crystal goblets, he held one of them out to her. The wine shimmered crimson in the flickering candlelight. Careful not to brush his fingers with her own, she took the glass.

Looking down at her, he held out his own goblet in toast. "To every delicious pleasure."

She clinked glasses and then drank deeply, tilting her head back and closing her eyes, waiting for the wine to hit her empty stomach. Her nerves badly needed bracing.

Stefano lifted a large silver lid off a tray and served them both. Annabelle looked down at her filled plate. Her stomach growled at the sight and mouthwatering smell of the country-style Spanish dishes: steaming hot *empanadas*, red rice and marinated chicken, spicy Basque *chorizo*, cheese and green olives. She realized that she hadn't eaten since breakfast—coffee and a granola bar she'd devoured at a gas station on the road from Portugal—and she was starving. She put down her glass and picked up her fork.

"It's delicious," she blurted out after the first bite of chicken.

"Gracias," Stefano said as he refilled her nearly empty wineglass with red Rioja wine. He took a sip of his own wine and Annabelle realized he'd barely had any yet,

while she was apparently on her second glass. She would need to slow down. *No more Dutch courage,* she ordered herself, and she dug into her *empanada* with gusto. He smiled, watching her with satisfaction.

She hesitated, suddenly self-conscious, but the baked Spanish pastry filled with fish and tomato was so flavorful and delicious she couldn't stop herself from taking another big bite.

"I'm probably making a pig of myself," she said with an embarrassed laugh. "But it's so good."

His lips curved with approval. "On the contrary. I like a woman with appetite."

Nervously, she wiped her mouth with a napkin and washed down the last bit of *empanada* with a bit more wine. "You're not eating?"

"I am," he said, taking a bite of chorizo. "I just keep getting distracted."

"By me?"

His dark eyes gleamed. *"Sí."*

Her cheeks went hot as she put down her fork. *He's not flirting,* she told herself fiercely. *He's probably just never seen a woman eat properly before. He's used to dating actresses and stick-figure models.* Annabelle gulped another long drink of wine, then picked up her fork again. She tried everything on her plate. When she looked up, she saw Stefano refilling her wine again. She hadn't even realized her glass was getting low.

"Are you trying to get me drunk?" she demanded with a laugh, only half joking.

"Would it be difficult?"

No. She felt half-drunk already just being near him. But she lifted her chin.

"I can handle my liquor," she said, although the truth was she handled liquor mainly by staying away from it.

She was famous for always sipping mineral water. She'd been teased for it, but having a drunkard for a father and drug addict for a mother tended to make a person more cautious.

And by the increasing dizziness in Annabelle's brain she was drinking too much wine, too fast. Candlelight flickered against the high stucco walls of the dining hall as she looked at him. She suddenly realized her body had shifted in the chair. Instead of leaning away, she was now leaning forward, almost touching him. He could move a few inches and touch her.

Her attempt to calm her nerves with wine wasn't working.

"You're different than people say," Stefano said in a low voice. His dark eyes caressed her face.

Annabelle stiffened, hating the thought of being the subject of gossip. She knew people called her an ice queen. People could be so vicious, even cruel, not caring whom they hurt in their own amusement. "I have no interest in hearing what people say about me."

He shook his head, smiling.

"Yet another way," he murmured, "in which you are different from any woman I've met."

"Because I don't swoon at your feet?"

Stefano gave that same low, sensual laugh.

"Sí," he said with visible amusement. "Most women do swoon, believe it or not. But it's more than that."

As he looked at her, searing her with his intense gaze, she felt her skin flush with heat and her body start to melt. *Please, don't let me swoon,* she prayed. *Don't let me make an utter fool of myself.*

Setting her wineglass down, she sat back in her chair. "You said you wished to talk about work. Let's talk about that."

"Is work really all you care about?"

"Yes."

"I can hardly believe such a beautiful woman would say such a thing," he said softly.

Was he flirting with her? Was he?

She started to reach for her wine, then caught herself and angrily pushed it away.

Stupid wine!

Stupid candlelight!

Stupid handsome man who was like a dark prince out of a sensual dream!

"My work is all that matters," she bit out forcefully. "It is all I care about."

He stared at her, his brow furrowed.

"That's wrong," he said. "You are a young, desirable woman. Enjoy your work, yes. But there's so much more to life."

"Not for me," she said, lifting her chin.

"*Especially* for you. I admire your work a great deal, Annabelle. You have an eye like no other photographer today. So take my advice or leave it, as you choose." He sat back in his chair casually, breaking the spell. "But you might consider taking pictures of the yearlings on the upper slope…"

As they discussed various aspects of the ranch, he gave her suggestions about people and animals and the best angles of his ranch's rugged landscape. They finished their dinner, but just as Annabelle started to relax into a business discussion, he suddenly asked with gleaming eyes, "So have you decided about me yet?"

"What do you mean?"

"Have you decided if I am *a brilliant huckster* or a saint?"

She flushed, then met his gaze steadily. "I haven't decided yet. Maybe neither. Maybe just a man."

He leaned toward her.

"I want you to know me," he said softly. "All of me."

She felt hot beneath his gaze, then he leaned back again in his chair. "I set the price of my horses high for a reason. No one buys them who is not prepared to treat them like gold."

She snorted. "Because they are just as expensive, pound for pound."

"You think I am greedy?"

"No. I think you are arrogant and proud."

His lips curved as he said softly, "What else do you think you know about me?"

Annabelle swallowed. She already knew too much. She knew he was impossibly beautiful, like a dark angel, and every time she was around him her body felt tight with her heart in her throat. She knew he made her feel the warmth of sunlight and a soft sultry breeze of awareness every time he was near. "I think you're a playboy who toys with women's hearts."

Frowning, he leaned forward.

"I do not toy with anyone's heart," he said sharply. "Women who come to my bed know it will be for a short time. I am always clear. If a woman deceives herself into believing our affair will last, she has only herself to blame."

Annabelle sucked in her breath. "So you actually admit you're a womanizer."

Stefano's gaze traced slowly over her in the candlelight. Prickles of heat spread across her skin beneath her linen suit. "Does it bother you?"

"Morally, you mean?" Setting her jaw, she shook her head. "No. Why would it?"

"It frightens you."

"Frightens?" She forced out a laugh, and then told the biggest lie of all. "I'm not the least bit frightened of you."

"But you are." His dark eyes glimmered. "I can see that. What I don't quite understand is why."

"Don't think you know me. We just," she bit out. "You don't know anything about me!"

He swirled his goblet, making the red wine gleam like rubies in the candlelight. "I've already learned a great deal by watching you." Tilting his head, he observed her. "I know, for instance, that you always behave rudely when someone's getting too close."

"Don't be idiotic!"

Stefano's black eyes burned through her. "Exactly."

Annabelle's cheeks went hot.

"You're being ridiculous," she mumbled, looking away.

He leaned his elbow against the dining table, looking at her in the candlelight. "Why are you so defensive? What have men tried with you?"

She stared at him, then said stiffly, "I don't see how that's any interest of yours."

"Oh, come on," he said with a cajoling smile. "Just this morning, Afonso Moreira was complaining to me on the phone, saying you were quite impossible to seduce. An ice queen, I think his words were."

"Moreira is a fool," she retorted. "His idea of seduction was to make smacking sounds with his lips every time I passed him in the hallway. When I ignored him, he slapped my backside."

Stefano's eyes widened. "What did you do? Slap his cheek?"

"I had no need to resort to violence," she said uncomfortably. "I simply let him know that his attentions were not appreciated."

His smile spread into a grin that made his eyes twinkle. "Yes, I bet you did," he said. "I can only imagine. He's probably still frozen solid in a chunk of ice from your response."

Annabelle felt a lump in her throat at the criticism. "You think I'm cold and horrible, then?"

"To the contrary, *señorita*." His dark eyes met hers. "I think you're magnificent."

Her breath caught in her throat. She looked at the floor. "So what has worked with you?" she mumbled. "With women?"

He took another sip of wine, then glanced at her with a playboy's careless smile. "Usually this is what works. Flirting, asking questions, drinking wine. Why?" His smile spread to a grin. "Is my charm starting to get to you?"

She felt her cheeks grow hot. "That's not what I meant. I know you think no woman can resist you. But what about you? Has any woman ever gotten under *your* skin?"

"Oh." The smile on his face faded. He lifted a dark eyebrow, then looked toward the faded paint of the crest of arms on the far wall. "Did you know, as a boy, I used to steal horses from this estate?"

Was he changing the subject? Frowning, she gave an incredulous laugh. "Really? I can't believe it."

"All right, not steal," he said. "*Borrow*. I felt sorry for the horses because the owners ignored them. I took them for exercise when my father wasn't looking. Then I was caught riding a stallion bareback by one of the guests—the coach of a famous show-jumping team. Instead of denouncing me to the owner, he invited me to join his team. I said no. I was only eighteen and didn't want to leave my family. Until…" His lips turned downward. "Until the coach's beautiful blond daughter asked me in a way I couldn't resist."

A dull ache filled Annabelle like a thud. Why? She couldn't be jealous! What did she care about some blond girl who'd once had power over Stefano? She didn't! "So what happened?"

Again that shrug. "Last I heard, she married a wealthy man in Mexico City. But I cared for her, once. When I was too young to know better. Until I discovered the kind of woman she really was."

"What kind?"

"The wrong kind." He looked at her. "Is that what you wanted to know?"

She licked her lips. "You speak of the coach and his daughter so scornfully. But…they took you from poverty, didn't they? They gave you your start?"

"In a way," he said grudgingly. "I used money from my year of show-jumping to buy this ranch sixteen years ago."

She shook her head, furrowing her brow. "Then I don't understand why you stopped your horse at the equestrian show. Why turn on the people who'd helped you?"

He looked away. "I had my reasons."

"And—"

"I answered your question," he said. "Now it's your turn."

"What do you want to know?" she said hesitantly.

"Why are you so alone?"

She stared at him in shock, her mouth open.

"You came here without an assistant," he continued silkily. "I'd imagined most photographers of your caliber would travel with an entourage."

Ah. So that was what he'd meant. For a moment she'd thought he'd meant…that he'd somehow seen…

The loneliness of her entire adult life.

Annabelle's lips turned down. "My assistant had a baby last week. She's with her husband in Cornwall. Until I replace her," she said in a small voice, "I'm on my own."

"Ah. *Que lástima.*" He held out his arms expansively. "But at least you are not the one to be tied down, *sí?* No dilapidated cottage garden for you to weed, no tiny babies crying and keeping you up all night. No husband to cook for every day, ironing his shirts and washing his socks. *Sí,*" he said approvingly. "An artist like yourself must always have solitude and freedom." He lifted his goblet, looking down at her. "To freedom."

Her throat hurt as she lifted her wineglass. "To freedom."

They clinked glasses, and he drank deeply. Annabelle took a tiny sip, but the wine now tasted sour. She'd had freedom, yes. For many, many years. Practically all her life.

What was the difference between freedom and emptiness? What was solitude, but loneliness?

Annabelle put down the glass, feeling suddenly weary. She placed her elbows on the long wooden table, leaning her forehead against her hands as she rubbed her eyes with her fingertips.

"Are you not feeling well?" he asked with concern.

"I think I've had too much wine," she said in a low voice.

"I will escort you to your bedroom."

Back to her bedroom? She looked up sharply. "No!"

He stared at her, his brow furrowed.

She exhaled. "What I mean is…I'm not ready for bed. I just need some fresh air."

"Of course." Tossing his linen napkin on the table, he

rose gracefully to his feet and held out his arm. "Let me take you outside."

Annabelle stared at the muscled, bare forearm revealed by the rolled-up sleeve of his shirt. She was afraid to touch him again, afraid of the reaction she knew it would cause. She placed her fingers as lightly as possible on his arm.

As her fingertips felt the rough dark hair of his warm skin, she felt the same sizzle as before. She could feel the strength and grace of his body as he walked beside her. She trembled, looking up at him through her lashes.

The sprawling house was quiet and dark as he led her down the hallway. Apparently, the stablehands and house-keeper had all gone to bed. The only sound Annabelle heard was the echo of their footsteps.

They were alone.

She nervously glanced up at him through her lashes. It took a great deal of willpower, all her pride, not to turn and run away. She thought again of her truck parked in the garage. She could be back in London in seventeen hours, less if she pushed hard on the gas pedal.

As soon as they were out on the terrace, she dropped his arm, exhaling in relief. Then she blinked in amazement at the view of the wide-open night sky and moon-drenched fields beneath.

She felt the cool air against her skin and took a deep, cleansing breath.

Then Stefano spoke from the darkness beside her.

"So Moreira failed to seduce you," he said in a low voice. He looked at her. "How would a man succeed?"

Silvery moonlight frosted his hard-edged cheekbones, the hard masculine edge of his jawline. She couldn't look away from the sensual shape of his mouth, illuminated in soft silver light.

"Annabelle," he said softly, and her name on his lips was like music.

With an intake of breath, she stumbled back from him, grabbing a stone column on the terrace for support. He grabbed her upper arm. She felt his warmth through the linen of her jacket sleeve and shivered.

"How could a man seduce you?" His voice was low, but his eyes were fierce.

Annabelle took a deep breath.

Like this, she thought. Everything about him seduced her. Candlelight and conversation. The comfort and beauty of his home. The strength of his body. The power of his will. The intensity of his dark eyes.

But she couldn't tell him that. He was probably just making small talk. How great a fool would she be to tell him she was already falling for his playboy charm? He didn't need another gullible female believing the lying promises of his gaze.

"I told you." She looked away. In the distance, she saw the dark shadows of the craggy hills against the pale violet of the moonlit horizon. "I am impossible to seduce."

He moved closer. "I don't believe you."

She pulled away, looking at him with narrowed eyes.

"Why do you care?" she said. "You have enough women queuing up for your bed. You certainly don't need one more falling at your feet."

Silence fell, the only sound the distant call of night birds. He looked down at her, his body absolutely still, so close and yet not touching her.

"Ah," he said quietly, "but you're the woman I want."

He wanted her?

With a sharp intake of breath, Annabelle looked up. He couldn't have just said what she thought he said! She felt the soft night breeze against her skin. Saw a wispy cloud pass in front of the full white moon above. She licked her suddenly dry lips and tried to contain the tremble of her body from within.

"But you said...you said I'm not your type," she stammered.

"You're not."

"Then—"

"You're not a *type,*" he cut in. "You're different than any woman I've met before. Beautiful, independent, talented, restrained. I've had many lovers. But never a woman like you."

Shaking, Annabelle stared up at him, feeling hot and cold all over. Her only armor against her own traitorous body's desire had been her belief that Stefano didn't want her. Hearing he *did* want her was the spark. It caused the dry timber of her lonely heart to burst into fire.

She tried to fight it. Crossing her arms, she turned away. "Why?" she said bitterly. "So you can brag about your conquest of the ice queen to your friends?"

He sucked in his breath. "Who made you like this?"

She lifted her chin. "Like what?"

He set his jaw. "I do not brag. I have no need to. And I do not see why you would even have such a fear. I've only ever heard one man boast about you. The rest of your lovers have been remarkably discreet. Even of such a glorious conquest as you."

The rest of my lovers? Annabelle thought over the lump in her throat. There were no *rest.* There was not even *one,* just Patrick, a spurned would-be lover, the former mentor whom she'd thought to be her trusted friend. Until the day he'd tried to drag her into bed, and when she'd refused, he'd struck back at her in the lowest way he could.

Annabelle sucked in her breath as Stefano cupped her

face with his large hands. The feel of his palms, rough and calloused against her soft skin, caused a tremble down her body.

"All other women fade into shadow beside you," he said. His dark eyes seared her. "I want you, Annabelle. And I intend to have you. I will seduce you slowly, bit by bit, until you cannot resist me. Until you are mine. In my bed. At my pleasure."

Her heart was hammering in her throat. Swallowing, she lifted her chin. "Many men have tried, Stefano—tried and failed."

"But I will not." His fingertips brushed her skin and it felt like the hot breeze of summer after a long winter. His thumb stroked her sensitive lower lip, and her whole body shuddered with repressed need.

Stefano lowered his head until it was inches from hers, and she closed her eyes, even as her body trembled for flight.

"Soon I will show you, *querida,*" he whispered huskily against her skin, his breath warm against her hair. "Soon, I will show you the depths of the fire inside you."

She felt his hands on her skin, felt his powerful body against hers, and her knees went weak. She sagged in his arms as warmth and the exquisite anguish of desire flooded her body.

She could not resist…could not….

Then one of Stefano's fingers brushed lightly over her raised scar. The effect was electric. She heard the harsh echo of a man's voice.

You're ugly beneath that make-up, Annabelle. A hideous monster. No wonder your mother overdosed on drugs when you were a baby. No wonder your father tried to kill you.

With a choked gasp, Annabelle ripped away from him.

"Never," she spat out. Her eyes glittered at him in the moonlight. "I don't care how charming or sexy or powerful you are. I'm no man's one-night stand." She lifted her chin. "You'll never have me, Stefano. Never."

CHAPTER FOUR

STEFANO SAT UP STRAIGHT in his bed.

For a few seconds, he stared across his empty bedroom, looking at the slanted moonlight on the wall. It was still the middle of the night. Had he heard a noise? Or just imagined it?

He held still for a minute, listening; but when he heard only silence, he lay back against his pillow with a disgruntled sigh.

I'm no man's one-night stand.

After Annabelle had stomped off the terrace last night, leaving him standing there alone, Stefano had been shocked. He'd never been refused by a woman before—and in such a way!

You'll never have me, Stefano.

Why was he failing? What had he done wrong? He'd been so close to taking her in his arms and kissing her senseless. He'd thought he read her body's signals correctly. He'd seen the flush of desire on her skin and the deep yearning of her eyes in the moonlight. Cupping her face in his hands, touching her soft skin, he'd felt her tremble. Even her words had confirmed what he'd already known from her body: she thought he was charming. Sexy. Powerful. In short, she'd been putty in his hands.

Then she'd run away from him, practically sprinting in those two-inch heels.

Scowling, Stefano tried to straighten the cotton sheets twisted around his feet. He generally rose early in the morning, taking the rhythm of sunrise and sunset for his work on the ranch. He only made exceptions when he had been up all night making love. But the exception had not been required.

Never.

Irritated by how much her words bothered him, Stefano plumped his pillow, turned on his side and tried to get comfortable. After her rude rejection, he'd gone to bed early, but it had taken him a long time to fall asleep. Now…he looked at his clock—2:00 a.m. And his mind was already filled with the way she'd mercilessly crushed his pride. How she'd exposed his arrogance for what it was—unfounded.

He set his jaw. She was even infiltrating his dreams. He'd awoken when he imagined he'd heard her scream. Clearly it was only his own injured pride that was so shocked by her rejection that—

Then he heard it again.

Annabelle was screaming.

He leaped to his feet and raced barefoot down the hall in only his boxer briefs, his feet slapping against the cool tile floor. Cold fear gripped his heart as he pushed open her door and ran across the darkened room to the four-poster bed.

He found Annabelle asleep, her eyes squeezed shut, as she twisted and turned on the mattress. Her fingers clutched the white blankets, her body tense. In the shadowy darkness of the room as she gave a sudden heart-breaking cry.

"Annabelle," he said urgently. Sitting on the bed beside her, he gripped her shoulders. "Annabelle! Wake up!"

With a gasp, she opened her eyes. Her gaze was wide, terrified. Then she saw him and burst into tears. Not quiet, ladylike tears, either, but great gulping sobs.

Stefano felt his throat go tight. He pulled her into his arms.

"Shh," he whispered, stroking her hair, comforting her like a crying child. "You had a bad dream, but it's over. You're safe. You're safe."

He repeated those words over and over as she clutched him like a life preserver that would save her from drowning in the cold ocean. She held him tight, weeping against his bare shoulder.

As Stefano held her, he looked down at her in the dim shadows, unable to clearly see her face pressed against his chest. "What did you dream?" he asked in a low voice. "What happened?"

She clutched him closer, her fingers pressing against the bare skin of his back. When she spoke, her voice was sodden and muffled. "I don't want to talk about it."

Seeking to comfort her, he reached for the small light on the nightstand. But her arm whipped around him, quick as a flash to turn it off.

"No light," she choked out.

No light? He frowned, looking down at her head. "I only want to chase away your fears. Whatever dark terrors filled your night, *querida*," he whispered, stroking her soft hair, "they cannot hurt you now. Not while I am here."

He felt her tremble. "Thank you," she whispered almost too softly to hear.

He held her for a long time; he did not even know how long. As the thin slant of moonlight slowly moved across the far wall, she gradually relaxed in his arms. Her breathing became steady and even. But still she held him tight, like a desperate child.

He could hardly believe this was the same woman who'd so coldly pushed him away just hours before. Where were all her vaunted defenses? Where were her armored walls?

He breathed the scent of her hair. She smelled like apples and sunshine with a hint of soap. And she felt even better, soft and womanly and warm. She was wearing only a button-down pajama top of thin cotton and—he groaned when he felt the brush of her bare thigh against his—no pajama pants.

They were both half-naked. Holding each other on her bed. In the dark.

His body tightened with need.

No! Stefano set his jaw. He'd come to comfort her, to make sure she was safe, not to seduce her when she was defenseless. Not to take advantage of her weakness like a coward! He took a deep breath.

"You are safe now, *querida*." He kissed her temple softly, over the sweaty tendrils of her hair. He started to push away. "I will leave you now, to your sleep...."

"No!" The cry seemed to come from her heart as her hands pulled him back to her. Her lovely, delicate hands. He could feel the stroke of her fingertips against his naked skin, against his back and hip, pulling him against her on the bed. Where he wanted to be. He nearly groaned.

"What are you asking of me?"

For a moment, she did not answer. Then she said in a low voice, "I want you to stay with me while I sleep. Please...won't you?"

He wanted to tell her no. He wanted to leave her and

return to his bed, far away from the temptation she offered. *Madre de Dios,* he was only a man.

But her request had been timid, almost fearful, as if she were already bracing herself for his inevitable refusal. As if she expected some cutting reply, and yet her need was so great she'd had no choice but to ask, anyway.

How was it possible that such a beautiful woman, an international star of photography, a wealthy girl from an aristocratic family, could sound so timorous and pitiable when asking for the merest human kindness?

Stefano exhaled. Swallowing, he put his head down on her pillow. Stretching out his long, lean body, he pulled her down beside him. He wrapped his arms around her, pulling her against his chest, and tried to ignore the feel of her soft, plump breasts beneath his arms. He closed his eyes, willing himself not to notice the feel of her sweetly curved backside pressing back against his groin, with only thin cotton fabric separating them. He took a deep breath.

"Go to sleep," he whispered against her hair. "I will watch over you tonight. I will keep you safe."

And he did. For hours. He held Annabelle, listening to the rise and fall of her breath as she slept. He breathed in the scent of her hair, their heads on the same pillow. He held her body in the darkness, caught between the need to protect her and the agony of not making love to her.

He'd never slept all night in bed with any woman. Even Rosalia, the subject of his youthful infatuation sixteen years ago. He always left a woman's bed after he was done making love to her. He'd never slept with a woman like this. As Stefano held Annabelle in his arms, listening to her rhythmic breath, even in his torment of sexual need he found himself lured into a strange sense of peace. Of home. He closed his eyes.

"Stefano." Annabelle suddenly turned around in his arms, wrapping her arms around him. She clutched him closer to her naked, nubile body as he tasted the sweetness of her skin, suckling her breasts as she moaned his name in bed.

He woke from the sensual dream with a start, realizing his hands had started to reach for her breasts in reality.

Maldita sea. He sucked in his breath, wiping his forehead as he glanced out the window. He was overwhelmed with relief to see the first pink curls of dawn appearing over the eastern horizon. Morning, at last. Thank God. He looked down at Annabelle. She was turned in the opposite direction, curled up with a pillow clutched in her arms. He was unable to see her face but knew she was asleep by the soft rhythm of her breath.

The night of torture was over.

He had passed his test.

Carefully, Stefano moved away from her, rising from her bed. He stared down at her for a moment, then fled on silent feet back to his own bedroom and the cold shower he sorely needed.

After toweling off and putting on clean jeans and a white T-shirt, he went downstairs to the kitchen. It was dark. Even Mrs. Gutierrez wasn't up yet. Making himself a breakfast of dry, slightly burned toast rather than wake the elderly housekeeper, he gulped down a *taza de café* drunk so black and hot it burned his tongue.

Grimly, he went outside.

The world was still quiet and dark in the hush of dawn. He went to the old stables and took a deep breath of the saddle soap, horse sweat and clean hay. He was desperate to start work, determined to grind out his body's tension through hard labor.

Annabelle.

How on earth had he managed to sleep nearly naked in her bed all night without touching her?

He exhaled. He'd wanted to kiss her and never stop, and yet...she'd been so bewildered, so frightened by her dream. More than making love to her, he'd wanted to protect her and keep her safe. He'd never felt this way about any woman.

Annabelle was so strong. And yet, vulnerable. Almost... *innocent*.

What dream could have possibly affected her so horribly?

Stefano looked around the old stables. The ancient stalls had been meticulously repaired. The tools and equipment that were always carefully put away in their place had been cleaned and brought to shine. He grabbed a pitchfork and furiously shoveled piles of fresh hay, putting his back into it.

He thought again of how she'd sobbed after her dream, how she had refused to tell him about it, how she hadn't even allowed him to turn on the light.

He paused, leaning on his pitchfork.

Perhaps he was making a mistake, getting involved with Annabelle Wolfe. His instincts were starting to warn that an affair with her would not be light. Or simple. Or easy. All the things he usually insisted upon in a brief relationship.

But she intrigued him. Her cold exterior was just armor to protect her vulnerable heart. She might be from an aristocratic English family, he thought, but she was nothing like the rest of her class.

As a boy, Stefano had once envied wealthy men such as his father's employer, who bought and sold horses and lavish estates, and could change other people's lives on a whim. It had taken Rosalia and her father's long-ago betrayals to teach Stefano how artificial and heartless those people truly were. Now, he despised the cold, glittering world of the international jet set. He stayed away from the cities and the racing circuits where the upper crust traveled, and only had to endure their company once a year.

His annual polo match and gala raised money for his charitable foundation. Important. Valuable. But, oh, how Stefano dreaded it. Just a few days more...

He exhaled, shoveling another pile of straw, and pushed his thoughts back to a more pleasurable topic.

How many lovers had Annabelle had? Not many, surely. She was too prickly for that. And she could certainly afford to be choosy. So how many men had she invited to her bed? Less than ten? Less than five?

Stefano scowled. It irritated him to think of Annabelle with other men. Hypocritical of him, surely, since he'd taken so many lovers himself. He could barely recall half of the women he'd made love to, any more than he could remember satisfying other physical needs over his lifetime. Sex was a physical need like any other. He couldn't remember every single blanket he'd used in winter, every glass of wine he'd drunk or every bite of food he'd eaten. Why would he remember every woman who'd warmed his bed?

But if he ever made love to Annabelle... He shuddered. *That* he knew he would remember.

But would he have her?

You'll never have me, Stefano. Never.

So she'd said. But training horses had taught him to pay attention to nonverbal cues. And in many ways body language was the same for women as horses. The way her eyes wouldn't meet his. The way she skittered from him, backing away. The way she resisted his touch. The way she seemed to tremble—and if he drew too close, the way she would lash out. Whatever she said with her words, he could read her body as clear as day.

Seducing her was going to be far more challenging than he'd thought. But he would not fail. Could not.

Stefano heard a noise and looked up. Through the stable window, he saw a shadow and recognized Annabelle's slim figure silhouetted against the gray-and-pink dawn.

Strange. He'd once thought of her color as gray, but now he realized he'd been wrong. She wasn't like winter twilight at all. Annabelle was a January dawn. Cold, brittle—and yet with a pale mist curling upon the edges, soft pink promise like a whisper, wistfully dreaming of spring.

My work is all that matters. It is all I care about, she'd said.

Madre de Dios, that a woman like Annabelle should think such a thing!

He wanted to free her from that tight self-control. He wanted to see her smile, give her joy, hear her scream with pleasure—

"Oh." With an intake of breath, Annabelle stood blinking in the stable doorway. Her blond hair was pulled back in her regular tight chignon, and she wore a soft pink linen pantsuit and plain, sensible shoes. She pulled her camera down from her face. "I didn't expect you to be up so early."

"I couldn't sleep." He looked her over, relishing the image of her slim body. "Not after I left you."

"Oh. Right." She bit her lip. "About last night. Thank you for staying with me. I'm rather embarrassed by the whole thing…."

"Don't," he said sharply. "You had a bad dream. It happens to everyone at times."

Turning away with an unintelligible mutter, Annabelle lifted her camera and snapped pictures of the wood-slatted ceiling, of the horse in the closest stall, of the dust motes floating in the air from the first light of sunrise flooding through the open door.

The camera was her protection, Stefano suddenly realized. *It was her mask.*

"Put the camera down," he said.

"I'm almost done," she replied, taking pictures of the well-swept wooden floor. "Then I'll leave you alone."

"I don't want you to leave me alone."

Reluctantly, she lowered her camera. "I did have a question."

"Si?"

She pressed her lips together. "I wondered…if there was any reason you left my bedroom this morning," she said finally. "If you…saw something…that made you leave."

He stared at her. "I left because of you."

She looked up at him, her lovely face stricken. "You did?"

"I wanted you so badly it almost killed me not to touch you." He gave a low, self-mocking laugh. "It was a new skill for me to learn, sleeping next to a woman I desire without seducing you. By dawn, my self-control was almost entirely lost."

"Oh." The creamy complexion of her cheeks turned the color of roses. "That was very…gentlemanly of you."

He snorted. "I'm no gentleman. But I know you did not ask me to stay in your bed last night for sex. You needed comfort. So that is what I gave you."

She lifted her eyes. "Thank you," she whispered.

He broke eye contact deliberately. He looked at her clothes. "Another elegant suit."

She looked down at her designer pantsuit in pale pink, then lifted her chin. "I always wear a suit. I've dressed like this in the Gobi Desert, Tahiti, everywhere. Why should I treat Santo Castillo any differently?"

"You might prefer jeans and a cotton shirt for the hard work we do here," he said frankly. "I could send for some new clothes for you in Algares."

She shook her head. "I'm fine as I am."

Stefano set down his pitchfork. He started to pull off his white T-shirt. "Work as you please, then."

She stared at him with an intake of breath. "What—what are you doing?"

"Working as *I* please." He dropped his sweaty T-shirt to the floor, leaving his chest bare. Annabelle's eyes fixed on his chest, her eyes the color of hot embers as her gaze slowly followed the trail of dark hair down his bare chest until it disappeared beneath the waistline of his jeans.

"Annabelle."

Her eyes looked up. "What?"

Her tone was belligerent, but beneath her defiance he could see the flush of her skin and the way she swayed forward—even as her feet inched away.

If he hadn't been hard for her before, he would be now. Painfully. "Come here."

"What do you want?"

He looked down at her.

"I want to kiss you," he said in a low voice. "I want to pull that suit off your body and kiss your naked skin all the way down to your feet. I want to take you right here. I want to push you down against the soft, clean hay and make love to you until we're both hot, sweaty and exhausted with pleasure."

Her jaw dropped.

"That is what I want," he said quietly. "But for the

moment, I will be satisfied just to talk to you. If you will come closer."

"I...I can't," she choked out, backing away. "I need to get back to work."

"Are you still afraid of me?"

She clutched her camera in one hand, staring up at him. Then she tossed her head.

"Why would I be afraid of some Spanish playboy?"

"If you're not afraid, prove it," he whispered. His gaze fell to her lips.

With a gasp, she jumped back two steps. Stefano wondered if she even knew she'd done it, or if it had been pure reflex.

The beam of morning light from the door illuminated Annabelle's hair, making it a million shades of gold. She licked her pink, heart-shaped mouth, staring up at him with her big gray eyes.

Stefano swallowed. He'd never felt desire like this before. It was magic. He was caught, ensorcelled by desire.

"You're so beautiful, Annabelle," he whispered. "I've never seen your equal."

She stared at him for a long moment, her eyes wide. Then she clenched her hands.

"Just because you comforted me last night, I won't fall at your feet now." She shook her head fiercely. "I won't let you seduce me."

Beneath her defiance, Stefano saw the increasing tremble of her body. He saw her nervousness and fear. He knew if he came closer to her, even a single step, she would flee. Even now, her feet were inching back toward the stable door. It was only the knife's edge of pride that held her.

"Why are you so afraid?" he asked in a low voice.

"I'm not!"

"You're trembling. You're so afraid of me, that if I take one more step toward you, you'll bolt for the door."

She tossed her head, but he saw the desperation hidden beneath the bravado. "Don't be ridiculous!"

Slowly, deliberately, Stefano raised his black leather boot above the rough wood floor in a single step.

With a hoarse intake of breath, Annabelle stumbled back, dropping her camera with a clatter as she turned and fled the stables.

Annabelle had barely taken a dozen pictures so far that morning, testing the early light, before she'd found him in the stables. The last person on earth she wanted to see.

Stefano.

He'd seen her at her worst last night when she'd screamed in her recurring dream, the horrifying nightmare that always clung to her like cobwebs after she awoke. Annabelle could never awake from it completely. She'd lived it.

"Please don't hit her! Stop it, stop it!" her little brothers had screamed and cried over the rhythmic *thwack-thwack-thwack* of the whip cutting her flesh as her drunken, enraged father savagely beat her in Wolfe Manor. Annabelle was curled up in a ball on the floor, too weak to protect herself from the continuing blows. She knew her father wanted her to cry and beg for mercy, but she couldn't do it. If she did, she feared his anger would turn on the little boys crying behind him.

She could barely see little Sebastian and Nathaniel through the sheen of blood as she gasped to them, "Stay away! Run, get out of here!" But they wouldn't abandon her, even at such risk to themselves.

Then Jacob had burst into the hallway. Her eldest

brother, so tall and strong at eighteen, had knocked their father aside with a shout, snatching up the whip as he punched their father away from her with a single resounding blow. Annabelle saw their father fall, fall, fall as if in slow motion. She heard a loud terrible bang as his head hit the bottom step of the staircase, and their father's violent life had come to an abrupt end.

It was always the same nightmare when she was under stress, ending with the same shocked look in her father's eyes.

His death hadn't been her fault. She'd told herself that again and again. But she didn't quite believe it. He'd stared straight at her as he'd died. Whenever Annabelle had the dream, she always woke with a sob, woke to loneliness and despair.

But last night, like a miracle, she'd woken to find Stefano's arms around her. She'd felt safe. Comforted. With him beside her, she'd fallen back asleep, knowing nothing bad could happen when he was keeping watch over her.

Then she'd woken up and he was gone. Her embarrassment that he'd seen her in a vulnerable state was bad enough. Then she'd wondered if he'd seen the scar on her bare skin in the morning light, and it had been her ugly face that drove him away.

You're ugly beneath that makeup, Annabelle. A hideous monster.

Rising from her bed, she had showered and dressed. She'd pulled back her hair and applied her makeup with a trembling hand. Then, not wanting to face Stefano at breakfast, she'd gone straight outside. She'd tried to focus on taking pictures, but amid the silence of the morning, his low, husky voice invaded her soul.

I want you, Annabelle. And I intend to have you. I will

seduce you slowly, bit by bit, until you cannot resist me. Until you are mine. In my bed. At my pleasure.

When she'd found him in the stables, when he'd challenged her after everything that had happened between them, she'd been overwhelmed. Blood rushed through her veins as she'd tried to hold her ground. She'd clung to her pride.

Then he'd taken off his shirt.

She'd seen a man's bare chest before. But looking at his tanned torso, taut and lean with muscle, with a scattering of dark hair pointed downward like an arrow, she hadn't been able to look away.

Stefano had taken that single step toward her, and a surge of fear had ricocheted down her body. She couldn't explain what happened next. She'd just bolted. Her feet had scrambled back, nearly tripping as she fled. She hadn't stopped running until she was across the farthest field and gasping for air.

Now, as Annabelle finally caught her breath, she became slowly aware of the morning songs of birds, the noisy rippling of the stream. She was alone in the forest, standing by a stream of water on a rocky hillside. She looked up at the beams of morning light shimmering through the dark, shadowy trees.

She blinked. How far and fast had she run?

Breathing in the fresh, cool air, she knelt by the stream and splashed cold water on her face. Gradually the rapid pounding of her heart slowed. As she rose from the rocky banks, she looked around the forest.

No doubt Stefano was still laughing himself silly back at the stables.

Why did he have this effect on her? Even now, she craved his touch. It frightened her. She couldn't allow herself to be vulnerable to any man—but especially not

Stefano! As protective and kind as he'd been last night, a playboy had only one objective. To bed a woman…and forget her.

Annabelle's cheeks became hot as she recalled the look in Stefano's dark eyes as he'd taken that single step toward her in the stables…and how, in spite of all her defiance, she'd fled from him like a coward. Like a pathetic virgin.

But a virgin was exactly what she was. She closed her eyes. A pathetic virgin.

"C'mon, don't act like some pathetic virgin," the older boy had said, leering at Annabelle's low-cut lace top. She was just fourteen, and she'd snuck out of Wolfe Manor to follow her twin brother Alex to a party in the village with his older friends. Then her brother had seen her.

"Damn it, this is no place for you, Annabelle!" Alex had marched her straight to the door. "Go home, where it's safe!"

Her brother hadn't known she would go home and walk smack bang into their father, who'd just returned drunk from a frustrating day of hunting. Alex hadn't realized that their father would take one look at Annabelle all tarted up and explode into murderous rage at his daughter for the first time—and the last.

Annabelle's hand went unwillingly up to her forehead and cheek, feeling the hard ridge of the scar beneath her makeup, the scar that had never completely faded.

Go home. Where it's safe.

Her lips twisted with bitterness. No place was ever safe. Especially not home.

And no person was safe, either. People died, like her mother. People turned on her, like her father. People left, like her assistant. Or they betrayed her, like Patrick.

Better to just be alone.

Closing her eyes, Annabelle took a breath of the fresh mountain air. She heard the ragged sound of her breath over the birds of the forest and stream.

"There you are," a deep voice growled behind her.

She whirled around. The cold feeling in her heart exploded into heat that almost brought her to her knees.

"Stefano," she whispered.

Still shirtless, he stood before her, his muscular body and jean-clad legs planted on the ground before her. He looked powerful, rugged. Dangerous.

She licked her lips. "What are you doing here?"

His dark eyes looked at her across the shadows of the forest. "I came for you."

"You followed me?"

"It wasn't difficult."

She tried to glare at him, but she was so tired of fighting. So tired of running. "I…I don't appreciate you sneaking up on me. Can't you see I'm here trying to…to work?"

Sunlight and shadows shifted over the muscular curves of his half-naked body as Stefano walked toward her. In the slanted sunlight, dust motes floated lazily through the golden air. He seemed like a handsome gypsy, a dark prince from a fairy tale.

Then, wordlessly, he held out her camera.

Looking at it, Annabelle felt the blood rush from her face. Reluctantly, she reached out to take the camera.

Their fingers touched, and the shock of his rough fingertips against her skin caused a seismic tremble through her body. She started to pull away.

With a low Spanish curse, he grabbed her hand. "Why are you so afraid?"

She felt like she was falling apart. Desperately, she lifted her chin. "Afraid? Of you?"

"Yes, of me, damn it," he said harshly. "Of everything. Of *life!*"

His words hung between them, echoing in the cool air. She took a shaking breath.

"Because I don't want you to seduce me."

"But you do." He lowered his face until it was inches from hers. "You want it badly."

He knew too much, saw too much. Her heart hammered in her throat.

He abruptly released her. "You didn't run into this forest to take photographs," he said harshly. "You ran away from me because I was getting too close. And that's how you use your camera, your rudeness, your coldness. To keep people at a distance."

She swallowed, looking away. When she spoke, her voice was almost too quiet to hear. "Yes."

"Why?" he demanded.

She took a deep breath, lifting her chin.

"Because," she whispered, "it ends badly if I let anyone close to me."

Stefano's eyes were suddenly gentle as he reached his hand toward her cheek. "But, *querida,* just because a journey sometimes ends badly, doesn't mean it's not worth taking—"

Annabelle jerked her head away before he could touch the makeup that hid her scar. She flashed him an angry glance. "I'm not like you, all right? I'm not promiscuous. I don't try to seduce total strangers. I don't have one-night stands in hotels, with anonymous lovers I don't even want to bring home!"

He sucked in his breath.

"No," he said in a low voice. His eyes glittered. "Instead, you have no home. You share yourself with no one, because you are afraid!"

She gritted her teeth. "You don't know me!"

"No?" His eyes narrowed. "Your body reveals the truth. You turn to me, *querida,* like a flower to the sun."

She gasped in outrage at hearing the truth spoken aloud. "No, I don't!"

His dark eyes electrified her as he stepped closer. "Even now, you want me to take you in my arms," he said. "You want me to kiss you so badly you're trembling."

"I'm not!"

His handsome face was brutal, his body lithe and powerful, and he moved closer until only an inch separated them. She could feel the warmth emanating off his naked skin, feel the dark hair of his chest brush against the fabric of her jacket.

"Are you sure?" he said softly.

Ruthlessly, he took her in his arms. His broad, rough hands cupped her chin, tilting her face upward. She saw his lips curve wickedly beneath the dappled sunlight.

And he lowered his mouth to hers.

She tensed, expecting him to ravish and plunder her mouth, almost expecting him to roughly take her with force.

Instead, to her shock, his lips were warm and tender. His sensual mouth moved against hers gently, luring her, tempting her to pleasure, and against her will, she melted into his arms. She felt dizzy, swirling in a whirlwind of bliss and need. She felt his hard chest crushing her breasts. His skin was hot and silky beneath the trail of hair. He was so powerful. He could have taken her at his will. But he had no need to force her.

Annabelle found herself kissing him back with trembling, innocent lips.

He deepened the embrace, pulling her more tightly into his arms. Her lips melded with his as he guided her, teaching her the rhythm. His hands softly stroked her back, up and down. He parted her lips with his tongue, and as she felt him brush inside her mouth, a gasp of pleasure came from the back of her throat.

Annabelle's knees trembled. She twisted her arms around his neck, holding on for dear life. His hands moved to her hips and he held her firmly, keeping her close and tight against his body.

His tongue teased her mouth, tasting the corners of her lips, entwining and dancing with her trembling tongue. Pleasure cascaded in waves down her body. His kiss was hungry, his body hot and hard against hers. He held her against him, not allowing her to escape or deny his sensual demand. As if she could...

Her first kiss. She was lost in sensation, overwhelmed with desire. The whole world seemed to shrink to their physical points of contact, to his strong arms around her, to his hard, naked chest, to the fiery heat of his lips against her own.

His kiss changed. His lips no longer softly lured her. They became more demanding. Stefano no longer tried to convince her. He simply took what he wanted. He kissed her savagely, hungrily, hard enough to bruise. Clutching his shoulders, Annabelle kissed him back with the same force, with all her pent-up need of her lonely life.

Her mind was long gone, her body possessed. She only knew she had to kiss him or die. And it was so good she almost wept....

It seemed minutes or hours later that Stefano pulled away.

"And you still say," he breathed against her temple, "that you did not need to be kissed?"

Eyes still closed, Annabelle pressed her cheek against his chest. Her heart was beating so fast. Her lips were bruised. She felt warm sunlight on her skin. His strong arms felt like a shield, protecting her from the hard, cold world.

He stroked her hair tenderly. "How long has it been, *querida?*"

"What?" she whispered, dazed.

He smiled down at her. "Since you last took a lover."

She blinked. Then she stared up at him in slowly dawning horror. Her heart pounded in her throat as all the passion and heat and fire turned to cold ash inside her.

You'll never have me, Stefano, she'd said. *Never.*

She'd lied. The playboy was seducing her.

Annabelle sucked in her breath as waves of fear whipped through her. She couldn't let it happen. She couldn't! If she gave her virginity to a playboy like Stefano, she would lose everything. Her heart. Her soul.

While thirty seconds after Stefano had possessed her, he would forget her and move on to his next conquest!

With a gasp, she pulled away. Turning, she started to stumble back through the shadowed forest.

"Where are you going?" he demanded.

She tossed back over her shoulder, "I quit!"

"Running back to London? The fearless Annabelle Wolfe?" he taunted behind her. "Over one small kiss?"

She paused, looking back at him, her heart still pounding. "It wasn't *small*."

Stefano stood motionless, staring at her. Overhead, the green trees swayed in the warm breeze, causing dappled sunlight to scatter over them both like topaz.

"You hated it so much?" he said softly.

Hated it? No. She hadn't hated it. That was the problem.

Stefano's kiss had exploded her world. For the rest of her life, her memory would be divided in a new *before* and *after*. Today would forever be the day when she knew, without a doubt, how deep her loneliness and hunger went. And that she'd always be alone.

Annabelle felt a painful sting beneath her eyelids. She wanted to rush back into the warmth of his arms, to cling to him and beg him to kiss her again, to hold her tight and never let go.

But she knew how it would end.

You won't be able to resist him. No woman can.

The broken hearts he's scattered are as infinite as stars.

All the warnings hadn't saved her. He'd still penetrated her defenses. If she stayed at Santo Castillo, he'd have her flat on her back in a week!

A week? She shuddered. She wouldn't last the night.

"I'll tell the magazine to send another photographer," she choked out. Clutching her camera, she whirled around, her eyes blinded with tears. Her foot stumbled over the uneven ground on the edge of the stream, causing her to trip forward into the shallow water.

She fell hard against the rocks. A wrenching pain in her leg made her gasp, clutching her ankle.

"Annabelle!" Stefano was instantly at her side in the cold stream. "Don't move."

His touch was gentle as he lifted her out of the water and set her gently down on the banks of the stream. Her calves were wet and cold as he pushed up her pink linen pant leg. As he ran his hands along her ankle, she was mesmerized by the feel of his fingers against her bare skin. Then he brushed her ankle and she winced.

He looked up at her. "That hurts."

It was a statement, not a question. Reluctantly, she nodded.

"I'll carry you back to the house," he said grimly.

She blinked. "Carry me? In your arms?"

He looked down at her with his ruthless dark eyes. *"Sí."*

Ohmygodohmygod. She shook her head vigorously. "No, I'm fine. Really! I can walk! See?"

Rising, she tried to show him how well she could walk, only to wince and stumble when she put too much weight on her right foot.

Stefano's black eyes blazed as he growled a Spanish curse. Without asking for permission, he swept her up in his arms. She felt the warmth of his bare skin, the fire of his touch as he held her against his chest.

He looked down at her, his eyes as hot as fire.

"No more arguments," he growled. "Now…you are mine."

CHAPTER FIVE

ANNABELLE FELT DAZED, in a dream, as Stefano carried her out of the forest. A soft wind blew through the trees, moving the dark branches high above as beams of golden sunlight moved in patterns against Stefano's face.

When they reached the field, she felt the warm Spanish sun against her skin. She felt the shifting muscles of his arms and bare chest as he held her, heard the rustle of jean-clad thighs as he walked through the swishy grass.

Annabelle looked at Stefano's tanned forearms encircling her. She closed her eyes, shivering as she pressed her cheek against his rough, hair-dusted chest. Over the sigh of the wind through the grass, she could almost hear his heartbeat.

She hadn't been this close to anyone. Not for twenty years. Even before that. She hadn't been held like this by anyone, not since her mother had died when she was a baby. She'd had no embraces by lovers, not even a long hug from a friend. She hadn't allowed it. She wouldn't have allowed it now if he'd asked her, but Stefano had simply taken it as his right.

She was overwhelmed with feelings. Of safety. Of longing. Of need…

As they grew closer to the hacienda, some of the young stablehands saw them. Three came running with a shout.

"Get a doctor," Stefano ordered in Spanish. "Miss Wolfe has been injured."

"I don't need a doctor," Annabelle said in English. "You're making too much of a fuss!"

Ignoring her protests, he took her inside the house and up the stairs. Carrying her as if she weighed nothing, he brought her to her bedroom and set her down carefully on the bed. Then he glowered at her.

"Wait here."

A moment later, he returned with an ice pack. Sitting beside her on the bed, he grabbed a pillow and put it in his lap. Pulling off her shoe, he put her bare foot on the pillow and pressed an ice pack gently against her ankle.

Annabelle's cheeks burned as she submitted to his care. Looking up at his face, all she could think about was the way he'd kissed her in the forest. The way his body had felt against hers as he carried her back to the hacienda beneath the warm morning sun. And the way he looked now, still shirtless, sitting on her bed. Annabelle's eyes unwillingly traced the muscles of his tanned chest. They were so close, alone in her bedroom. It would be so easy to...

No! She couldn't even think that!

But her gaze fell to his mouth. His sensual, masculine lips had taught her to kiss. Taught her to *want*. With one heartbreakingly fierce embrace, he'd taught her the meaning of the word *desire*. Her lips tingled, spreading heat down her limbs to the molten core between her thighs.

"Annabelle," he ground out.

She looked up. "What?"

His dark eyes burned through her. "Don't look at me like that."

"Like what?"

"Like you want me to push you back against this bed. And make love to you until you scream."

She sucked in her breath, then licked her lips nervously. "I…I don't. Want you to kiss me."

"So you keep saying. *Lying.* To me. To yourself." Moving the pillow and her ankle off his lap and onto the bed, he stood. He handed her a blanket and said tersely, "The doctor will be here soon."

She felt vulnerable, lying in the large bed with him standing over her like a giant. "I told you, I don't need a doctor."

"You'll do as I tell you."

"You're not listening to me." She started to rise from the bed. "I don't want your help. I don't need it. I don't want *you.* I already quit this job. I'm going back to London—"

With a low snarl in Spanish, Stefano pushed her back against the bed. For a long moment, he held her there, his hands holding her shoulders against the mattress, his half-naked body hard alongside hers.

Their eyes locked, and Annabelle couldn't breathe. She was lost in his dark gaze, in the sensation of his body pressing her forcefully into the bed. They were alone, and if he chose, he could strip her bare—in every way.

Stefano's eyes fell to her lips.

"Why do you fight me so constantly?" he said in a low voice. "Why do you refuse to let me take care of you?"

Annabelle's heart pounded in her throat. "I can take care of myself."

"It's all right to rely on others for help," he bit out.

"No, it's not." She looked away. "I'm better off on my own."

"Do you really believe that?"

Against her will, Annabelle looked back at him. She could smell his woodsy masculine scent, like saddle leather and scorching sun. Like heat and hardness and fire. *And she yearned.*

With a softly muttered curse, Stefano pushed away from her. He stood beside the bed, glaring down at her. "Stay here until the doctor comes. Don't make me lock the door."

"Fine," she said, still shaking from her desire.

"You give me your word?"

"Yes," Annabelle said. "I'll see your doctor. Then I'm gone."

He moved slowly around her bedroom and sitting room, closing all the blinds until it was quiet and dark. A soft breeze blew from the ceiling fan high above, moving the air against her skin.

A moment later, there was a knock at the door. The elderly Spanish doctor inside gave her a kindly smile. As the man checked over her ankle, she submitted to the examination stoically, aware at every moment of Stefano watching her.

The gray-haired man finally turned and spoke in the Galician dialect of Spanish to Stefano, who suddenly smiled down at her as he translated.

"It's fine. A mild sprain. He says to keep ice on it and stay off it for the rest of the night."

"I told you," Annabelle said, exasperated.

The doctor patted her hand and left. As she started to rise, Stefano came to the bed.

"Where do you think you're going?"

"Like I said, back to London."

He sat down on the bed beside her. "Because I kissed you?"

"Yes."

His dark eyes glittered in the shadowy light from the

shuttered windows. "Are you saying I kissed you against your will?"

Annabelle remembered the way her knees had trembled as he'd kissed her, how she'd wrapped her arms around his shoulders as waves of pleasure had exploded down her body. She remembered how she'd gasped, how she thought she'd die with need.

Swallowing, she looked away. "I can't work with a man who clearly thinks all women are his own personal toys."

"I don't think that," he said in a low voice, his body inches away from hers on the bed. "I respect you, Annabelle."

Sure, she thought bitterly, he respected her. And he would keep on respecting her, right until the moment she surrendered in his bed.

When he'd comforted her last night after her nightmare, she'd felt cherished, protected, even safe.

Safe? She mocked the thought. Stefano Cortez, *safe?* He was the opposite of safe. He was a heartless, selfish playboy. If she allowed him to seduce her, if she gave him her virginity, he might give her pleasure, yes. But he'd be gone by dawn. And she'd have sold her soul for that brief illusion of being cherished and protected.

"You don't respect me." Annabelle shook her head stonily. "I'll have the magazine send another photographer."

"You're the only one I want."

"You should have thought of that before."

"You can't drive to London," Stefano said roughly. "You heard what the doctor said. You need to stay off your feet."

"I'll take a taxi to the airport and send for my truck later."

"I won't let you go."

Folding her arms to hide the tremble of her hands, Annabelle glared at him. "You can't keep me here against my will."

In the gray shadows of the shuttered bedroom, Annabelle felt warm air blow against her skin from the ceiling fan. She felt the dark power of Stefano's gaze and shivered. Maybe she was wrong. Santo Castillo was his own private estate, the empire he ruled, with a staff loyal to him alone. For all she knew, Stefano *could* keep her here against her will.

The air between them hummed with electricity as he started to move toward her.

Swiftly, Annabelle swerved her feet around the side of the bed, starting to rise to her feet. Stefano stopped her with a heavy hand on her shoulder.

"Don't go," he said quietly. "Rest. We'll talk later."

"There's nothing to talk about. Let me go."

He exhaled. "Please."

That single humble word stopped her as nothing else could. His dark eyes gazed at her with passion, yearning.

He looked at Annabelle as she'd dreamed her whole life of a man looking at her.

"You've had a difficult time," he said in a low voice. "Traveling from Portugal. Your bad dream last night. You're exhausted. Please. Stay. Rest. Then we'll talk."

Annabelle looked at the hard lines of his body. She thought of fighting past him to call a taxi, or physically trying to hop her way on one foot downstairs to her truck in the garage. Not appealing. Nor was it a happy thought to imagine dropping out of her assignment at the eleventh hour. Aside from what it would do to her professional reputation, she would personally know she'd fled here like a coward.

She could just imagine the juicy gossip that would be whispered behind her back. *The stud of Santo Castillo,* people would nod knowingly, *has claimed even the ice queen as his victim.*

Annabelle hissed through her teeth at the thought—of having the whole world think Stefano had seduced her.

He stared down at her. "Please, *querida.*"

Crossing her arms, Annabelle glared at him.

"Fine. I'll stay. For a while."

He gave a single nod. "Did you have breakfast?"

She shook her head.

"I'll bring you a tray." Rising to his feet, he pointed toward a button beside the bed. "Ring if you need anything." He paused. "You promise you won't try to leave?"

"I won't try to hop down the stairs on one foot or fling myself out the window, if that's what you mean."

"Bien," he said. "As long as I have your word." Taking her hand, he started to lift it to his lips. A deep tremble went through her, but he stopped before his lips touched her skin.

"Ah," he said. "I almost forgot. You do not wish me to kiss any part of you." Looking down at her with his inscrutable dark eyes, he straightened with a mischievous grin. "Rest now."

Rest? She fidgeted. "What am I supposed to do in bed all day?"

His lips curved. "I'm sure you'll find a way to keep busy." He brought her laptop and printer from the desk over to her side table. "Here. Now you can work. Although—" he tilted his head, his dark eyes bright "—if you ask me, there are far more interesting ways you could spend a day in bed...."

She scowled. "I'm not interested in hearing what you like to do in bed!"

"You're already thinking about kissing me, aren't you?"

"No!"

He gave her a wicked half grin. "You're wondering what it would be like, how it would feel, if I pulled you into my arms and stroked your skin." He leaned forward. "If I slowly kissed up and down the length of your body. Your breasts. Your thighs. If I tasted you with my tongue."

Heat roared through her, and she couldn't breathe. "I…"

With a low laugh, he turned away. "Perhaps I can't kiss you, *bella*," he said, "but I can dream of you tonight. All night long." His voice was almost a purr as he walked away from her. "Ah, *querida,* the things you let me do to you in my dreams…"

"I wouldn't do any of that!" she cried after him. But he'd already left, closing the door behind him.

Annabelle stared at the closed door sulkily.

The things you let me do to you in my dreams…

Lying in bed, with her ankle still propped up and wrapped in ice, she stared out through the open French doors of her veranda. Even from here, she could see the green forest where he'd kissed her. Her lips still tingled from the memory of his mouth on hers. She could still feel how he'd held her against his hard, naked chest as his lips had seized hers, pushing her mouth wide, taking her as his right—

Stop!

She would work. Yes. Work. Booting up her laptop, she opened up her email and scanned new messages. There were invitations to various lavish parties in London and work-related notes from *Geography World* magazine about her upcoming trip to Patagonia and Tierra del

Fuego. Annabelle blinked when she saw an email from Mollie Parker, the daughter of their former gardener at Wolfe Manor. Mollie was a kindhearted soul, one of the few friends that Annabelle still remained in contact with from her old village. She opened the message.

Just got back from Italy, and I'm feeling like a new woman. Except I'd barely decided to change my gardening business to landscape design when your brother Jacob insisted I make Wolfe Manor my first project. I'll spare you the gory details, but he left me no choice. After so many years, it's strange and a bit overwhelming to see him every day now. But he has thrown himself into renovating the house like a man possessed.

Wolfe Manor had fallen into disrepair after Annabelle had left to study photography in London, but it was now being renovated. Jacob was back in England after all these years. Annabelle hardly knew which surprised her more.

Jacob. Annabelle closed her eyes. If he hadn't saved her from their father almost twenty years ago, she would have died at fourteen. She had no doubt of that. Someday, she would have to thank him. But after all these years, she was afraid to even speak of those terrible days. The last time she'd tried to talk to Jacob about it, he'd left Wolfe Manor the next morning, and disappeared into two decades of exile.

She'd driven him away with her heartbroken tears that night. She drove everyone away, somehow.

With a deep breath, Annabelle looked back at her laptop screen.

It's strange and a bit overwhelming to see him every

day now, Mollie had said. Annabelle remembered the helpless schoolgirl crush the gardener's daughter had once had on Jacob. Her eldest brother, the Wolfe heir, had barely noticed her.

Annabelle wondered morosely if any woman ever knew how to love a man in a way that was good for her.

Staring through the window at the blue Spanish sky and distant green forest, she touched her lips. After thirty-three years, she'd finally been kissed. And her first kiss had been from a master.

For the second time in her life, there would always be a mark. Another *before.* Another *after.* All because Stefano Cortez had kissed her.

Work, she ordered herself. She turned resolutely back to the screen. She typed a reply to Mollie, then, plugging her camera into her laptop, she transferred the newest images to her computer. She looked through one shot after another of wide golden fields, cragged green mountains, horses galloping through the slow-rising mist of dawn.

Annabelle paused, her fingers stilled over one image.

The single picture she'd taken of Stefano in the stables that morning shone with vividness and energy. She'd caught him unaware, while he was shoveling straw. The slant of dawn's golden light from the windows illuminated the sheen of his tanned skin. Dark hair laced the muscles of his bare, muscled chest. His masculine beauty made her catch her breath.

She paused. She closed her eyes.

And she deleted the picture.

She nearly cried doing it. Her photographer's soul screamed not to destroy the beautiful image. But it was her only hope of survival—to erase Stefano from her heart.

There was a knock on her door. She looked up, her cheeks hot with guilt and grief. "Come in."

"Here's breakfast." Stefano brought in a tray and put it on her lap. She looked down to see ham and eggs, toast and fruit. "I got this from the kitchen. I brought both coffee and tea, since I didn't know which you'd prefer."

"Thanks." Mechanically, she took a bite of toast. She poured cream into her tea, then drank a sip of the hot black coffee. She looked up at him and said in a dead voice, "I've decided to stay and finish my assignment."

A smile lit up his handsome face. "*Bien*. I knew you would—"

She held up a hand, cutting him off. "You must never kiss me again."

His brow lowered. "Why? You disliked it?"

She sucked in her breath. "No. That would be a lie. When you kissed me…" She swallowed, then tried to keep her voice even as she said, "You kiss very well. Of course you do. You're famous for it."

He blinked at her cool tone.

"But being close to you impairs my judgment," she said. "It impairs my ability to do my job with clear eyes. And like I said…my work is what matters."

"But, Annabelle, surely…" He reached to take her hand, but she pulled it away, folding her hands tightly in her lap.

He stared down at her, his eyes dark.

"Do not pursue me," she said. "Please. Let me finish the job I came here to do." In spite of her best efforts, her voice trembled and broke as she looked up at him with tears in her eyes. "If you have any mercy in your heart," she whispered, "leave me alone."

CHAPTER SIX

STEFANO RUBBED HIS HAIR with a towel as he got out of the shower. Lathering his face in front of the mirror, he shaved with a straight razor. He froze at the sight of his haggard face.

He'd had three days of staying away from Annabelle now. Three days of leaving her alone. Three days of telling himself it was all for the best.

Three days of hell.

Setting his jaw, he toweled off the rest of his body and left the en suite bathroom, padding naked across his bedroom to the closet. He was still furious with himself.

He should have known better than to kiss her in the forest. He'd tamed enough horses to know that rushing Annabelle into a kiss, after she'd just run away from him in blind fear, was a mistake.

And yet he hadn't been able to stop himself.

What a kiss. When she'd kissed him back with her trembling heart-shaped mouth, it had been heaven. He'd very nearly ripped off her clothes right then and there in the forest, and taken her against the rocks. Against a tree. In the water. Anywhere.

Annabelle's kiss had been so raw, so unpracticed, so real. She'd clearly taken very few lovers in her life, a chosen, sacred few. He'd felt it when he'd kissed her, in her shaking lips as they separated beneath the force of his caress. She did not surrender herself lightly. He'd felt her shock, her hesitation. Then, like a miracle, he'd felt her fire.

A man would die for a kiss like that.

Stefano should have felt privileged beyond imagination. Instead, he greedily wanted more. Hungered for it. Thirsted.

If once he'd been intrigued by her, now he was obsessed.

But Annabelle's face had been so wan as she lay stretched out on the bed, her injured ankle extended and wrapped in ice. She'd looked up at him, her expression heartbroken as she'd whispered, "If you have any mercy in your heart, leave me alone."

He'd sucked in his breath at the pain in her eyes.

"Is that truly what you wish?" he'd replied.

She lifted her chin fiercely, her gray eyes glittering with tears like melted ice.

"It is."

"Then I give you my word," he'd said in a low voice.

And he'd left her, when all he'd wanted to do was take her in his arms and kiss away the gleaming tears he'd seen in her eyes. It had been the first moment of hell, and since then, it had only gotten worse.

For three days, he'd had only glimpses of Annabelle as she photographed the ranch. He'd seen her laughing with the boys in the dining hall, even chatting with the elderly housekeeper about her grandchildren in the nearby village.

Annabelle Wolfe, an ice queen? He gave a single hard laugh. She was charming and warm with everyone.

Everyone, except him.

When she passed Stefano in the hall, if she met him in

the stables, her eyes seemed to glaze over as if she saw right through him. He'd become invisible to the woman he wanted most on earth.

Now, setting his jaw, Stefano pulled a clean T-shirt and jeans from his wardrobe. Sitting on his bed, he put on his black work boots. Then he paused, staring blindly across his masculine, Spartan bedroom.

For three days now, he'd tried to convince himself it was better this way—better for her, better even for him. He shouldn't risk getting more involved with a woman who cried out with nightmares she wouldn't explain, a woman so powerful on the outside but so fragile inside.

He'd already slept an entire night at her side. He'd put her needs ahead of his own. Shocking. He'd never wanted a weighty affair. All he'd wanted with Annabelle Wolfe was a pleasant challenge and bit of fun. This was getting too serious. He should let her go.

But his body wouldn't listen. *He wanted her.*

Gripping his hands into fists, Stefano rose to his feet. Going downstairs, he went to the dining hall for breakfast.

He found the plump, gray-haired housekeeper, Mrs. Gutierrez, setting down bowls of freshly baked rolls on the long table. All the young stablehands bounced around her, noisy in their hungry eagerness. The teenagers, as usual, stacked food on their plates perilously high as they cheerfully wished him *buenos días*. Stefano growled out a reply and went straight to his usual chair, where he poured himself some black coffee. He drank deeply of the hot, bitter brew, burning his tongue.

"Good morning," he heard Annabelle's sweet voice say. Stefano put down his cup on the table and looked up.

The sight of her took his breath away.

She was sleek and professional as always, wearing a

pantsuit in creamy ivory and glossy black shoes beneath. Her blond hair was pulled back in her usual tight chignon. Small gold hoops gleamed in her ears and she carried a black leather case.

But the ivory of her suit was nothing compared to the creamy color of her skin. The gold of her earrings was dull compared to the lustrous blond gleam of her hair. Her bare lips were naturally pink and full, her big gray eyes fringed with light blond lashes. And it was all Stefano could do not to fall to his knees before such beauty.

Annabelle froze when she saw him. Then her soft gray gaze became inscrutable. She turned away.

He wondered what she was thinking. If the past three days had been as difficult for her as they'd been for him. Usually women fell over themselves to share their thoughts. But Annabelle didn't say a word.

The young stablehands saw her and rose to their feet to greet her, clustering around as they asked about her welfare in Spanish and accented English.

"*Señorita,* good morning!"

"Miss Wolfe, did you bring the pictures?"

"You fool, don't ask her yet. Let her sit down first!"

Annabelle gave a laugh like the ripple of cool water in a mountain stream. "Yes. I brought the photos. Just let me have a bit of breakfast and I'll be glad to show you."

The boys cheered, then escorted Annabelle to her seat on the other end of the long table. Stefano tightened his hands on his coffee cup, willing himself into self-control.

At any other time, he would have been proud of the teenagers for showing such good manners, falling over themselves to make a guest comfortable. But as he saw the delighted, warm smile that Annabelle bestowed upon them, something like a growl rose to the back of his throat.

Stefano wanted to be the recipient of that smile.

He wanted Annabelle to look at *him* like that.

It was a strange feeling for him to be ignored by the woman he wanted most. Mrs. Gutierrez, smiling, brought her a plate and she calmly served herself. Stefano watched Annabelle eat pastries, cooked eggs and ham with gusto while he drank only black coffee, feeling surly. He saw her smile and laugh as the boys entertained her with jokes, tossing rolls at one another. As usual, the teenagers were rowdy and full of laughter as they gobbled down their food and drank gallons of milk.

Beneath the dining hall's high ceilings of vaulted wood, Annabelle sat in her tall wooden chair at the end of the table, holding court like a princess, laughing at the boys' antics. And Stefano suddenly wondered why, at almost thirty-four, she had no children of her own. She would make a wonderful mother. Why had she never settled down and started a family?

Because she couldn't commit? Because she was a workaholic? Because she was constantly on the road and didn't need, or want, a real home?

All good reasons, he thought.

All bad reasons.

Annabelle finally finished the last of her tea.

"Now?" the boys demanded.

She smiled. "Clear the table."

The long wooden table was clean in seconds. As the boys clamored around her, even Mrs. Gutierrez came over to see what all the commotion was about. Annabelle reached into the black leather case at her feet and withdrew a stack of colorful printed images.

"Here's a sampling of the pictures I've taken so far. Just preliminary pictures off my travel printer," she warned. "The final versions will be far better."

She placed the stack on the table, and the boys snatched them up. Immediately, they started exclaiming with praise over the beauty of the photographs she'd taken of Santo Castillo.

"You are truly a wonder, s*eñorita*."

"*Sí*—you even made Juan look less ugly in this one!" another boy snickered, only to be punched in the shoulder by the first boy.

"My goodness, these are beautiful," Mrs. Gutierrez cooed. "The prettiest pictures I've ever seen." The housekeeper looked over at Stefano. "Don't you think so, s*eñor?*"

Annabelle's gaze met Stefano's across the table, and he heard her intake of breath. The smile on her face fled.

Setting his jaw, Stefano walked toward her. Reaching for the papers, he looked through the images. He saw Santo Castillo's landscapes, the golden fields around the hacienda, the dappled forest, the horses in the stables, even the boys working. He saw Mrs. Gutierrez cooking in the modern kitchen as she made a meal for seven hungry men.

Technically, the pictures were all perfect. And yet... they didn't move him. Something was missing. Something like passion. *Like life.*

"Well?" He looked up to see Annabelle biting her lip. "What do you think?"

It was the first time she'd spoken directly to him in three days. He could not tell her the cold hard truth—that these pictures did not touch his heart. What did he know about photographs? What did he know about art? Nothing.

Waiting, she licked her lips nervously. He had the vision of that pink tongue flicking at the corners of her full mouth. He felt himself tighten as he imagined those

sweet pink lips against his rough skin, gasping her pleasure, crying out his name.

No—he had to stop torturing himself!

But he'd never experienced anything like this, being so
close to a woman he desired without being able to possess
her. Did she even know the power she had over him?

"Stefano?"

"The pictures are fine," he muttered. Roughly, he
pushed the stack of photographs aside and turned away.

"No." The sharpness of Annabelle's voice stopped
him. "Don't be polite, Stefano. I want to know what you
actually think."

He slowly turned back to face her.

"I think they are unremarkable," he said quietly. "*Verí-
dicamente,* I expected better from you."

She blinked, clearly shocked. "What?"

"There is no passion in your photographs. No heat or
wildness." Lifting the stack of printed pictures from the
table, he placed them gently back into her hands. "I'm
sorry, Miss Wolfe. But you have completely failed to capture the essence of my ranch."

She stared at him numbly. "You…you don't like them?"

"I didn't say that."

"Then—"

He shook his head. "The pictures are beautiful, but
have no life. They are like a beautiful corpse." He looked
her straight in the eye. "Your pictures are frozen, Annabelle. They are dead."

Annabelle choked out a gasp. He might as well have
slapped her in the face.

Your pictures are frozen. They are dead.

She'd never felt so empty or so alone as she had for
these past three days. Mrs. Gutierrez had taken care of

her almost like a mother, packing snacks and tea for her when Annabelle went up to the old Moorish ruin, now just a pile of rocks overlooking the valley. Even the boys had looked after her, reminding her of her own brothers in childhood. It had almost been like…a family.

Except for the constant ache in her heart.

She missed Stefano.

She hadn't had any more nightmares to wake him. She hadn't dreamed at all, in fact. Her mind was blank. She had nothing but emptiness in her heart as she tried to throw herself into her work. She'd dragged her heavy camera bags and lighting equipment all over the ranch, taking photographs with her camera tripod and long-lensed cameras, using her lights for closer portraits inside the house.

But the truth was that she'd barely noticed the images she photographed. Not when it took all of her focus not to rush back into Stefano's arms.

So with a trembling heart, Annabelle had waited for Stefano's verdict as he looked through the pictures spread across the table. She'd prayed that somehow, by some miracle, he would think they were good. Instead, she'd never had her skill so thoroughly scorned.

I'm sorry, Miss Wolfe. But you have completely failed to capture the essence of my ranch.

Now, as his brutal judgment still echoed across the dining hall, Annabelle stared up at him in horror.

The boys started mumbling out excuses in Spanish.

"Better check on the new colt."

"Need to go shovel something."

"Need to be…somewhere else."

The teenagers grabbed the last pastries from the table before filing out of the room with surreptitious back glances.

After one last reproachful look at her employer, Mrs. Gutierrez followed them, closing the door softly behind her.

Annabelle looked up at him with wide eyes.

"Why would you say something so cruel to me?" she whispered. She felt like she was floundering, drowning. "You're—you're just trying to hurt me, because of… before."

Stefano set his jaw. "Do you really think so little of me?" he said harshly. "It gave me no pleasure to tell you this. Believe me. But you wanted the truth."

The truth. The truth was Annabelle felt like her heart was being ripped out of her chest.

But she could see in his face that he wasn't trying to hurt her. He truly thought that her work was frozen and dead. A beautiful corpse. Just like Annabelle herself.

She'd always known she would someday be exposed as a talentless fraud. Barely holding back tears, she turned away. "I…I should go…"

Stefano grabbed her wrist. "Don't."

The pressure of his hand on her wrist left her lightheaded as the pace of her heartbeat quickened. She ripped her hand away. Stuffing the pictures back in her bag, she lashed out, "What more can you possibly say?"

He looked at her. "You are a brilliant photographer, Annabelle. I have seen your work. You can do better than this."

"Maybe I can't."

"You have observed Santo Castillo from a distance. But you need to feel it. You need to live it." His dark eyes plundered her soul. "You need to come work with me."

She stared at him in confusion. "Work? With you?"

"*Sí*. With the horses."

Annabelle thought of shoveling hay, rather than watching through the safe cool distance of her camera lens.

She thought of the sweat, the hard work, the risk of her makeup smearing and revealing her scar. And worst of all, she thought of being so close to Stefano, when it took all of her effort not to throw herself in his arms and beg him to make love to her.

She pressed her fingernails painfully into her palm. "Why would you want my help with the horses?"

"It is you who needs the help." He brushed against her in a touch that seemed accidental, but she knew was not. The slow burn of his nearness sent tingles down her spine, causing her lips to tingle and her toes to curl. "To understand the ranch, you must feel it—" reaching up, he put his hand over her heart, not quite touching her blouse "—right here."

She looked up at him. She could feel the radiant heat of his hand. Annabelle's heart pounded even harder, slamming against her ribs.

Then he took both her hands in his own.

"Will you come with me?" His fingers enfolded hers, his bare skin against hers. He did it gently, like a lover's tender clasp, and yet her limbs burned, as if coming back to life after a long winter.

Annabelle knew she was in danger. Knew it to her bones. He wasn't trying to seduce her body now, but her heart. Even as she shook with need for his warmth, his touch, she was scared of his power over her, and the knowledge that if she surrendered, a love affair could come to only one sad end: her own destruction.

She swallowed. "I…"

He cupped her cheek with his hand. "Come with me today, Annabelle," he whispered. "No camera. Just you." His hot, dark gaze fell briefly to her lips, and her mouth tingled, making her feel dizzy. "For one day, leave your camera behind. Look with your eyes. Look…with your heart."

"Why do you care so much?"

A smile traced his sensual mouth. "I want your photographs of Santo Castillo to shine. To leave no doubt that my ranch is the best in the world."

"The best in *Europe*."

He gave her a grin. "That is a difference of opinion."

She laughed at the gleam in his eyes, then sobered. "Is that the only reason?"

"No," he said quietly. "I look at you and see an innocent, bright young woman that's been hurt by the world. Beneath your cold exterior, Annabelle, I see a broken heart."

She nearly gasped. How did he know? How did he see?

Setting his jaw, he shook his head. "It infuriates me. Like seeing a promising yearling with its spirit broken."

Annabelle tried to hide her emotion beneath sarcasm. "So you're comparing me to a horse?"

He put his hands on her shoulders. "Let me help you," he whispered. "Let me at least try."

Pressing her lips together, she looked up into his gleaming dark eyes. "But what if I fail?"

He gave a low snicker. "Fail? You've already failed."

She choked out a laugh. "You have a funny way of trying to reassure someone."

"Failure is liberating. It sets you free. If you are brave enough to fail and still do not quit, you will prevail," he said softly. "And I do not take you for a coward, *querida*."

A breathless, almost painful hope filled her. "You don't?"

He shook his head.

"In fact," he said huskily, moving closer, "I think you

are a woman who would rather die before you'd give up—on anything."

Their eyes locked. She swallowed, feeling prickles of fire spreading down her body.

"You just need to remember," he said, touching her cheek.

"Remember what?" she breathed.

"Who you were before your heart was broken." He lifted her chin. "And who you were born to be."

CHAPTER SEVEN

"WHERE ARE WE GOING?" Annabelle asked as he led her across the courtyard.

As they walked, Stefano smiled down at her, looking confident and completely irresistible as he pushed open the door to the old stables. "To the paddock on the upper slope. It's where we train the colts."

She halted inside the door, looking with trepidation at the monstrous-size horses inside the wooden stalls.

"You should change your clothes," he said yet again, looking down as her designer pantsuit and glossy black heels.

"If I leave now, I'll lose my nerve," she breathed.

It had been nearly twenty years since Annabelle had last ridden a horse. The same August day she'd decided to sneak out to the party in the village. She'd felt so powerful that day. Fearless. Free.

But by the end of that night, she had been in the hospital, and Jacob arrested for their father's murder. Her brother was acquitted, the verdict being accidental death in self-defense, but their family—and Annabelle—had never been the same.

She swallowed. The last time she'd ridden a horse, she'd been so innocent. So unafraid. *So young.*

Coming up behind her, Stefano put his hands on her

shoulders. She felt his warmth and strength like a burst of sunshine through rain. "Do you know how to ride?"

"I used to." She slowly reached up to stroke the horse's nose. "I used to race to keep up with my older brothers." She stopped her hand in midair, not quite touching the animal. She whispered, "I used to be fearless."

"You can be again."

She swallowed, then looked back at him. "Can I? Can I ever be that girl again?"

"Yes," Stefano said steadily.

With a deep breath, Annabelle turned back toward the horse. Then she hesitated. "But what do I do? How do I start?"

Coming closer, he smiled down at her. "First, you will choose the right horse. Not Picaro, he is a brute for all of his innocent face. Do not believe his deceit." He pulled her farther back into the stables. "Now this is Josefina, she is gentle. She will care for you like a mother."

He swiftly saddled the horse, then turned back to her.

Her eyes locked with his, and suddenly, climbing on the horse's back seemed easy compared to being this close to Stefano, to enduring the searching intimacy of his dark eyes.

Ignoring his hand, Annabelle went around him. Putting one foot in the stirrup, she threw her leg over the back of the saddled dapple-brown mare. To her surprise, she discovered that she hadn't forgotten how to do it. Her body somehow still remembered how to use her thighs to grip the saddle, her hands to hold the reins lightly.

"*Excelente,*" Stefano said approvingly. "You have not forgotten how to sit a horse." Swiftly saddling a horse in the nearby stall, he swung up on the black gelding in a single movement of beauty and grace. "Follow me."

Annabelle couldn't take her eyes from Stefano as he

led them out of the stable. He moved so well, and never more so than on horseback. She stared at his muscular backside, at his tree-trunk thighs splayed across the saddle. Then as he rode away from her, she blinked and clumsily urged her horse to follow. The gentle mare took pity on her and obeyed.

The wind blew against them as they rode away from the hacienda. Stefano glanced back at her with a wicked smile, then urged his horse faster with a low whistle. Watching him ride ahead of her, Annabelle was mesmerized by the image of the darkly handsome Spaniard riding the black horse across the wide golden field.

He looked back at her, his horse rearing back on two legs.

"What are you waiting for?" he shouted.

Annabelle felt a fierce answer in her own heart. Leaning low over her mare, she lightly tapped her heels and her horse raced forward with excitement that matched Annabelle's own. She soon caught up with Stefano. Smiling at him coquettishly, Annabelle gave a wild, joyful laugh, and raced past him.

She heard Stefano's shocked laugh behind her, then the rapidly approaching pounding of hooves as he caught up with her.

"The upper paddock," he called to her. "It's this way."

Annabelle felt strangely free, her heart light. *She felt young again.* They raced their horses side by side and, in the distance, she could see the far-off ocean echoing deep blue into the sky above, as the fields shimmered and waved around them like a golden sea. They rode side by side, hooves flying beneath them as Annabelle looked at him.

Stefano was laughing, his dark eyes alight with joy.

"How could you ever give up riding?" he shouted to her. "How could you ever give this up?"

"I don't know," she cried. She felt like she'd been sleeping for twenty years, and in this moment, *she awoke*.

They reached a plateau high in the green cragged hills. Following his lead, she tied her reins as she climbed down from the horse, feeling slightly sweaty but exhilarated as her feet touched the soft earth and her weary legs nearly buckled beneath her. The ride had tired her more than she'd expected. But it was worth it.

Was this all it took for Annabelle to reclaim the girl she'd been? One ride across the fields with a handsome man? If so, why hadn't she done it before?

Stefano went inside a large shed, and she surreptitiously checked her hair and makeup in the compact mirror from her jacket pocket. Her hair was ruffled but her makeup still in place. Perhaps working on the ranch wouldn't be as difficult as she'd feared.

Stefano came out of the shed with a rope lariat hanging around his neck, then brought out the first of the young foals from the nearby paddock out into the large pen.

"Stay close," he told Annabelle when she tried to move back to the shade. "You're going to do this."

For hours, he worked tirelessly to train each young colt to respond to his command, whether given by voice or gesture—to walk, to stop, to change direction or speed. When he returned each colt to the paddock, he brought out another, then another. Some of the animals obeyed. Some refused at first. But Stefano never lost patience. He worked each foal hard, and as the sun beat relentlessly down on them, his skin soon glistened with sweat.

Annabelle felt a bit sweaty herself, watching him with trepidation. He finally turned back to her, holding out the rope. "Now you."

She felt a surge of terror. "No, I really…"

"Here." He pushed the rope into her hands. "Now walk him," he ordered in a quiet, soothing voice, as if training *her* as much as the horse.

Annabelle tried her best to follow Stefano's instructions, but it was physically demanding work. The wily young horse didn't obey her commands as it had Stefano's. He kept pulling away, resisting her, yanking hard on the rope until it ripped out of her hands, chafing her skin.

When he was done, Stefano brought out another horse, then another. He kept forcing Annabelle to try again, until all she wanted to do was return to the house and collapse weeping in her bed.

But his words kept echoing in her mind. *I think you are a woman who would rather die before you'd give up on anything.* So Annabelle didn't give up. She grimly kept trying. She didn't want to prove him wrong. Stefano's regard had become important to her, as had the hope he'd given her for a different kind of life, a life of fearless passion and joy.

But by the time they took a lunch break, Annabelle's whole body was shaking with exhaustion. The white-hot sun beat down upon them as Stefano took the rope from her. "I'll take the colt back to the paddock."

Annabelle exhaled, nearly crying with relief. "We're done?"

But Stefano barked a laugh. "The day has barely started, *querida*. But the color in your face suits you." He smiled down at her. "I think you're starting to understand what it means to feel alive."

Agony flooded through her. "I don't…" she whispered, then swallowed. "I can't…"

He looked down at her. "You can."

They sat down at a table beneath a shady tree to eat the

sandwiches from Mrs. Gutierrez, but lunch was over all too quickly. It was all Annabelle could do to hold back her tears when they went back to work. As the afternoon wore on, her body ached and her head throbbed from dehydration and heat exhaustion. She could see why he'd wanted her to wear jeans. Her designer pantsuit was dirty and ripped, her black glossy heels impossibly muddy and scuffed.

Surely they'd be done soon, she told herself desperately. Surely they couldn't do this much longer. Could they?

The sun beat down on them, growing hotter by the minute. And the more exhausted Annabelle felt, the less the foals seemed inclined to obey her. Her hair was a mess, her clothes covered with sweat and grime and her pale skin was turning pink in the sun.

Worst of all: she knew with sickening certainty that the makeup covering her scar was starting to melt.

When Stefano brought out yet another new yearling to train, she wanted to scream.

"See this mare?" he said softly. "You wouldn't know it, but she was beaten by her first owner. I have trained her for months, to help her learn not to be afraid." He thrust the mare's rope into her hands. "Hold tightly to the rope."

Looking up at Stefano, Annabelle imagined she saw pity in his eyes. A hard lump rose in her throat as she choked out, "I'm meant to be like the horse, right?"

He frowned. "What?"

"Come on. The poor old horse who was once beaten and afraid. She's me. You're winning my trust, taming me as you did her. That bit about making me fearless—it's a trick! It's all a trick!"

"I'm trying to help you!"

"I don't believe you!" she cried. Part of her knew she

was being unfair but as she felt tears rise behind her eyes, she was beyond being reasonable. "Are you torturing me for your own amusement? To finally get me into bed?"

His eyebrows lowered. "*You're* tortured?"

"I don't need your pity!" She felt vulnerable and raw. "I'm not going to fall for you. I'm not. You can just… forget it!"

With a choked sob, she dropped the horse's rope as she covered her face with her hands.

"Don't drop the rope!" he said tersely, but it was too late. As soon as the mare was free, the animal immediately took off at a run, the rope flying behind her in the wind.

Stefano chased the horse down, caught the rope, soothed her with his touch and soft words, then led her out of the pen. When he finally came back to Annabelle, she could see the grim line of his body, the way he clenched his hands at his sides.

"I've saddled your horse. Go back to the house."

He was sending her away? "Fine," she said over the lump in her throat.

He came closer, his jaw set, his voice hard. "I was trying to help you, you know," he said. "I was trying to be unselfish for once in my damned life. But have it your way. Go back to your solitary, lonely world. Enjoy being alone and closed off from the world."

She flinched. She'd gotten what she wanted—she'd driven him away. He'd given up on her. Just what she expected. She drove everyone away sooner or later.

"Fine," she repeated. She rubbed her aching temple, then wiped away tears with an angry fist as she turned away.

"What happened to your face?" he demanded harshly behind her.

Annabelle froze.

She realized she must have rubbed off the last of her makeup. Now, to top everything else, he'd seen her scar. He knew how vulnerable and ugly she really was.

"It's nothing," she said. She quickened her pace, desperate to get away.

She heard him come up swiftly behind her.

"Stop," he said roughly. "Let me see your face!"

Annabelle wanted to collapse on the ground and sob. He'd given her the kiss of a lifetime. For the space of a few hours, she'd almost thought they were friends. Now... this is all he would remember of her. The ugly scarred monster.

Slowly, Annabelle turned.

"Oh, my God," he breathed, coming closer. "What happened to you?"

Beneath the merciless sun, she lifted her bangs, turning her face upward so he could see the deep red scar stretching down her face.

"Are you satisfied?" Tears streamed down her cheeks. "This is who I really am. *A monster.* Why did you have to give me hope I might ever be more than this?"

Stefano stared down at her, his expression a mask of shock. Annabelle looked up at his wide, dark eyes and saw horror and disgust.

With a choked sob, Annabelle turned and ran blindly, streaking over the wooden fence toward the forest.

This is who I really am.

Her choked, tear-sodden words still echoed in Stefano's ears as he stared after her, overwhelmed by the vision of her ruined, lovely face. The ugly red line had slithered down her forehead and cheek like a poisonous snake.

A monster.

His heart pounded in his throat. What had happened to her? Had she gotten the scar by accident? Or by the hand of man?

With a sob, Annabelle had turned and run.

With an intake of breath, Stefano ran after her. But this time, she was faster than he'd ever expected. She didn't want to be caught. Grimly, he crashed through the underbrush and into the forest. He saw Annabelle just ahead, her long blond hair streaming behind her. His stride was longer, his legs were faster, his stamina greater. He caught up with her on the other edge of the forest, pushing her into the bright, open meadow beyond.

"Let me go!" she cried.

"No," he said, tightening his grip on her wrists.

Annabelle struggled and kicked as he pushed her past the trees into the vivid field of red poppies. Shackling her wrists with his large hands, he looked down at her.

She looked half-wild. Her cheeks were flushed, her chignon gone as her blond hair fell in waves down her shoulders. Her pant leg was ripped, her ivory jacket dirty with splattered mud.

From this close, he could see every detail of the jagged scarlet line slashing down her beautiful face. But that wasn't what disturbed him the most. It was what was beneath the scar: the anguish in Annabelle's trembling face.

"What do you want?" she cried. "Why do you keep trying to hurt me?"

"I'm not! I want to help you!"

"You can't." She shook her head as tears streamed down her sunburned face. "No one can."

Amid the waving flowers, she looked so beautiful that his heart turned over in his chest. He took a deep breath. "How did you get your scar?"

She looked up at him with big eyes, like pools of gray after rain.

"Please." His hands gentled their hold. "Tell me."

"It hurts too much," she whispered. "It's better to be numb."

"No," he said urgently. Looking down at her, he put his hands on her shoulders. "Pain is how you know you're alive," he said, searching her gaze. "If you are too afraid to feel pain, you'll never know joy."

Annabelle turned toward the green mountains jutting into the wide blue sky. With a deep breath, she looked back at him.

"You think I'm hard and distant and cold." She shook her head, her eyes bright with unshed tears. "I wasn't always like that. My father had eight children by five different women. He hated all of us. He drove each of our mothers away, by force, death or insanity. But we children couldn't leave." Blinking fast, she looked down at her hands. "He hit my brothers for the slightest excuse. But not me, never me. I looked too much like my mother, you see. I thought I was lucky. And then…"

Swallowing, she looked away. "At fourteen I decided it would be fun to sneak away to a party, dressed in a low-cut shirt to see if any of the village boys might notice me."

Stefano set his jaw. "And did they?"

Annabelle sank to her knees abruptly, sitting in the field of red poppies and purple flowers. Her eyes stared blindly at the blue sky.

"My brother sent me home early from the party to protect me. But I found my father drunk, just returned from an unsatisfactory day of hunting." She blinked. "He was furious when he saw me. He screamed at me as he raised his whip. 'You whore,' he said, 'no boy will ever look at you again!'"

Stefano felt a sickening rage inside that nearly turned his vision to black. But she was looking up at him through her lashes, nervously waiting for his reaction. Clenching his hands into fists, he forced himself to sit down beside her amid the flowers.

"Go on," he said tersely.

She exhaled. "My brother saved me," she said. "Jacob knocked my father aside and pulled the whip out of his hand. My father fell and hit his head on the bottom stair. He died almost at once. And we were glad," she said dully. "We were all of us glad."

"I'm sorry," Stefano said in a low voice. His hands were still clenched, wanting to punch someone long dead.

"Now you know." Annabelle looked down at her own hands, and for the first time he saw that the tiny red lines he'd thought were scratches were actually scars. "Now you know how ugly I really am inside."

Stefano stared down at her.

"Ugly?" A warm breeze ran through the meadow, causing the flowers around them to dance softly in waves of red and purple. Fiercely, he grabbed her by the shoulders. "You are not ugly. You are beautiful and strong. Far stronger than the past actions of a coward like your father."

She looked away. Blinking back tears, she whispered, "You were right about what you said. I like being behind a camera. It makes me feel…like I'm invisible. So after living alone for years at Wolfe Manor, I went to university to study photography. But my most trusted mentor, the one I thought was my friend, turned on me after my first success. He was twice my age, but tried to seduce me. When I refused him, he called me a monster. He said no one would ever love a scarred woman like me. He said he'd only tried to seduce me out of pity."

Stefano sucked in his breath. "Was that Patrick Arbuthnot?"

She looked away, not meeting his eyes. That was answer enough.

"I met him once, did I tell you?" Stefano said flatly. "The man came to my charity event a few years ago. When I refused to sell him a horse he wanted, he bragged about being your first lover. I think he was trying to impress me." He set his jaw. "Say the word and I'll go hurt him for you."

Annabelle gave a surprised laugh, then shook her head tearfully. "He was thirty years older than I was, and weighed over twenty stone. He died last year of a heart attack while in bed with a Ukrainian model." She took a deep breath. "But still. What he said about me was true. No one can ever truly love a scarred monster like me."

Stefano cursed in Spanish, so loudly and fluidly that her eyes went wide. "You are beautiful. Talented. Lovely and kind. I've never wanted any woman as badly as I want you, Annabelle," he said harshly. "I've been tortured with wanting you."

He saw her blink, heard her ragged intake of breath. "You really think I'm still beautiful?" she whispered. "Even like this?"

He took a shuddering breath. Reaching forward, he traced her scar with his fingertip. "This is only a small part of you. You are more than this. You are also *this*," he said, lightly running his fingertips down her soft, unblemished cheek. "And this," he said, stroking her long, creamy neck. He moved his hand to her sensitive lower lip, unable to look away from her pink, full mouth. "And this."

He felt her tremble beneath his touch. He wanted to

kiss her so badly he couldn't bear it. But he forced himself not to do what every cell in his body screamed to do.

He'd given his word not to kiss her. So dropping his hand, he turned away.

Then, like a miracle, he felt her soft hand on his cheek, turning him back to her. He had a brief vision of her eyes, shining like a summer mist.

And she kissed him.

He felt the tremble of her mouth as her lips parted. He felt the softness of her skin. *Dios mío.* His body shook as he kissed her back ferociously, with all his pent-up need.

A gasp came from low in his throat. He needed more of her. *All of her.* He'd never wanted any woman like this. Feeling her slender body against his own, wrapping his arms around her, was like embracing pure fire.

With a shuddering intake of breath, he wrapped his arms around her. "I want you, Annabelle," he breathed. "I think I'll die if I don't have you."

Her gray eyes shone at him with trust and desire. Placing her hands on his cheeks, Annabelle kissed him with sweet, trembling passion. He tasted her tongue in his mouth and gasped.

Roughly, he pulled her down against him. Kissing her with every ounce of force he possessed, he rolled her beneath his body, laying her down amid the waves of purple and red flowers.

Now. He could wait no longer. *Now.*

CHAPTER EIGHT

AS STEFANO PRESSED HER back into the flowers, Annabelle felt the cool damp earth beneath her ripped suit, felt the warmth of his hard body over hers. She'd fallen into a dream.

When he'd told her she was beautiful, when she'd seen the truth shining in his handsome face, she hadn't been able to stop herself from kissing him. Now, she felt his hands move over her skin, caressing her sunburned face. Poppies blew against them, red and purple petals tangling and twisting in her hair.

He kissed her so deeply that she didn't know where he ended and she began. His lips moved against hers, his fingertips lightly stroking down her neck, beneath her bare collarbone. His tongue flicked inside her mouth, teasing hers like a sensual whirlwind. A tingle of sensation flooded her body. Her nipples tightened as she gasped, clinging to him. His calloused hands moved downward, stopping at the edge of her neckline. She held her breath, waiting for him to reach beneath her silk camisole. Instead, after a pause, his hands moved over the linen jacket, cupping her high, firm breasts.

Electricity ricocheted down her body, jagged and raw. Her breasts felt heavy, straining against the camisole, her nipples pebbling to tight aching points.

With a shuddering breath, he pulled away to look at her.

"You think you're not beautiful, Annabelle? You think you're not lovable?" he whispered. "Let me show you."

His hands cupped her breasts before he moved the weight of his body against her, kissing her so long and hard that she felt lost in her own fiercely answering need.

Annabelle looked up at his face. Above him she could see the wide blue sky as the wind fluttered purple flowers and red poppies down upon them. He was so handsome, so impossibly handsome, with his tanned skin and lean, muscular body. Tendrils of chin-length black hair had escaped the leather tie at the base of his neck and hung down around his face, giving him the look of an eighteenth-century pirate.

His dark eyes were hungry for plunder. For her.

Somewhere in the back of her mind Annabelle knew that giving her virginity to a Spanish playboy would do worse than break her heart—it would destroy her. But she couldn't push him away. Not now. She needed his warmth, his light, his touch. She needed to feel. *She needed to live.*

Stefano stroked her face with the pads of his thumbs, making her shiver in the hot sun. He cupped her face, looking down at her amid the flowers. "Never hate your scar. It is a badge of honor. It is beautiful."

She choked out a disbelieving laugh.

"Sí," he insisted. "It reveals your strength and courage, a far greater beauty than flawless skin. I would kiss your every scar if I could."

Annabelle's heart pounded in her throat. Could her scar really be something to be proud of, rather than something to hide?

She swallowed, licking her lips. Trembling at her own

boldness, she lifted her hair to reveal a scar on the base of her neck.

"I have one here," she whispered.

He smiled at her. Then, lowering his head, he kissed her neck.

She felt his lips against the scar, leaving a trail of hot and passionate kisses down her neck to the crook of her shoulder. Prickles spread down her body like wildfire, crackling with need, burning through her like a dry forest.

When he drew back, she shyly pulled off her ripped linen jacket, revealing the white silk camisole beneath. She pointed at a long, jagged scar along the length of her right upper arm.

"And here."

Taking her slender arm in his rough hands, Stefano slowly kissed up her scar. She felt his lips caress her skin, felt his slick tongue along her puckered flesh as he nibbled her with the edge of his teeth.

Again, he drew back. His dark eyes devoured her, as if only the barest thread of will held Stefano back from ripping off her clothes and making love to her amid the flowers.

Annabelle should have been afraid. Terrified.

Instead, she felt strangely fearless, like the fourteen-year-old girl she'd once been. The girl who wasn't afraid to pursue what she wanted most.

She pulled the neckline of her silken camisole down to reveal a single extra inch of skin. "Here."

Slowly, so slowly, he kissed the long-faded scar that stretched along the top of her naked breast. She nearly gasped at the new waves of pleasure, of tension and need. No man had ever done so much to her.

The white sun beamed down on them, the flowers

blowing softly in the hot wind. On the distant hillside Annabelle could see the ruined pile of rocks of the old Moorish castle. She felt out of time, out of place. Ancient magic, a sensuality older than memory, wove through her. It made her weak; it made her strong. It flooded her body with sharp euphoria and a breathless hush of expectation.

"I want you," Stefano breathed, cupping her face. "I've never waited so long for any woman. *Annabelle*."

His lips were hard and hungry as he kissed her. She felt his fingertips stroking softly down her body, her neck, her waist, and she forgot to breathe. She needed him more than she needed air. She gasped as he slowly kissed down her neck, tasting her bare shoulder as his hands cupped her breasts beneath the fabric. Her nipples tightened, and he moved his mouth to suckle her through the silk.

Her fingers gripped his shoulders as she gasped aloud.

He pulled her arms upright and yanked the silk camisole up off her body. Her white lacy bra came next. Her upper torso was completely bare as he pushed her back amid the flowers. She shivered in the hot sunlight, beneath the dappled shadows of tree branches swaying in the wind, as he looked down at her.

For several seconds, he stared at her in awe, whispering incomprehensible words of reverence. Then he swiftly pulled off his shirt. He looked like an ancient god of passion and war. Dark hair laced the tight, hard muscles of his chest and the flat plain of his belly. His shoulders were powerful and wide, his arms strong enough to fight a thousand men for her.

His body fell against hers. She felt his hard chest crush her breasts as he moved against her, the heavy weight of his body pinning her against the cool earth. His lips plundered her mouth in a kiss of seduction and fire. His hands moved down her half-naked body, stroking and caressing every bare inch of her skin. He suckled her earlobes, kissing along her neck to the hollow between her breasts. Her breaths came quick and fast as he slowly kissed down her naked belly. He flicked his tongue into her belly button and she moaned, shifting her weight beneath him. Desire pooled low in her belly. She felt a driving need for more....

He wrapped his hand around the mound of one breast and suckled her taut, naked nipple. She felt him take her inside his wet, warm mouth and arched her back with a soft cry. He swirled his tongue against her, teasing her nipple gently with the sharp edge of his teeth. As she gasped, writhing beneath him, he moved to her other nipple, licking and suckling her. She felt his hands move down her naked waist, down to the waistline of her pants. Over the fabric, he stroked her hips, grazing lightly over her thighs.

He lifted her legs around his hips.

She felt his hardness through multiple layers of fabric. It was unmistakable. He felt so hard and huge, pressed up against her. He swayed, moving between her legs, and her breathing came in haggard gasps.

She'd never known it could be like this. *She hadn't known....*

Suddenly, Stefano choked out a low, guttural curse. As the sun moved behind a cloud, a shadow shifted across Stefano's face as he ripped away from her.

It took a minute before she remembered how to speak, before her lips could even form words. "What—what's wrong?"

He stared down at her furiously, his jaw hard. "We have to stop. I never thought... I'm not prepared. Damn me to hell!"

Even through her pants and his jeans, she'd felt him

against her, rock hard and huge. "You seemed pretty prepared to me."

"I didn't bring a condom," he bit out, scowling in fury.

Looking at him, a laugh escaped her. "You mean you don't carry one in your wallet? You? The playboy everyone warned me about?"

"A mistake I will soon rectify." Standing, he yanked her camisole back over her chest. Wadding the rest of their clothes into a ball, he picked Annabelle up from the flowers. Carrying her against his bare chest, he strode swiftly out of the meadow and back through the forest.

"Put me down!" she said. "I can walk!"

"Not until you're in my bed," he said grimly, never breaking stride as he crashed through the forest. "I'm not giving you the chance to change your mind."

Back at the paddock, he carried her to the gentle mare he'd saddled for her. As if she weighed nothing, Stefano lifted her onto the dappled horse, then swung onto the saddle behind her. Thrusting their crumpled-up clothes into the saddle's pack, he wrapped both of his arms around Annabelle. With a flick of the reins, he tapped his heels against the horse's sides.

The mare leaped forward, and Annabelle rested her head back against Stefano's chest. She closed her eyes, hearing his heartbeat, feeling protected in his arms. They flew forward through the trees and back down the hillside, back toward the golden fields that surrounded the hacienda.

Sitting in Stefano's lap astride the horse, leaning against his muscled chest with his arms wrapped around her, Annabelle drowsed in a sensual dream. Her lips were bruised from his kiss. Her silk camisole clung to her bare skin where he'd suckled her with his wet mouth. Red and purple flower petals flew from her loose blond hair, whirling in the breeze as the horse soared over the ground, sharp hooves flying.

With every leap of the animal's long stride, Annabelle felt the warmth and strength of the powerful man who held her. She felt how much he still wanted her.

Annabelle twisted her head to look back at him as he guided the horse. His dark eyes were focused intently on the horizon. He looked like a knight, she thought, riding a charger to save a medieval castle. She felt every jarring step of the horse's fast gallop against the earth. She saw the sharp hooves and the distance to the ground, but in Stefano's arms, she wasn't afraid. Not even of what waited for her.

His bedroom.

His bed.

When they arrived in the courtyard, Stefano pulled the mare to a stop with a low whistle. Tossing the reins to one of the young stablehands, he leaped down. Not bothering to explain, he lifted Annabelle into his strong arms. She had a single vision of the teenager's shocked face as Stefano carried her to the house.

His fast stride never wavered as he took her upstairs. They were inside his bedroom before Annabelle's eyes had adjusted from the bright sunlight to the cool darkness inside. She blinked and saw his bedroom, the mirror of her own but with Spartan, masculine furniture.

Stefano put her down on his enormous bed. He looked down at her, bare-chested, dark-eyed and impossibly handsome. The rest of the world disappeared. She could see only him. Wanted only him.

Even if it destroyed her.

Stefano pushed her back against his pillows. He kissed her, his lips deliciously hard, and she felt his hands reach for her camisole. Roughly, he ripped the silk apart in his bare hands and dropped it to the floor.

"Don't rip my clothes!" she gasped.

"I want it all off," he growled. "Now."

Flinging himself on top of her, he moved his hands down her body, stroking her naked breasts to her flat belly. His gaze locked with hers as he undid the zipper of her pants and yanked them down over the curve of her hips, past her feet, before tossing them to the floor.

Annabelle's mouth parted in shock as he knelt at the foot of the bed.

Roughly pushing her legs apart, he kissed up the inside of her naked thighs. He cupped the mound between her legs over her underwear, causing her to tremble and arch her back, rising to meet him. She closed her eyes, gripping the white cotton sheet in her fists, as if she were afraid she might otherwise go spinning upward into the sky. His mouth moved to the edge of the cotton fabric, licking just beneath the elastic with a flick of his tongue. Then he ripped it off her body entirely, and she gasped.

She realized she was naked, spread-eagled across his enormous bed. No man had ever seen her naked before. She opened her eyes.

Looking at the hunger in his eyes, she sucked in her breath. Slowly, never taking his gaze from hers, he took off his jeans and dark boxers. Naked, he knelt before her on the bed. Staring up at him in the half shadows slatted with streaks of light from the blinds, Annabelle sucked in her breath at his masculine beauty. He was so hard, and so ready for her. But he was so huge. How would he ever fit inside her? How badly would it hurt?

Biting her lip, Annabelle looked up at him, her eyes dazed with wonder and desire and fear. With a groan, he lowered his head to kiss her. He kissed her softly on the forehead, her eyelids, then finally her mouth with a long, intense kiss.

"Look at me," he whispered, biting her lower lip, "and ask me if I think you're beautiful."

He pulled away, his knees braced on the mattress as he straddled her hips, and even as the question rose to Annabelle's mouth, she had no need to ask. The physical proof of his desire jutted hard from his body.

"Touch me," he said roughly. "And ask if I want you."

She'd never *seen* a naked man before, let alone touched one. Timidly, she reached out a fingertip and stroked him from the tip along the shaft. He jerked beneath her touch. Gaining confidence, she took him fully in her gentle grasp. He exhaled. He was so huge in her hand, and so hard. When she looked up in wonder at his handsome face his expression was strained, as if he were fighting to keep control.

"You want me," Annabelle said softly. It was a statement, not a question.

Stefano looked down at her, spread across his bed. His dark eyes seared her skin. She realized he could see all the scars on her whole body. Everything that surgery and time had not healed, everything she'd hidden for twenty years, *he could see.*

But to her surprise, she wasn't afraid. She wasn't ashamed. Beneath his eyes, she was beautiful.

He lowered his body over hers, and as he kissed her, she felt it all over her body. The intensity of his embrace felt like Christmas, like home, like love itself. She felt the hard roughness of his thighs against hers, felt his muscled, hair-covered chest slide against her plump breasts. They were so different and yet, as he held her beneath him, they were the same. They were one.

She felt him between her legs, sliding over her most

secret core, demanding entrance. His hands cupped her breasts as he suckled her nipples and stroked her breasts. She gasped as she felt his fingers move down her flat belly to her hips and finally between her thighs, closer and closer to the sweet aching place that begged for his touch. He teased her, making her tight with longing and desire as he licked and stroked her body. Finally, when she was nearly half-mad with need, he brushed her molten core with his fingertips, in the barest whisper of a touch.

Her hips jerked forward in the explosion of sensation, and she gasped. He touched her again, so softly. With his other hand, he pushed a single exploratory fingertip inside her, and she gripped the sheets in her hands, twisting back and forth, wanting deeper. Wanting more, but not knowing how to ask.

But he already knew. In a swift motion he moved down her naked body, placing his head between her legs. Pushing her thighs apart, he tasted her with the full width of his tongue.

She cried out, arching her back beneath the electric arc of pleasure. The shock was intense. She tried to move away. He held her down with his hands, making her submit to incredible pleasure such as she'd never known.

He slowly licked her, his tongue lapping the hot wet center of her need, flicking against her hot aching peak, swirling in progressively tighter circles until she was writhing in sweet agony. Her body was so tight and taut, and climbing higher still. Her breathing came in ragged, short gasps as the edges of her vision started to go dark. The tension was unbearable, making her shake and twist beneath the savage, ruthless lapping of his tongue. The pleasure was building. Exploding. She clutched the back of Stefano's black hair, trying to pull him away before she…before she…

But he wouldn't let her escape—he wouldn't—

Her world exploded and waves of bliss poured over her like colors, the blue of the Spanish sky, red poppies, deep brown earth and the black of her lover's eyes. She screamed out his name and Stefano moved, sheathing himself in a condom in a fast movement before he braced his hands on either side of her body, positioning himself between her legs.

In a single rough movement, he pushed himself inside her.

Pain shot through Annabelle as he ripped through her, splitting her apart. She heard the intake of his breath as he broke the unexpected barrier inside her.

"Annabelle?" he said in a strangled voice. "How is it possible…how can you be a virgin?"

She twisted her head away, her eyes tightly shut at the shock and revulsion she imagined she heard in his voice. He started to pull away from her, but she couldn't bear for it to end, not like this!

"I'm not a virgin," she whispered, gripping his shoulders, holding him inside her. "Not anymore."

She heard his low, hoarse gasp. "Look at me."

Shaking, Annabelle opened her eyes, waiting to see scorn in his handsome face. Instead, she saw only shock and something else—wistfulness?

"I don't want to hurt you," he said quietly.

"It's too late," she said in a low voice. "It's done."

"If I'd known you might be a virgin—"

"Don't stop now," she choked out. She shook her head, blinking back tears she struggled to hide. "Please don't leave me like this."

Stefano closed his eyes, then with a ragged intake of breath, he slowly pushed back inside her. The movement was slow, impaling her inch by inch. His jaw twitched with the tight ferocity of his control.

She gritted her teeth, bracing against expected pain.

But instead, as he moved slowly inside her, she was shocked by a new feeling that rose above the pain. Pleasure rebuilt inside her like dark clouds of a thunderstorm on a hot summer day. Darkening. Building. Ready to explode.

He filled her so deeply. With each thrust, he went deeper still. She saw by the tension of his body what it cost him to hold back like this. He was so careful—so gentle. His eyes were closed, his jaw twitching with the effort of self-control.

She loved him for that. Reaching up, Annabelle pulled him down and softly kissed his lips. The last vestiges of her body's pain dissipated and the tension coiling low in her belly started to fill her with every thrust. She gripped his shoulders as he rode her, digging her fingernails into his skin, desperate for more, to feel him harder, deeper. And with a ragged gasp, he obliged her. Annabelle's head fell back as she gasped for breath, lifting her hips to accept each hard thrust as he rode her. He was so huge, so hard, and as he held her down with his weight, slamming into her so deeply, she cried out from pleasure so intense it almost felt like pain.

His low growl built to a roar as he gripped her hips, pushing inside her with one final shattering thrust. He was so deep, deep, deep inside her that when he shouted her name in the hard ecstasy of his release, joy exploded through her and she screamed as her world went black.

When Annabelle came back to herself moments later, she found herself cradled against Stefano's naked body, wrapped in the powerful shelter of his arms. She looked around in amazement. The bed looked as if it had been hit by a tornado, with white sheets and covers twisted and ripped around them. Everything else was chaos, but she and Stefano were at peace, the eye of the storm.

Annabelle exhaled in wonder, hardly able to believe what she'd experienced. She pressed her cheek to Stefano's naked chest and felt the rhythm of his breath. She closed her eyes, listening to his heartbeat, feeling closer to Stefano than she ever had to anyone on earth. Nestled in his strong, protective arms, Annabelle smiled in wonder and joy as happiness washed over her.

Then her heart almost stopped in her chest.

Her eyes flew open. Stefano was a playboy. Every joy he'd just given her was sweet sugar laced with poison. She'd let her inhibitions go and surrendered everything to his conquest. Her feelings were in his hands now, but how long would he be interested in her? A day? Two? Or was he already done?

She'd just given herself to a man who always lost interest in every woman after he bedded her.

She'd given him her virginity. Her trust. Her...heart?

No. Annabelle shuddered. Please God, she couldn't be that foolish. She wouldn't give her heart to a man who would betray and desert her in a matter of days, if not hours.

Would she?

"So what happens now?"

Still half-asleep, Stefano opened his eyes lazily at the trembling sound of Annabelle's voice. Both of them were still naked and lying across his bed amid the ransacked white cotton sheets. He smiled to himself. *Dios mío*, he'd never felt such passion for any woman. Beneath that cool reserved exterior, she had even more fire than he'd ever imagined.

When he'd first kissed her in the meadow beneath the wide blue sky, breathing in the scent of the flowers— the scent of her—Stefano had thought he would die if he didn't have her. But making love to Annabelle had exceeded his wildest expectations.

Now, to his shock, he wanted...more.

"What happens now?" he repeated, a tender smile on his lips as he looked down at her cradled to his bare chest. He frowned as if in thought, then grinned. "We go downstairs for dinner?"

"We slept together," she pointed out.

"Yes," he murmured, kissing her temple. "I noticed that."

But Annabelle's beautiful face had an unhappy, pinched expression. "You must have a usual procedure after you've bedded a woman. How does this end?"

Stefano blinked. A usual procedure? *Sí,* he did have one. After he made love to a pretty woman who was barely more than a stranger, he always got dressed, told the woman he'd never forget their night together, left the hotel room and promptly forgot her.

But this...this was different. This was *Annabelle.*

She was a virgin. He'd made love to her in his own bed. Most of all: he knew her. For the first time in his life, he'd become friends with a woman before he'd slept with her. He'd been forced to wait so long to seduce her, he'd had to fight so hard to win her, that he'd actually started to...care.

"So." Annabelle took a deep breath, her lips turning downward unhappily in the deepening shadows of his bedroom. "What happens now?"

"I don't know," Stefano said slowly. Trying to brush aside her question, he gave her a sudden wicked grin. "We could always do it again."

But she pulled away from him. "I'm serious," she insisted.

"So am I." Looking at her now, soft and naked in his bed, was the culmination of all his dreams. He stroked her soft skin, caressing her naked body. He could see the faintly pink pattern of scars on her skin, like the veins of a flower. She was so sweet and soft, like a pale pink rose.

He would never forget the taste of her. He would never forget the feel of her pebbled nipple in his wet mouth or the soft pleasure of her breasts. He'd never forget the sound of her gasp when he'd pushed her legs apart and licked her, when he'd thrust himself to the hilt inside her tight sheath. The pleasure of that had nearly overwhelmed him. He would never forget how it had felt to fill her, to hear her cry out his name, to bring her to gasping fulfillment before he'd shuddered and shattered inside her with his own orgasm.

He was already hard for her again. How? How was that possible? Usually, he lost interest in a woman immediately after he'd bedded her. But this time, instead of being satiated, he didn't want to let Annabelle go.

He softly kissed the top of her head, and even that small movement caused a new shudder of desire to course through his body. He said in a low voice, "How is it possible that you were a virgin, Annabelle?"

She swallowed. Folding her arms, she looked up at the white plaster ceiling. "I know. It's a bit pathetic, isn't it? Most women my age have boyfriends, husbands, children. I've never had anything. Or anyone."

"So—why did you choose me?" he whispered hoarsely, hardly able to believe it.

She looked at him for a long time, then finally said, "I've been chased by many men, but never one like you. You pursued me with such single-minded passion. Such…

devotion. And such skill. I could not resist you. In the end, I didn't want to resist, no matter what it might cost me." She took a deep breath. "How long do you want me to stay?"

He frowned, not understanding. "In bed? Stay as long as you like."

She looked at him in the shadows of twilight, then gave a harsh laugh. Abruptly, she sat up. Her gray eyes became hard and flat as slate.

"Let's be honest and call this what it is," she said coldly. Her cheeks flushed red over her faint pink sunburn. "A one-night stand."

"No." He immediately sat up beside her. "Not a one-night stand. That's not what I want."

She exhaled, and the coldness in her eyes fell away. She suddenly looked vulnerable and painfully young. "It isn't?"

Swearing softly in Spanish, he snorted a laugh. "*Dios mío,* Annabelle. I don't want any other woman. I want you. Don't you know that by now? I've never had to try so hard to win a woman. I don't want you to leave my bed. I've barely had a chance to enjoy you yet."

Looking at him, she licked her lips. Then slowly, she lifted troubled gray eyes. "Then…I'll stay." She took a deep breath and added quickly, "Just until my assignment ends here on Saturday. When your charity gala is finished, I will leave Santo Castillo."

He scowled at her. "You can stay longer than that."

She laughed at his expression, then sobered. "No, I'd better not."

"Why?"

Annabelle rose from the bed. Naked, she reached for her linen skirt and silk camisole now crumpled on the floor, ripped and dirty from her work with the horses.

"I want an answer," he said steadily.

She stopped, then. Folding her arms over her naked breasts, she looked at him with clear gray eyes.

"People can't change who they are, Stefano," she whispered. "I've learned that the hard way. My father was a brute. My mentor was a liar. They both treated me differently at first. My father beat my brothers, but not me. Patrick lied to other people, but not me. I thought I was special. But ultimately they treated me like all the rest."

"I'm nothing like Arbuthnot or your father," he said angrily.

She shook her head sadly. "You're wrong. Whatever you might think now, you will someday treat me just as you treat all other women. You will hurt me. And I've already given you too much." Turning away with her clothes in her arms, she whispered, "If I were smart, I would leave now…."

Leaping to his feet, he caught her wrist.

"No," he growled.

She looked down at his hand, then gave him a trembling smile. "You are a playboy, Stefano. It was the first thing I heard about you. You will someday leave me for another."

"Maybe," he exploded. "But not today! Not next week!"

"No, not today." She gave him a wan smile. "But soon. How could you not? We are all wrong for each other. You love this ranch and hate to leave it, while I will never settle down and have a home."

"So? I could visit you in London, you could visit me here…."

She shook her head. "It's more than that." She looked down at the floor unhappily. "I know you will betray me. I can't bear to just wait for it to happen."

"But, Annabelle." He stared at her. "We could have

weeks, months, together. Why do we have to decide now how it ends? Why not just enjoy it while it lasts?"

Blinking back tears, she gave him a tremulous smile. "You asked me how I could be a virgin at thirty-three. It's because I don't let anyone close. I don't give my heart easily."

Her heart? He frowned. "We haven't said anything about love. We're talking about sex."

"For you, I know they are not the same. But for me…" She shook her head. "That's why I need to leave. Before I…" Her eyes glimmered in the light as she took a deep breath. "Before I love you."

His eyes went wide.

Staring at him, Annabelle shook her head with a laugh. "You needn't look at me like that. Don't worry, I know you are the worst possible man I could choose to love. You will never be faithful to any woman. And I couldn't take another betrayal, Stefano. I really couldn't."

He scowled. "Annabelle—"

"Stop." She put her finger on his lips. "There's nothing more to say. You know I'm right. We'll just enjoy the rest of this week and then…we will part."

Stefano swallowed.

People can't change who they are, she'd said. And in his heart of hearts, he knew she was right.

And yet…

And yet…

In this moment, Stefano couldn't bear the thought of her leaving him. Not now. Not yet.

For the first time in his life, he wanted more of a woman after bedding her, and she was pushing him away!

He shook his head angrily, not wanting to accept her decision. "Stay an extra week after the gala," he argued.

"Surely a week won't hurt." He tried to smile. "That won't make you love me. I'm not that adorable."

She snorted, then shook her head. "I can't," she said. "I'll need a week in London to edit and develop the photographs of Santo Castillo for *Equestrian,* then I immediately leave for Argentina on assignment for *Geography World* magazine. No." She took a deep breath. "Our love affair—whatever you want to call it—must end when I leave on Saturday. It'll be a clean break. For both of us."

He swallowed. "I don't want you to go."

"It's for the best." Her eyes were luminous in the fading light. "Let's enjoy the four days left. Then we'll say goodbye before it gets serious. Before anyone gets hurt. All right?"

He sucked in his breath.

"All right," he said heavily. "Four days."

He didn't like this. Didn't like it at all. But he couldn't argue with anything she'd said. He didn't want to hurt her, but knew he probably would.

Four days would have to be enough. He'd somehow make it be enough. Then he would forget her, like all the rest.

Wouldn't he?

Standing beside her, Stefano entwined his fingers with hers. "Only four days," he said softly. "Let's make every minute count. We still have the rest of the evening. We still have all of the night."

Her gray eyes flashed up at him, looking breathless and mysterious. "After all our hard work today—"

Taking her hand, he pulled her back toward the bed. "I couldn't exactly call it work."

She giggled, allowing him to draw her two steps toward the bed before she stopped. "But I'm starving."

"Me, too," he growled, pulling her into his arms. Holding her against the length of his naked body, he kissed her.

With a sigh from the back of her throat, Annabelle melted. Her wadded-up clothes fell from her hands as she wrapped her arms around him. Stefano smiled to himself, knowing he'd get his way. He relished the feel of her soft body against his, the feeling of paradise.

Then they heard a loud shout downstairs, as the young stablehands headed noisily into the dining hall.

Annabelle pulled away from his embrace. "We should go downstairs," she said, blushing. "Everyone might wonder what we're doing if we don't show up for dinner."

"Let them wonder." Smiling down at her, he stroked her cheek. "We'll ask Mrs. Gutierrez to bring up dinner. We have no reason to even get dressed."

She looked scandalized. "We couldn't!"

"Why not?"

"Well—" she bit her lip "—it would set a bad example for the boys. I wouldn't want them to think it's acceptable behavior to sleep with their girlfriends before they're married...."

"Ah, *querida*," Stefano said tenderly, laughing. "You're an old-fashioned girl."

She stiffened in his arms. "I suppose I am."

He stopped her with a kiss, then looked in her eyes. "I meant it as a compliment."

Naked, they faced each other. But for once, Stefano wasn't looking at her body. He took her hands in his own, staring in wonder at her beautiful face. Her gray eyes were endless pools of light.

He felt her warmth, heard the hush of her breath in the shadowy room. He realized he couldn't see the scar on her face anymore. All he saw was her beauty—inside and out.

He'd never felt like this before.

He...cared for her.

You are the worst possible man I could choose to love.
The echo of her voice rang hollowly in his ears. *You will
never be faithful to any woman. And I couldn't take another betrayal, Stefano. I really couldn't.*

A cold jolt went through him, but he pushed the feeling away. He would just enjoy their four days. It would be
a short, hot affair. That was all he ever wanted, anyway.
Right?

Right?

He dropped her hands and turned away. "If we're going
downstairs to have dinner, I'd better go take a shower."

"I'll miss you," she said wistfully behind him, then
gave a goofy laugh. "Isn't that ridiculous? How can I
possibly miss you for ten minutes while you're in the
shower?"

Four days. Only four days. And the clock was ticking.

Ignoring the lump in his throat, he turned back and
crossed the room in three steps.

"You won't miss me, *querida*." He looked down at her,
and his body went hard as his heart turned over in his
chest. "I'm taking you with me."

CHAPTER NINE

ANNABELLE LISTENED TO Stefano's even, quiet breathing as he held her naked against his chest, lying in his bed. She looked down at their intertwined fingers. Even though he slept, his hand was wrapped around hers, their intertwined clasp lit with soft gold in the fresh morning light.

Every new hour, every new minute, Annabelle spent with Stefano over the past two days had increased the depths of her joy. She'd never known life could be so wonderful.

Her camera bag and expensive photography equipment had been left in her bedroom, gathering dust. Instead, she'd lived the warm, busy, physically demanding life of the ranch, caring for the horses, going on long rides through the fields, feeling the wind and sunshine on her face. She'd even pulled vegetables from the garden and felt the earth against her fingertips. She'd taken lots of pictures, but only using her smallest digital camera, the one she could easily tuck into the back pocket of her oversize jeans. Being Stefano's mistress took precedence over everything else.

At midnight last night, long after the rest of the staff was asleep, she and Stefano had been suddenly starving after four solid hours of lovemaking. So they'd scampered down to the kitchen, where Stefano had insisted on show-

ing her how to prepare his favorite Spanish rice dish of
paella.

"Just in case you ever want to cook for me," he said
with a wicked grin, his hands stroking over hers as he
helped her stir the pot.

"Cook for you? The very idea!" she'd teased, flashing
him an indignant look. "I'm a busy woman. You should
cook for *me!*"

For answer, he'd grabbed the belt loops of the oversize jeans hanging low on her hips and turned her to face
him. Her wooden spoon had clattered to the tile floor as
he pulled her close to him in the kitchen.

"I'd love to cook for you," he'd whispered. "Every time
I look at you, I boil."

He'd kissed her hungrily. Then, shoving aside the
empty bowls and shattering them to the floor, he'd
roughly pushed her back against the kitchen counter. As
he lifted her into his arms, she'd wrapped her legs around
his waist as he held her against him, pressing her back
against the counter.

They'd very nearly made love right then and there,
but Annabelle had suddenly remembered Mrs. Gutierrez, who was a light sleeper and probably heard the bowls
smashing to the tile floor, and the impressionable teenagers who slept through anything but might wake up and
wander into the kitchen for an extra meal.

Stefano had tried to reassure Annabelle that the housekeeper and boys were all exceedingly deep sleepers, long
abed in a distant hallway, but she'd been steadfast. So
with a growl, he'd carried her in his arms, running up the
stairs to his bedroom, where they'd made love for another
two hours behind closed doors.

It was only later they'd remembered the *paella* in the
cold pot downstairs. Throwing on robes, they'd gone back

to the kitchen and reheated their late-night dinner in the microwave, washing it down with a cold bottle of white wine at the tiny table in the dark kitchen.

Then they'd gone back upstairs, and again, one thing had led to another....

Annabelle sighed, wriggling her toes in pleasure at the memory. Her body felt wonderfully sore and she kept yawning from lack of sleep, but she'd never been so happy.

There was only one shadow on her happiness. The future.

Half their time together was already gone.

After the first time they'd made love, Annabelle had wanted to be with him so badly, she'd made a compromise with her soul: bargaining for four days of happiness at the expense of a little pain in the future. She'd told herself she couldn't possibly fall in love with Stefano in four days. As he'd said himself—surely he wasn't that adorable!

She still had two days left, she tried to comfort herself.

Two days. But only one night.

Tomorrow night, she would be the official photographer at his annual charity polo match and gala. Then, late at night, she would pack up her equipment and drive back to London. She'd go edit the photographs of Santo Castillo for *Equestrian,* then catch a flight to Argentina.

She'd looked forward to visiting Patagonia and Tierra del Fuego. But now, she couldn't bear the thought of leaving Stefano, her first lover. Her only lover.

The man she loved.

No! Annabelle's hands flew to her head in consternation. She couldn't let herself love him. Stefano Cortez would never commit to any woman. She would have to be barking mad—or utterly masochistic—to let herself love a man who'd never love her back!

Trembling, Annabelle carefully pulled away from his arms and crept out of his bed. She took a shower in his en suite bathroom, then got dressed in clothes she'd borrowed from his wardrobe: an oversize white cotton shirt and jeans cinched to her hips with his leather belt.

Looking down at her clothes, Annabelle smiled. Stefano had been so gleeful to finally get her out of her dressy suits. She'd finally given up her sleek and professional outfits as impractical, and instead relished the comfort and good sense of Stefano's oversize cotton shirts and rolled-up jeans.

He'd sent for new work boots for her in the village. He offered to get her new clothes, as well. But she'd refused. She loved wearing Stefano's clothes. It was intimate. She sometimes thought she caught his scent of saddle soap and sunlight. Feeling the worn, soft cotton against her skin felt like being in his constant embrace.

Now, she looked at herself in the bathroom mirror. And for once, it wasn't the angry red scar across her face that drew her eyes. It was her mouth.

She touched her bruised lips. She could still feel Stefano's kiss. His perfect body. She'd been sleeping in his bed every night. His sensual, powerful body commanded her without words. He gave her such pleasure, made her feel so *alive*....

"There you are," she heard him growl behind her. "Why did you leave bed so early?"

Annabelle looked up at the mirror and saw him behind her, standing naked in the open doorway. In spite of their many days together, she blinked in astonishment at his masculine perfection. His shoulders were so broad, his body muscular and lithe. She couldn't look from his image in the mirror as he walked into the gleaming white bathroom. Her eyes traced downward from his handsome face and dark, chiseled jawline to his hard chest and flat belly and lower still….

He wanted her to come back to bed. A lot.

His darkly amused eyes met hers in the mirror and she licked her lips, blushing. Coming behind her, he turned her around in his arms.

"I missed you." He looked down at her. "I was disappointed to wake up alone."

Closing her eyes, she breathed in his woodsy, masculine scent, in the pleasure and comfort of his embrace.

Only one night left.

Swallowing, Annabelle pushed away from him, tucking her smallest digital camera into the back pocket of her oversize jeans. Trying to hide the emotion on her face, hiding her desire to cling to him forever, she said sadly, "I have to work today."

"Forget work," he commanded, stroking her cheek. "Stay in bed."

She shivered with longing, staring up at his handsome face. "I've forgotten work too much already," she said. She shook her head. "*Equestrian* will wonder what on earth I've been doing all week here."

"Then let's both give back their advance," he said, nuzzling her neck. "I would happily lose a hundred thousand euros for a single hour of having you in my arms."

Annabelle sighed. Looking up at his handsome face, she was beyond tempted. She wanted nothing more than to stay here, in the warmth of his bedroom, with its rustic furniture and incredible view of the vast fields and horses outside. She wanted nothing more than to stay here in his arms forever.

No. No, she couldn't give in to that feeling! *I don't love him,* she told herself desperately. *Absolutely not...*

A loud bang came from outside the house. Crossing to the bedroom window, Stefano peeked through the blinds, then winced at the roar and hum of moving vans and the shouting of men outside.

"We're under siege," he said grimly, pulling away from the window.

She grinned. "You invited them here."

"I hate this time of the year."

"You only gave the party planners a single day to set up for tomorrow. What did you expect? What else could they do but send an army? And it *is* for charity."

"I still hate it." He scowled, then lifted a dark eyebrow with a wicked half smile. "Come distract me."

She tilted her head as if considering. "I suppose I could use your services today..."

"Aha—"

"...as my assistant," she finished.

He pouted, then brightened. "Taking any photographs in the meadow today?" he suggested sweetly.

She snorted, then turned back to the mirror and reached for her simple diamond stud earrings, which she put on one at a time. Her makeup and toiletries had already taken up residence across his private bathroom counter. Grabbing her small collection of tiny brushes, she put on her makeup, carefully covering the scar on her face. "Sadly, no. I need to go to the village. For my story."

"Go to Algares? Why?"

"You grew up there—many of the young stablehands you now employ came from there."

"So?"

"It's the first village you helped with your charity

foundation, long ago. I want to see how it's changed. The village is part of the story. I have to include it."

Stefano looked irritated, and was just opening his mouth to argue when they heard another loud bang outside, and the sound of a truck's loud, incessant beep as it backed up in the courtyard. Men started yelling in Spanish and they heard a woman's loud voice in French telling them they were setting it up all wrong. The men answered angrily in Spanish, and the multilingual dispute had the ranch's dogs barking in a cacophony of noise.

"On second thought," Stefano growled, "I'll come with you."

"You will!" Annabelle said, thrilled she didn't have to leave him in order to finish her work. So much for guarding her heart, she thought to herself sourly.

Stefano swiftly showered and put on a cotton shirt and jeans that fit him far better than they fit her. He didn't need a belt to keep the jeans snug against his lean hips. After he pulled on his boots, they walked to his six-car garage, where he climbed into an old 1950s Willys Jeepster. Getting in beside him, Annabelle looked at the rare open-topped truck with appreciation. "Nice," she said. "Not flashy. Real."

"Glad you like it." He started the engine. Maneuvering his truck around the vans and trucks sprawled all over his lawn, past people unloading supplies from food to flowers to polo equipment, Stefano drove past the chaos and down the peaceful tree-lined avenue. They passed the old stone gate, crenellated and covered with moss in the shade, and Annabelle realized it was the first time she'd left the ranch for almost a week.

She wasn't sure she wanted to go back into the real world, to be honest. But the village was only a few miles away, down the slender road clinging to the edge of the

rocky green hills. All too quickly, they arrived at Algares,
a tiny, prosperous village of whitewashed houses tucked
in the valley.

The moment they arrived, a crowd of children appeared,
rushing from the houses, running in the dust behind the
Jeepster. They joyfully shouted Stefano's name.

"Children are following us," Annabelle said, looking
back in amazement.

Stefano glanced back in the mirror. A smile lifted the
hard edges of his mouth. "I know."

Parking the truck on the street, Stefano climbed out
and held out his arms. *"¡Hola, mis amigos!"*

The laughing children ran to him eagerly. Bending to
their eye level, he patted one little girl on the shoulder as
he smiled at another child and asked him something in
Spanish.

Annabelle climbed slowly out of the truck. Children
were bouncing all around Stefano, a little girl in pigtails
and a pinafore tugging on his shirt to get his attention, an
older boy excitedly telling him a story in Spanish about a
football game. From nearby doorways, she saw mothers,
young and old, coming out the doorways of their gleaming, tidy homes to smile at their children who held the
total attention of the tall, powerful Señor Cortez.

Annabelle slowly looked around her. *This* was Algares,
which ten years ago had been called the poorest village
in Spain? Now, it was charming, picture-perfect, a scene
of warmth and domestic happiness. With a slow intake of
breath, she raised her camera and took pictures of the village, the children and the tall, handsome man smiling at
them.

Stefano and Annabelle spent hours visiting different families in the village, all of whom clamored for the
honor of making their lunch. The people were so warm

and friendly, she thought. Both children and parents clearly thought the world of Stefano. Annabelle took tea in more than one snug house, and when they heard she was doing an article, they insisted on telling her all about how Stefano had saved their jobs or improved their lives, how his foundation had built a playground for the old park and bought supplies for schoolchildren. About how he'd helped their sons, after the boys had gotten into trouble with the law and started down the wrong path, by hiring them as stablehands and giving them not just a job...but a vocation.

Stefano had helped them, as he helped everyone he cared about.

Annabelle took pictures of everything. She took photos of Stefano most of all. When he looked at her, she lost her breath. When he smiled, her heart lifted to her throat.

After they'd visited practically every house in Algares, Annabelle's arm was wrapped companionably around his as they walked down the street. He was so much more than a playboy, she thought, sneaking sideways glances at him. She'd known his charitable foundation was important to him, but she'd never realized what a difference he made.

What an amazing man, Annabelle thought. She swallowed. The way she really felt about him now...

Clumsily, she stumbled over her feet.

"Careful, *querida*." Stefano caught her before she fell face-first into the street. "You seem tired," he said, tilting his head at her. He pointed at the village pub. "Why don't we stop and have a drink?"

Trembling, Annabelle looked at the building across the street. The tavern was two stories high, on a corner lot with a painted sign dangling cheerfully from the eaves. It was charming and cheerful and, as Annabelle stared up at it, she hated it on sight.

If I wish to, as you say, take a lover, I go to the village tavern and rent a room for the night.

"One drink before we leave," Stefano suggested. "You can even take a picture or two, if you like. This place is a local landmark."

"I just bet it is," she muttered with a surge of bitterness, and lifted her camera.

When she was done, they went inside. The pub was fairly empty and very well-swept. Annabelle tried to hide the way her body was shaking as Stefano led her to the small table in the window. As she sat down across from him, she wondered how many women had already joined him at this very table. And how many more would sit with him here in the coming weeks.

"Your usual, *señor?*" the bartender called in Spanish.

"Si," Stefano replied with a grin. "And the lady will have…" He turned to her, waiting.

"I'm not thirsty," Annabelle said.

"Come, you must have something. One drink."

"What are you having?" she asked him listlessly.

"A beer."

"I'll have the same."

He lifted an eyebrow in approval, then relayed her drink to the bartender. Turning back to her at the small table, he asked abruptly, "Can I see the new pictures you've taken?"

She bit her lip. "Will you tell me honestly what you think of them?"

"Do you really want me to?"

Reluctantly, Annabelle handed him her digital camera. The camera seemed tiny in his large hands as he looked slowly through the digital images she'd taken of the village, and the ranch before that.

Watching him, she licked her dry lips. She adored these new pictures. The photographs she'd taken over the past few days seemed rich and vibrant, full of life, even to her artist's critical eye.

But would he scorn them as he had her last pictures? Would he call them *frozen* and *dead*?

Trembling, she peeked over his shoulder as Stefano went through picture after picture. And Annabelle suddenly noticed something she'd never seen before. Her eyes went wide with shock.

No wonder she loved these pictures.

There was Stefano in the village, bending on one knee as he talked to the children. Stefano tilting his head back, giving advice to the young stablehands at Santo Castillo. Stefano standing alone in the paddock at sunset, training a yearling. Even her pictures of the wild, vast landscape somehow had his blurry elbow on the edge of the frame.

Every single picture had Stefano in it.

She'd even taken one of him last night, at a private moment in his bed. She'd wanted to capture the tenderness and passion of his dark eyes, and so she'd taken a picture of him as the red-and-orange sunset from the window cast a halo over his dark head, like fire.

Stefano was in all her pictures now. He was in her soul. In her heart.

Annabelle gave a strangled, silent gasp.

She was in love with him.

She'd tried desperately to fight it. She hadn't wanted to love him. For days, she'd denied her feelings, even to herself, because she knew loving him would destroy her.

But her photographs didn't lie.

Stefano had become the center of her whole world. The only man for her.

She loved him.

The bartender came over with their two drinks, and stared at her openly. She tried not to notice his knowing smirk before he left. He clearly thought she was Stefano's newest easy woman, here today and gone tomorrow.

Which was exactly what Annabelle was. She blinked, hard.

With a quick sip of his beer, Stefano continued to turn through the digital images. Ignoring her own drink, Annabelle stared at him, fighting back tears.

Would he notice he was in every picture? Would he understand what it meant?

Please, God, she prayed. *Don't let him notice.* If he did, her humiliation would be complete.

Finally, he looked up at her, and his dark eyes glowed.

"These pictures are perfect, full of passion and life," he said with a smile, handing back the camera. "I see your love and appreciation for my ranch in every image. Well done," he added softly.

Not just her love for Santo Castillo. She swallowed, her cheeks feeling hot. "Thank you."

They show my love for you. All for you. Her breath caught in her throat as she waited in agony for him to say something more, anything.

Annabelle, why am I in every picture?

Annabelle—surely you have not been stupid enough to fall in love with me?

Stefano cleared his throat.

"There were some good pictures of Mrs. Gutierrez and the boys. Perhaps you could make copies and send them to the boys' parents."

She blinked. "Sure."

His brow furrowed as he looked down at her, his dark eyes warm and tender. "Everything all right?"

"Yes," Annabelle whispered over the lump in her throat. But it wasn't all right. It would never be all right again.

He threw some money on the table to pay the bill and rose from his chair. "Let's head home."

On the drive back to the ranch, Annabelle stared out the window at the sunset shimmering in the west. The light turned the undulating green hills into silken ribbons of scarlet and coral and magenta.

Rolling down the window to lean her elbows against the frame, she closed her eyes and took a deep breath of the fragrant air, redolent of oranges and earth and the distant sea. She loved this beautiful, wild, half-arid landscape.

As they drove back, the simple brush of Stefano's hand against her knee as he shifted the gears caused a thrill through her body, even as it caused a jagged pain through her heart.

Then he spoke.

"Don't leave tomorrow, Annabelle," he said in a low voice. "Stay here. With me."

She looked at him with an intake of breath. "I wish I could."

"Why can't you?"

Because her heart was already breaking, and she didn't know how much longer she could hide her love for him, love he would never return. "Because…I can't."

His eyes looked black, then he turned back to the road and switched gears, hard. She sat in stricken silence as they drove back through the gates of Santo Castillo.

The chaos at the ranch had only increased. He navigated past the delivery vans and horse trailers parked along his gravel drive, skirting around the people setting up for the polo match and gala dinner afterward. By noon tomorrow, Annabelle knew, Santo Castillo would be overrun by the world's most beautiful, sophisticated, experienced women. Just thinking of it, she felt sick inside.

Stefano parked the truck in the garage and turned off the ignition. Setting his jaw, he faced her.

"Come to my bedroom," he said. "So we can discuss this."

"I'll come to your bedroom, but there's nothing to discuss."

"There is."

"Don't ruin our last precious night by trying to change things that cannot be changed."

"Anything can change. We are the ones who know what we want and how we want to live. You have three minutes to get to my bedroom." The hard set of his jaw frightened her. "Or I'll carry you. Right now."

"Everyone would see!"

"Three minutes."

He got out of the truck, slamming the door behind him.

Annabelle sat in the darkened garage in shock. When she finally got out of the truck and left the garage, Stefano's broad, muscular back was disappearing behind a brightly colored horse trailer as he pushed through the throngs of caterers and party planners and hired help.

She stared at him, and felt like crying.

Leaving him was the last thing she wanted to do. But she had to do it. The longer she stayed now, loving him, the more vicious her heartbreak would be. She'd never loved anyone like this. If she let herself stay, his ultimate betrayal might kill her. Her only hope of saving herself was to leave. Immediately.

Annabelle slowly started to walk through the crowds toward the house. But she had a sinking feeling that it was already too late.

CHAPTER TEN

THREE MINUTES FELT LIKE an eternity.

Stefano paced across the cool tiles of his bedroom floor. He was not going to let Annabelle leave tomorrow. Not now. Not yet.

He had to persuade her to stay. With words. With his body. Whatever it took. The more time he spent with Annabelle, the more he knew they were meant to be together—if not forever, then at least for longer.

Stefano heard her knock, and flung open the door.

Annabelle's beautiful face looked both sad and determined as she folded her arms. "All right, I'm here," she said. "But I'm not going to change my mind about tomorrow. So let's not talk about it, we have so little time left already…."

Stefano held open the door. "Come in."

He could see the uncertainty and longing across her lovely, expressive face as she entered his bedroom.

"Sit down," he said. "I want to tell you something."

She stood in front of him with a spine straight as steel and shook her head. "I'll stand."

"I want to tell you," he said quietly, "the real reason I gave up my show-jumping career at nineteen, in the middle of the London International Equestrian Show."

Her mouth fell open. Her gray eyes were wide as she sank onto the bed.

Stefano looked down at her. He hadn't wanted to ever explain this, but it was the only thing that might help her understand. He forced himself to speak, and the words came slowly.

"I told you I was lured into joining the show-jumping team by the coach's daughter. Rosalia," he said in a low voice. "I thought she loved me, and we would someday marry. The night before the horse show, I was unable to reach my parents back in Spain. My mother hadn't answered her phone for weeks. I was worried so I went to see my coach, who I believed cared for me as a son."

"What happened?"

Stefano's lips curved sardonically. "He thought I was asleep in my hotel room. I overheard him laughing with another coach about how he'd convinced my parents to keep my mother's illness a secret. *Stupid peasants with no money,* he called them. He'd convinced them it would be selfish to ask me to leave my team and be with my mother before she died."

"Oh, no," Annabelle whispered, her face stricken.

He took a rough breath. "I left without him knowing I'd overheard. I went to Rosalia's room, to tell her what happened. I found her in bed with the captain of the show-jumping team." His lips twisted. "I'd never even slept with her. I was still a virgin with this idealistic goal of marrying this perfect woman. But she'd never given a damn about me, just for the pretty trinkets I bought her. The next day, I got my revenge. I stopped my horse before the jump and went back to Spain. I used my small savings to buy Santo Castillo for my mother. She lived for a year, and my father did not live long without her. But I never forgave myself…for foolishly valuing a woman's lies over what really mattered. My home. My family."

"Oh, Stefano." Annabelle reached for his hand, and he saw tears in her eyes. "I'm so sorry."

Standing beside the bed where she sat, he held her hand for long moments of silence. His hand tightened over hers as he looked down at her.

"I know you think you can't trust me, Annabelle," he whispered. He lifted his chin. "But you can. Being with you, for the first time since I was nineteen, I have found a woman I trust. A woman I believe in. I believe in you."

Visibly trembling, Annabelle rose to her feet.

Pulling her into his arms, he nuzzled her temple. "Don't leave tomorrow, Annabelle," he whispered against her hair. "Stay here with me."

He felt her hesitate, felt her start to melt in his arms. Then she pushed away angrily. "How dare you use your charm on me!"

He blinked. "Charm?"

"You know you have power over me!" she raged. "You always make me do anything you want!"

Stefano liked the sound of that. He came closer to her. "Do I really have such power?"

"You know you do," she whispered.

He hid a smile. Wrapping his arms back around her, he pressed his lips to her ear. "Then before you make any decisions about leaving tomorrow," he whispered, "listen to the rest of the argument in my favor…."

Cupping her face in his hands, he kissed her with all the emotion he could not express in words.

He felt her hands try at first to push him away. But he held on to her forcefully, kissing her passionately, until her hands grew still, then gripped his shoulders as a sigh of pleasure escaped her.

Her lips were sweet magic, luring him with the promise that he could be the man she needed, if only for a while. A few weeks. A few months. A year?

Her small hands reached beneath his black shirt, stroking his bare chest. *Teasing him*. With a growl, he turned on her and ripped her white shirt open, popping off the buttons. He pushed her against the bedroom wall.

Kissing down her neck, he stroked her breasts until her head fell back with a gasp of pleasure. He unhooked her bra and dropped it to the floor, licking the valley between her breasts as if they were covered with sticky sweet jam.

But Annabelle was no longer a shy, timid virgin. She loved this game and reached for his shirt, yanking it up over his head. He pushed against her, his bare chest to her breasts, hungry to feel her heat, her warmth, her softness. He nipped at her neck, sucking and biting her until he knew he'd left his mark. He felt her nails in his back as he kissed her mouth, hard and deep. He felt her teeth bite his lower lip and he gasped. He nearly exploded right then and there.

His innocent mistress had become a fiery, fearless temptress.

Moving his hands down her naked belly, he undid her belt. Her oversize jeans dropped to the floor. Kicking them aside, he ripped off her panties.

He needed her. Right now. He barely got his jeans unzipped and grabbed a condom and he was roughly inside her, shoving her against the wall, plunging deep as she wrapped her legs around his hips with a hot gasp. She was so wet, three thrusts and she gasped out her climax in the same instant that he pumped deep inside her with a shout.

Afterward, they were so spent they collapsed onto the bed. There, he held her, stroking her without words in the early-evening shadows. He kissed her softly, gently, stroking her cheek as he gazed down at her. He could not get enough of looking at her face.

But within minutes, he was hard for her again. This time, after taking her like an animal, he intended to go slowly. Rolling Annabelle gently back against the soft pillows, Stefano slowly kissed down her neck, her breasts, all the way down her belly and thighs and knees to the hollows of her feet. He kissed and sucked and stroked every inch of her body with his lips and fingertips until she shook all over, begging wordlessly for him to take her.

Moments earlier, he'd done so with rapid, explosive violence. Now, he moved slowly, torturing her with an hour of teasing and touching and suckling. Only when she begged for release from her agony did he finally show mercy. But even then, he tortured her. He gradually thrust inside her, impaling her inch by inch, until she wept with need.

Then…he slammed inside her. Hard. Fast. Her fulfillment came almost instantly and she arched her back in a sharp cry like the sun bursting through dark clouds.

That was the moment. The best moment. Stefano watched her luminous face, and knew if he lost her, he would lose the sun.

He would convince her to stay. He would find a way.

Hours later, as the pale light of dawn crept through the blinds of his bedroom window, Annabelle woke up smiling from a delicious dream. Except it wasn't a dream.

She was still in Stefano's arms, lying against his naked body as he slept. She exhaled, exhausted to her toes. Sore. And yet so happy. She couldn't remember ever feeling so happy.

They'd made love three times last night. Or was it four? She counted.

One. Shocking. Rough. Hard and brutal against the wall.

Two. She shivered. He'd tortured her with his sensual hands for hours, it seemed, before he'd finally thrust inside her.

Then, putting on robes, they'd snuck down to the kitchen for sandwiches, giggling like children trying to stay quiet and failing miserably before they returned to his bedroom with a tray.

After the brief repast of sandwiches and wine and strawberries in bed, they'd slept in each other's arms before she'd been woken by the touch of his hand.

Three. He'd kissed her, deep and hot, then as she'd moaned with pleasure he'd rolled her over to take her from behind, plunging inside her, wrapping his hands around her body to hold her breasts as he thrust inside her like a stallion covering a mare. He was so deep inside her, touching her womb, stretching her to the hilt, she'd exploded almost at once.

Sweaty and sticky, they'd fallen back against the twisted cotton sheets. Laughing at the way their bodies seemed to stick together, they'd decided to take a shower.

Inside the enormous glass shower of his en suite bathroom, they'd washed each other's hair, scrubbing each other's bodies until they were pink with heat and fragrant with soap. He'd lightly massaged her shoulders and she'd closed her eyes, leaning back against him with a sigh as the hot steam surrounded them. Then abruptly, he'd turned her to face him.

Four. He'd fallen to his knees before her. Lifting one of her knees over his shoulder beneath the warm spray of water, he'd licked and suckled between her legs until she'd had a fourth explosion of shattering pleasure.

Afterward, she'd been exhausted, utterly spent. He'd

tenderly toweled her off and carried her back into his bed, cradled in his arms.

He'd set her, damp and naked, gently on the white sheets, and she'd briefly had a glimpse of his dark eyes in the moonlight. He'd looked obsessed, almost haunted.

For an instant, she'd wondered if he could be falling in love with her, too. If a miracle could happen and Stefano would tell her, *You're the only woman I want. For the rest of my life.*

Then the moment had passed. Stefano had pulled away, kissing her softly in bed and pulling her against his naked body as they slept the few remaining hours before dawn.

Now, as Annabelle blinked in the early dawn light, the smile slowly slid from her face.

Today was their very last day.

The last morning she would wake up in Stefano's arms. Tonight, after the gala, she would leave for London.

Today was the last day Stefano would be hers.

And even today, he wouldn't truly be hers, she realized with a sinking heart. Within an hour or two, guests would start to arrive for the late-morning pre-polo breakfast. Annabelle closed her eyes, imagining beautiful, sultry socialites swathed in diamonds and miniskirts, and no doubt experienced in the ways of luring and pleasing a man.

Annabelle swallowed, blinking back tears. She'd never know again how it felt to be Stefano's woman, to have him kiss her, to have him hold her in his strong arms as his dark eyes burned through her soul.

It had taken her thirty-three years to fall in love. Now, there'd be no more warmth. No more fire. No more Stefano.

Unless...

Unless what? a cold voice mocked. *Do you think if*

you tell him you love him, he'll miraculously say he loves you, too?

Annabelle took a deep breath. Maybe.

Forget it, the voice mocked. *All he'd feel would be pity.*

I don't know that. His eyes tell me he could love me. His body tells me he could love me. We might have a chance.

If you want to keep your dignity, the voice said scornfully, *you'll stay silent. You'll walk away.*

Stefano stirred in bed beside her, yawning. Still half-asleep, he instinctively pulled her close to his chest, wrapping her tightly in his arms. And how was it possible he already wanted her again? She could feel him hard behind her. Smiling in spite of her turmoil, she turned around in his arms.

She found his dark eyes looking down at her. His whole face shone with contentment.

"Buenos días, querida," Stefano said huskily. He leaned forward to kiss her.

She pulled away.

"I have to tell you something," Annabelle said, entwining her hands in his. She licked her lips. "For all my adult life, being a photographer has been the only thing that made me feel alive and safe." She looked back at him. "Until I met you."

Stefano gripped her shoulders. "Does that mean you'll stay?"

She stared at the floor. Her eyes stung as if pricked with needles.

Tell him, her heart pleaded.

Don't tell him! her brain ordered.

"Forget about London," Stefano said. His dark eyes glowed in the early gray light. "Forget your assignment in Argentina. Don't leave, *querida*," he whispered. "Stay with me."

Annabelle's whole body trembled. She didn't know what to do. All she knew was that her choice at this moment would change the rest of her life.

Pushing away from him, she sat up in bed and rose unsteadily to her feet. Feeling dizzy, she paced five steps, then turned back to him. "Before we talk about that, there's something I need to tell you first," she said unsteadily.

"Si?" He looked up at her.

Shivering, she grabbed her short silk robe with the colorful dragon and tied the silk sash around her waist. Pacing past the window, she glanced through the blinds. The delivery trucks were gone. Instead, she saw two polo players, and three young women in hats walking across the field toward an enormous white tent. Some of the guests were apparently so eager for the day's events that they'd arrived unfashionably early.

Annabelle took a deep breath. "It will feel odd to have strangers here." Her lips turned down grimly. "Your guests are starting to arrive."

His voice was low. "I know."

Annabelle turned away. "I should really get ready. I have a lot to do today…."

He stopped her with his stark question.

"Annabelle, what did you want to tell me?"

She didn't turn around. "Why should I tell you?" she whispered. "What more is there to say?"

Except I love you. I love you.

She closed her eyes. Her heart was beating so fast she thought it might explode.

She heard him rise from the bed and walk toward her.

"Whatever it is," he said, putting his hands on her shoulders, "you can tell me."

Annabelle tried to hide the tremble that went through her at his words. She took a deep breath and opened her eyes.

He was standing in front of her, naked and so brutally strong, even as his dark eyes shone with tenderness. She looked up into his face, and could no longer keep silent.

Slowly, she lifted her chin.

"I love you," she whispered.

Stefano sucked in his breath. Drawing back, he searched her face. Fear and hope coursed through Annabelle like a storm, leaving her knees weak.

"You love me?" His voice was husky and low.

Unable to speak, she nodded. "And I need to know... how you feel about me."

He blinked, then looked down at the floor.

"I care about you, Annabelle," he said. "More than I've ever cared about any woman."

His last words were quiet. But she could hardly hear anything over the loud thrumming of blood rushing through her ears.

Suddenly, she was freezing. The air in the bedroom was icy. She was surprised she couldn't see her breath. The soft woven rug felt sharp as rocks beneath her feet.

He didn't love her.

The mocking voice had been right. *It was happening again.* Every time she loved someone, they hurt her. Every time she gave someone her heart, they crushed it into dirt.

She felt like she was going to faint.

"You *care* for me?" she whispered. "I just told you I'm *in love* with you!"

Stefano's fingers tightened around hers.

"Yes," he said sharply. "I care. It's all I can offer you right now." Looking down at their intertwined hands, he took a deep breath. "And it's the most I've ever offered any woman. I care for you. I want to be with you. And as long as we are together, I will be faithful."

"Faithful?" She tossed her head, looking at him coldly. "For how long? A day? A week?"

He lifted his head, and his dark eyes glittered like a January midnight. "I don't know," he whispered. "But as long as we are together, *querida,* you will have all of me."

Staring at his handsome, tortured face, Annabelle wanted to fall to her knees and weep. Of course it had ended this way. *Of course* it had.

She folded her arms, willing herself to feel as numb as everyone believed her to be. But bitter anguish seeped through her soul like acid.

"*All of you* would mean love. Commitment. A promise. What you offer me is a long series of one-night stands. *That* is all a man like you can offer any woman!"

With a harsh intake of breath, Stefano stumbled back from her words, as if she'd shot him with a rifle.

Heartsick, stricken with tears, Annabelle turned to go.

"Wait. Don't go." His voice was low and hoarse. "It's all happened so fast. I never expected this. I need more time. You have to give me more time."

"No. I don't." Turning away, she started toward the door, desperate to escape before she collapsed into humiliating sobs.

"Wait!" He raced across the room. Gripping her shoulders, he looked down at her fiercely. "Just wait, damn it!"

"I don't need to wait," she whispered. "I already know how this ends."

"You don't!"

"And I hate feeling like this, feeling I can't live without knowing if—if—"

"If what?" he ground out.

She exhaled. "If loving you will kill me."

Stefano paced in front of her. He stopped, his jaw clenched. Furiously, he raked his dark hair back with his hand.

"What do you want from me, Annabelle?" he said. "Should I give you a list of pretty promises to keep you here with me? I'm telling you the truth! Should I lie and tell you I love you, when I don't even know what I feel right now?"

Annabelle choked out a gasp.

Should I lie and tell you I love you?

Turning with a sob, Annabelle went to his wardrobe and grabbed the tattered linen suit she'd worn the first day he'd made love to her. Dropping her robe, she yanked on her underwear and suit and shoes as fast as her trembling body would allow her.

"What are you doing?"

Grief ripped through her. "Leaving." Tears fell unheeded down her cheeks. "Right now."

"You can't leave! You're the official photographer today. It's part of your cover story for *Equestrian*—"

"I don't care," she choked out. "I can't stay another minute!"

"You're being ridiculous!"

"I know," she choked out. "See what you've made of me?"

"Annabelle!"

But she didn't listen. She ran down the hall to her bedroom. Leaving her equipment and camera bag, she grabbed her wallet, passport and car keys and fled down the stairs.

She could hear his heavy footsteps behind her. She could hear his shout. But her vision was misty with tears as she went to her old Land Rover in the garage. Starting the engine, she roared out of the garage.

Stefano ran in front of her truck, stopping her. Their eyes locked through the windshield.

"Don't go. I know you think I will hurt you, you think I will betray you, but…you've changed me," Stefano said hoarsely. "Can't you believe that?"

She looked at him.

"No," she whispered, and she drove away.

CHAPTER ELEVEN

BY THE time HER LAND Rover approached the French city of Châtellerault that afternoon, Annabelle had cried until she had no tears left.

A loud honk from a passing truck made her focus her attention on the road. Sweat broke out on her forehead. She'd just nearly had an accident. Had she wanted to crash?

Had she?

Her heart pounded. She saw an exit and pulled off the motorway. Parking beside a gas station, she turned off the ignition and cried, leaning her head against the steering wheel.

She wished she could talk to someone who'd give her a reason why she shouldn't crash her truck into a tree right now. Her heart yearned for Stefano. But he was lost to her now forever.

Who else could she turn to for comfort? Who? Her ex-assistant Marie was busy with her husband and newborn baby. Annabelle's brothers were getting married and settling down. They didn't need to be bothered by their poor pathetic sister yet again.

Then she thought of one person who'd remained at Wolfe Manor all these years, even after Annabelle's brothers had left. One person who'd refused to completely let Annabelle fall off the face of the earth.

Mollie Parker.

Annabelle turned on her mobile, and sudden hope rose to her throat. She looked to see if Stefano had left any messages, messages like *I changed my mind. I love you. I need you.*

But there were no messages.

And Annabelle realized she did have tears left, after all.

She was being stupid. She'd be back in London by midnight, she told herself, wiping her eyes. Soon, she'd be home.

Except her empty flat didn't feel much like a home anymore. Now, home meant blue skies and wide golden fields, laughing teenagers and a kindly, plump-cheeked housekeeper keeping them all in line. And most of all, home meant Stefano.

Gone. All gone.

Huddled in the driver's seat of her parked truck, she wiped her eyes even harder. She'd throw herself back into her career just like always. She'd forget Stefano. She'd bury herself in work until she died.

But the thought just made her cry harder. Once, she'd been numb and content in such a life, with her heart frozen and dead. Stefano had changed that. He'd brought her to life.

Then…he'd taken it all away.

With a shaking finger, Annabelle dialed Mollie's mobile number in the U.K. But she reached only voice mail. "Hi, this is Mollie…"

Annabelle didn't leave a message. Desperately, she rang the main house instead, praying that Mollie would be there.

Instead, she heard a man's deep voice. "Hello?"

"Jacob?" she said in shock.

"Annabelle?" Her brother sounded surprised, too. "Is that you?"

"I didn't expect you to be at the house," she stammered. "Mollie said you were in London all week...."

"I was, yes, but then something happened and—"

Nervously, Annabelle spoke over him. "Actually, I was ringing for Mollie...."

"She's not here." He paused. "But can I help you with anything, Belle?"

Her first instinct was to say no, to make an excuse and ring off. But instead, something made her grip the phone to her ear and take a deep breath, which came out as a sob.

"Have you been crying?" Jacob demanded. "What's happened?"

"No..." She choked in answer to his first question, then, "Yes. But I can't tell you."

"Why?"

"Haven't I already done enough to you?" she said fiercely. "Everything you did to save me, with Dad..." She took a shuddering breath, remembering that awful night her father had nearly killed her in a drunken rage. "It wasn't enough that I forced you to protect me, and made you go through those horrible months of the trial. Then I finally drove you away from England with all my whinging and complaining."

"You weren't whinging." His deep voice was gentle. "You were going through a hard time. You felt scarred and isolated and alone. I never blamed you for that, Belle. Never."

She looked up at the busy gas station nearby. The colors of the cars blurred. "But you left!" she cried. "The next morning you were gone. You didn't come back for twenty years!"

She heard his deep intake of breath.

"All this time, you've thought it was your fault?" he said. "You came into the study seeking comfort. I was drinking and nearly... I could see myself turning into..." He choked back his words. "You all were better off without me."

"But can you forgive me?" she whispered. "For ruining your life?"

"You never ruined my life," he said in a harsh voice. "I left because it was the only way to protect you—all of you."

"Protect us—from what?"

He paused. "From me."

Something about his dark, bleak tone reminded her of another man's voice.

What do you want from me, Annabelle? Should I give you a list of pretty promises to keep you here with me? I'm telling you the truth! Should I lie and tell you I love you, when I don't even know what I feel right now?

"Oh, my God," she breathed aloud.

"Belle? What is it?"

Stefano hadn't taken her home away from her.

She'd done it to herself. Her fear and lack of faith had demanded a promise for him that he wasn't ready to give. She'd accused him constantly of being a faithless playboy, but the truth was that, for Stefano, a commitment was a sacred thing. He hadn't wanted her to go. But he'd accepted her decision, rather than lie to her.

She'd been so afraid he would someday hurt her, but she'd beaten him to the punch. She'd deserted the only man she'd ever loved. All because she was afraid.

Pain is how you know you're alive, he'd once said

to her. *If you are too afraid to feel pain, you'll never know joy.*

Closing her eyes, Annabelle took a shuddering breath. Her life had been so full of pain already. It was a cold, cruel world. She'd learned the only way to be safe was to be alone.

But what if…that wasn't true?

What if playing it safe just was playing dead?

Memories came through her like the burst of dawn. The sound of Stefano's joyful laugh. The depth of his black eyes. The way he'd held her so tight against his naked body in the tender, sacred night. He made her feel safe. He made her feel loved.

I care for you, Annabelle. More than I've ever cared for anyone.

He'd wanted her to stay. She was the one who'd run away.

For too long, she'd lived in fear. But from now on, she would be brave enough to become the woman she was born to be.

Annabelle gripped her mobile phone. "I have to go."

"What? Why?"

"Bless you, Jacob," she whispered. "I love you. Talk to you more soon."

Her hands shook as she started the engine of her truck. Backing it out of the parking lot, she got back on the motorway—headed not north toward Calais, but back toward the Spanish border. Back home. Back to Stefano.

People didn't change, she thought.

Except…when they did.

Stefano had lost that afternoon. Lost big.

And as he walked through the enormous white tent

that night after dinner, his teammates were not being terribly forgiving about it.

"Nice going," his polo team's number-two player snarled as Stefano passed by in his tuxedo.

"Did you have to take us all down with you?" his number three growled from the dance floor.

"Were you drunk?" the fourth member of his polo team jeered from the bar.

"Not yet," Stefano muttered, heading toward the opposite bar. "But I will be."

The enormous white tent, erected in the biggest field near the hacienda, had been turned into a glamorous ballroom. Lilies and greenery decked with fairy lights overlooked the dance floor, which was filled with guests now that the surrounding dining tables had been cleared of dinner plates. Four different bars lined the edges of the tent and everyone was guzzling champagne like water. People would dance all night, Stefano knew. They'd dance till the music stopped.

But for Stefano, the music had already stopped hours ago.

"Bartender," he growled, holding out his hand. Fifteen seconds later, he took a long gulp of a double Scotch.

The polo game should have been close. On paper, the players were evenly matched. Instead, it had been a rout. Stefano's team usually won but this time, for him, each chukka had been worse than the last. Even Stefano's pony kept rolling his eyes at his rider's pathetically weak performance.

Stefano's heart hadn't been in the game. His heart had left the ranch that morning in a battered 1973 Land Rover.

Ignoring all the sexy women who were, even now, trying to get his attention, Stefano turned away from the frivolity of the dance floor. He stared bleakly at the white canvas of the tent behind the bar and loosened his tie. He could still hear her sweet, trembling voice.

I love you.

Should I have lied to her? he snarled at himself. *Should I have told her I love her when it's not true?*

At this moment, he almost wished he had. He took another gulp of Scotch, and the amber liquid burned down his throat like fire. Setting the glass back onto the bar with a hard clink, Stefano wiped his mouth. Yes, he wished he'd lied. He wished he'd said any damn thing to keep her at his side.

Because he missed her. He missed her like he'd miss his heart if it had been ripped out of his chest.

He had the sudden destructive urge to smash his glass against the bar. To insult his famous guests and order them off his ranch. To sell all his horses for a single euro. What difference did it make, when he'd lost everything he'd cared about the instant Annabelle Wolfe had disappeared through his gate?

He felt a small hand on his arm. For an instant, he held his breath. Then he turned.

Instead of Annabelle's angelic face and blond hair, he saw a brunette in a slinky red dress. The woman seemed familiar. Maybe he'd slept with her before. Or maybe all women just looked exactly the same now—none of them were Annabelle.

"Care to dance?" she said in a sultry voice.

Stefano finished off his drink and slammed the empty glass down on the bar. "Sure," he said harshly. "Why not?"

As he led the brunette onto the dance floor, she pressed against him. "Don't feel bad about losing the game," she purred, softly stroking his upper arm. "There are other prizes to be won tonight."

Her offer couldn't have been more blatant. Stefano stared at her. What better way to draw the line, to put Annabelle forever behind him, then to accept her offer?

But the thought of it sickened him. Even as self-destructive as he felt right now, there was only one woman he wanted. Only one woman he would ever want. Ever.

He stopped.

Annabelle was his first thought in the morning. His last thought at night. She was his sunlight. His moonlight. She lit his way. Her goodness. Her vulnerability. Her heart.

Ever since he'd been betrayed at nineteen, Stefano had been unwilling to commit to any woman. He'd thought he'd never love anyone again.

But his youthful infatuation for Rosalia had meant nothing. The truth was, he'd been waiting all these years for the right woman. The woman who would be his heart. His home.

He'd been waiting for Annabelle.

With an intake of breath, Stefano suddenly knew he could be faithful forever. But only for her. Only Annabelle. She was his woman. The woman he wanted. The woman he adored.

The woman he loved.

His hands clenched. He loved Annabelle. He loved her. And...*he'd let her go.*

"Well?" the brunette murmured as she swayed her body against his, barely in time to the music. "What do you think?"

Looking down at the woman, he stopped.

"Sorry," he said roughly. "I changed my mind."

Turning, he left her on the dance floor. He had to find

Annabelle. Right now. He would drive to London. Fly around the world. Cross the Sahara or climb Mount Everest. *He would find her and make her his own.*

As he walked off the dance floor, he heard a man give a low whistle behind him. "Look at that woman, mate. Great pity that."

"What? Who?" another man said.

"At the door. Beautiful woman scarred across the face."

Sucking in his breath, Stefano turned.

There in the parted doorway of the tent, beneath the beams of fairy lights from above, Annabelle stood dressed in a white gown. Her wavy blond hair cascaded down her shoulders.

He saw her pause, watched her search the crowd with her eyes.

Then she saw him.

Stefano couldn't wait. He went toward her, shoving recklessly through the crowds.

Once they were in front of each other, in the moving shadows beneath the swaying fairy lights, Stefano stopped. Looking at her beautiful face, the rest of the crowds disappeared. And he sucked in his breath.

For the first time in public, Annabelle wore no makeup over her scar. He could see the harsh red line slashing her lovely face, but it did not hide her incredible beauty. Nothing could.

"You—you're showing your scar," he whispered.

"Yes." Her gray eyes were shining. "I'm not afraid anymore. I'm not afraid of anything, except…losing you."

She held out her hand.

Stefano stared at it, then looked up at her face. She looked like an angel. Like a dream.

She looked like the answer to the question of the rest of his life.

Stefano took her hand. He exhaled, almost shuddering at the exquisite bliss of her touch. He hadn't realized how much he'd feared she was a mirage, a ghost who would disappear if he tried to touch her. The feel of her hand proved otherwise. She was no ghost. She was flesh and blood.

Like a miracle, she'd come back to him. *Dios mío.* Stefano's hand tightened over hers. What had he done, what good thing had he ever done in his life, to deserve this second chance?

"Forgive me, Annabelle," he said in a low voice.

"Forgive you?" Her voice was gentle and soft as water as she shook her head. She laughed, and it was like the chiming of bells. "I am the one who is sorry. I tried to force you to make a promise you weren't ready to give—"

"But I am." He took a deep breath. "I thought I'd lost you, and it nearly killed me," he whispered. "I never want to feel that way again. I never want to lose you."

He pulled her into his arms, and passionately kissed her.

Around them, he heard shocked whispers and gasps. He pulled away from Annabelle, and from the corner of his eye, he saw the people in the tent starting to elbow one another and point.

Stefano didn't care. He fell to his knees before her.

Annabelle gasped. Her gentle hands brushed against his hair. "What are you doing?"

The whispers built in noise. The dancers halted on the dance floor. Even the musicians stopped playing their instruments.

Or maybe Stefano just couldn't hear the music over the pounding of his own heart.

Closing his eyes, he pressed his cheek against her waist. Then he looked up at her.

"Annabelle, I love you."

She bit her full, pink lip. Putting her hands on his cheeks, she looked down at him, her face bemused and uncertain. "Are you sure?"

Rising to his feet, he cupped her face, stroking her tearstained cheeks. "Look at my face. And ask if it's true."

She searched his gaze, then tears filled her eyes. "I love you, Stefano," she whispered. "So much."

Her lips trembled and it was too much for him to resist. He kissed her with passion so searing and pure it burned through his heart, and he knew his love for her would last forever.

He heard whistles and ribald comments from nearby guests. Pulling away, Stefano looked down at her beautiful face. Her eyes were still closed, her lips still swollen from their summer days of endless kisses. He wanted to kiss her forever.

But what he felt for Annabelle was private. Tucking her hand over his arm, he led her away from the gossiping, chattering, madding crowd.

Outside the white tent, the warm Spanish night was dark with illuminated stars like scattered diamonds. Stefano heard the distant call of birds and whinny of horses. He loved this land with all his heart.

No. It now took second place in his heart. His guiding star, his love, stood before him now in a white dress.

"I have a question for you," he said, pulling her into his arms.

Beneath the night sky, she looked at him. She didn't push. She just waited, her gray eyes glowing with trust and love. He stroked her cheek, tilting her head back beneath the dark canopy of stars. Her sweet, innocent, beautiful face held such love and promise that it brought tears to his eyes. He loved her more than life. He never wanted to be without her....

"Marry me," he said.

Her lips parted. She looked up, searching his face.

"Marry me," he demanded, more forcefully.

With a choked gasp, she threw her arms around his neck.

"Yes," she said. "Oh, yes." Pulling away from him, she vowed, "I will cancel my assignment in Argentina. I will cancel everything. I never want to leave you again."

But he frowned, furrowing his brow. "But photography is your passion."

She pressed her cheek against his chest. "*You* are my passion."

He stroked her hair softly, his heart aching with love. But he could not allow her to make the sacrifice. Looking down at her, he took a deep breath. "I will come with you."

She looked up in shock. "But I'll be away for a month."

"So?"

She shook her head, tears in her eyes. "I can't ask you to leave your home!"

"Oh, Annabelle." Holding her face in his hands, Stefano looked down at her with adoration. "Don't you understand? It's you, *querida*." With a low laugh, he shook his head. "You...*you* are my home."

A month later, flying first class back from Buenos Aires to London, Annabelle was so nervous that she could barely hold still in the white leather seat.

"Champagne, Señora Cortez?" the flight attendant asked, holding out a silver tray.

Señora Cortez. She and Stefano had married in a simple ceremony at Santo Castillo, the day after she'd turned in her photo essay to *Equestrian* magazine. When the magazine's editors had seen her pictures, they'd instantly forgiven her for missing the polo match and gala. They'd retitled the cover story to *Stud Ranch Wedding: Stefano Cortez Elopes with Equestrian Photographer in Whirlwind Affair.* The publishers had already ordered a double printing as they expected the gossipy exclusive to be their best-selling edition ever.

Fortunately, Annabelle and Stefano had left it all behind, spending the past few weeks in Tierra del Fuego and Patagonia. Had it already been a month since she became Mrs. Cortez? Annabelle's new name still sounded like music to her. But Annabelle shook her head at the flight attendant's question, refusing the champagne.

"Sí, gracias," her husband said beside her, and took a sip from the flute before leaning back in his chair with a satisfied sigh. *Her husband.* Looking at him still made Annabelle flutter inside—as did the memory of the lavish four days they'd spent at a luxury hotel in Buenos Aires for a belated honeymoon.

Annabelle shivered. They would have to go back to Buenos Aires sometime and actually remember to leave their hotel suite. All she'd seen of the city had been from their veranda at midnight, when she'd gone out to see the twinkling lights and feel the cool breezes of the Rio de la Plata against her skin. But even then, she'd been swiftly distracted when her new husband followed her on the veranda wearing only a robe. He'd kissed her passionately in the darkness and, well, one thing had led to another....

She blushed. Stefano was an amazing lover. And even more—an amazing partner. He'd worked well as her assistant as she'd photographed the Pampas, and seeing his innocent wonderment over the beautiful landscape had given her such pleasure. Though hardly an equal recompense to the pleasure he gave her at night.

Annabelle's smile spread to a grin. She would accept fewer photography jobs from now on, taking only the truly fascinating assignments. She craved time nesting at Santo Castillo. She was even, at this moment, feeling the strange urge to learn how to sew and bake.

Her old assistant, Marie Thompson, had sent flowers to the Buenos Aires hotel yesterday when she'd heard of their marriage. Annabelle had immediately telephoned her in Cornwall for a nice chat. Just six weeks ago, she'd envied Marie for being loved by an adoring husband. Now she knew what that felt like.

And she would soon know something else Marie had experienced, as well….

Annabelle's legs bounced with nervous energy as she glanced out the airplane window. She looked down at the scattered, wispy clouds over the green continent of South America beneath them. She tried to gather her thoughts, but her heart was soaring higher than the plane.

Stefano stopped the bounce of her legs by putting his hand on her knee. "Are you really so nervous?" he murmured, smiling. "Just by the thought of going back to Wolfe Manor?"

"I am excited to see my brothers again," she admitted. "We haven't all been home together for almost twenty years. I can't wait to see how Jacob has fixed up Wolfe Manor. And tell them all the news."

Stefano's smile spread into a grin. Putting his arm around her, he kissed her on the temple. "You mean the news that you're my wife?"

"Yes." She looked at him with a sudden smile. "And there's more."

"More?" he said lazily, stroking her knee. "You mean

that I can't keep my hands off you? They'll see that for themselves."

"More than that." She took a deep breath. "We're going to have a baby."

Stefano's jaw dropped as he stared at her. Then his joyful shout reverberated across the first-class cabin as he gathered her in his arms.

"Oh, *querida*... Are you sure?"

She nodded, smiling through tears of happiness. "It must have been our very first time...after."

"A baby." He looked awestruck, then adorably anxious as he demanded, "But how are you feeling? Can I get you anything? Should you be resting?"

She wiped tears from her eyes. "I'm wonderful."

"You're crying," he said accusingly.

She shook her head, laughing. "I'm pregnant." Reaching up, she stroked his cheek and looked up into his ruggedly handsome face. "But I've never been so happy."

Pulling her into his lap, Stefano kissed her, so long and hard and passionately that it made the people around them in first class smile. When the kiss ended, Annabelle closed her eyes as he held her in his arms, tenderly against his heart.

She'd once been warned about Stefano Cortez.

Be careful, Miss Wolfe, they'd said. *You won't be able to resist him. No woman can.*

All the warnings had been true. He'd taken her body. Her heart. Her soul.

"I love you, Annabelle," Stefano whispered. Lowering his mouth over hers, he breathed, "I will love you forever."

As he kissed her tenderly, his hands resting protectively over her flat belly, she had never felt so cherished, so adored. The plane flew them back to England, back to Wolfe Manor. And it was somewhere over Brazil that Annabelle knew for certain that she would be safe, and loved, for the rest of her life.

* * * * *

CLASSIC

Quintessential, modern love stories
that are romance at its finest.

❦ Harlequin *Presents*

You can find more information on upcoming Harlequin® titles,
free excerpts and more at www.HarlequinInsideRomance.com.

HPCNM0112

REQUEST YOUR FREE BOOKS!

◆Harlequin *Presents*

PASSION GUARANTEED SEDUCTION

2 FREE NOVELS PLUS
2 FREE GIFTS!

YES! Please send me 2 FREE Harlequin Presents® novels and my 2 FREE gifts (gifts are worth about \$10). After receiving them, if I don't wish to receive any more books, I can return the shipping statement marked "cancel." If I don't cancel, I will receive 6 brand-new novels every month and be billed just \$4.30 per book in the U.S. or \$4.99 per book in Canada. That's a saving of at least 14% off the cover price! It's quite a bargain! Shipping and handling is just 50¢ per book in the U.S. and 75¢ per book in Canada.* I understand that accepting the 2 free books and gifts places me under no obligation to buy anything. I can always return a shipment and cancel at any time. Even if I never buy another book, the two free books and gifts are mine to keep forever.

106/306 HDN FERQ

Name _____ (PLEASE PRINT) _____

Address _____ Apt. #

City _____ State/Prov. _____ Zip/Postal Code

Signature (if under 18, a parent or guardian must sign)

Mail to the **Reader Service:**
IN U.S.A.: P.O. Box 1867, Buffalo, NY 14240-1867
IN CANADA: P.O. Box 609, Fort Erie, Ontario L2A 5X3

Not valid for current subscribers to Harlequin Presents books.

**Are you a current subscriber to Harlequin Presents books
and want to receive the larger-print edition?
Call 1-800-873-8635 or visit www.ReaderService.com.**

* Terms and prices subject to change without notice. Prices do not include applicable taxes. Sales tax applicable in N.Y. Canadian residents will be charged applicable taxes. Offer not valid in Quebec. This offer is limited to one order per household. All orders subject to credit approval. Credit or debit balances in a customer's account(s) may be offset by any other outstanding balance owed by or to the customer. Please allow 4 to 6 weeks for delivery. Offer available while quantities last.

Your Privacy—The Reader Service is committed to protecting your privacy. Our Privacy Policy is available online at www.ReaderService.com or upon request from the Reader Service.

We make a portion of our mailing list available to reputable third parties that offer products we believe may interest you. If you prefer that we not exchange your name with third parties, or if you wish to clarify or modify your communication preferences, please visit us at www.ReaderService.com/consumerchoice or write to us at Reader Service Preference Service, P.O. Box 9062, Buffalo, NY 14269. Include your complete name and address.

HP11B

Louisa Morgan loves being around children.
So when she has the opportunity to tutor bedridden Ellie,
she's determined to bring joy back into the motherless
girl's world. Can she also help Ellie's father open his
heart again? Read on for a sneak peek of

THE COWBOY FATHER

by Linda Ford,
available February 2012 from Love Inspired Historical.

Why had Louisa thought she could do this job? A bubble of self-pity whispered she was totally useless, but Louisa ignored it. She wasn't useless. She could help Ellie if the child allowed it.

Emmet walked her out, waiting until they were out of earshot to speak. "I sense you and Ellie are not getting along."

"Ellie has lost her freedom. On top of that, everything is new. Familiar things are gone. Her only defense is to exert what little independence she has left. I believe she will soon tire of it and find there are more enjoyable ways to pass the time."

He looked doubtful. Louisa feared he would tell her not to return. But after several seconds' consideration, he sighed heavily. "You're right about one thing. She's lost everything. She can hardly be blamed for feeling out of sorts."

"She hasn't lost everything, though." Her words were quiet, coming from a place full of certainty that Emmet was more than enough for this child. "She has you."

"She'll always have me. As long as I live." He clenched his fists. "And I fully intend to raise her in such a way that even if something happened to me, she would never feel like I was gone. I'd be in her thoughts and in her actions every day."

Peace filled Louisa. "Exactly what my father did."

Their gazes connected, forged a single thought about fathers and daughters…how each needed the other. How sweet the relationship was.

Louisa tipped her head away first. "I'll see you tomorrow."

Emmet nodded. "Until tomorrow then."

She climbed behind the wheel of their automobile and turned toward home. She admired Emmet's devotion to his child. It reminded her of the love her own father had lavished on Louisa and her sisters. Louisa smiled as fond memories of her father filled her thoughts. Ellie was a fortunate child to know such love.

Louisa understands what both father and daughter are going through. Will her compassion help them heal—and form a new family? Find out in
THE COWBOY FATHER
by Linda Ford, available February 14, 2012.

Love Inspired Books celebrates 15 years of inspirational romance in 2012! February puts the spotlight on Love Inspired Historical, with each book celebrating family and the special place it has in our hearts. Be sure to pick up all four Love Inspired Historical stories, available February 14, wherever books are sold.

nocturne™

NEW YORK TIMES AND USA TODAY
BESTSELLING AUTHOR

RACHEL LEE

captivates with another installment of

The Claiming

When Yvonne Dupuis gets a creepy sensation that
someone is watching her, waiting in the shadows,
she turns to Messenger Investigations and finds herself
under the protection of vampire Creed Preston.
His hunger for her is extreme, but with evil lurking
at every turn Creed must protect Yvonne from the
demonic forces that are trying to capture her
and claim her for his own.

CLAIMED BY A VAMPIRE

Available in February wherever books are sold.

HN61876

HARLEQUIN® HISTORICAL:
Where love is timeless

INTRODUCING

LOUISE ALLEN'S
MOST SCANDALOUS TRILOGY YET!

Danger & Desire

Leaving the sultry shores of India behind them, the passengers of the *Bengal Queen* face a new life ahead in England—until a shipwreck throws their plans into disarray....

Can Alistair and Perdita's illicit onboard flirtation survive the glittering social whirl of London?

Washed up on an island populated by ruffians, virginal Averil must rely on rebel captain Luc for protection....

And honorable Callum finds himself falling for his brother's fiancée!

Take the plunge this February!

Ravished by the Rake
February 2012

Seduced by the Scoundrel
March 2012

Married to a Stranger
April 2012

www.Harlequin.com

HHLA29676